MATHEW HAYWARD

EGO
check

WHY
EXECUTIVE HUBRIS
IS
WRECKING COMPANIES
AND
CAREERS
AND HOW TO
AVOID THE TRAP

KAPLAN) PUBLISHING

This publication is designed to provide accurate and authoritative information in regard to the subject matter covered. It is sold with the understanding that the publisher is not engaged in rendering legal, accounting, or other professional service. If legal advice or other expert assistance is required, the services of a competent professional should be sought.

Editorial Director: Jennifer Farthing
Senior Managing Editor, Production: Jack Kiburz
Typesetter: Todd Bowman
Cover Designer: Design Literate

Published by Kaplan Publishing,
a division of Kaplan, Inc.

Printed in the United States of America

07 08 09 10 9 8 7 6 5 4 3 2 1

Library of Congress Cataloging-in-Publication Data

Hayward, Mathew.
  Ego check : why executive hubris is wrecking companies and careers and how to avoid the trap / Mathew Hayward.
    p. cm.
  Includes index.
  ISBN-13: 978-1-4195-3535-2
  ISBN-10: 1-4195-3535-8
  1. Success in business--Psychological aspects. 2. Entrepreneurship--Psychological aspects. 3. Business failures. 4. Decision making. I. Title.
  HF5386.H348 2007
  658.4'09--dc22   2006029694

Kaplan Publishing books are available at special quantity discounts to use for sales promotions, employee premiums, or educational purposes. Please call our Special Sales Department to order or for more information at 800-621-9621, ext. 4444, e-mail *kaplanpubsales@kaplan.com,* or write to Kaplan Publishing, 30 South Wacker Drive, Suite 2500, Chicago, IL 60606-7481.

Dedication

For my friend, father, and fellow author, Don Hayward

Acknowledgments

I owe a great deal of thanks to a great many people.

I have been blessed to be a student and professor of business. Blessed to do my doctoral studies at Columbia University's Business School, where I learned the potential and power of theory-driven research from Warren Boeker, Don Hambrick, and Mike Tushman. Blessed to start my academic career at London Business School with Sumantra Ghoshal, Costas Markides, Peter Moran, and Don Sull, who know how to make research more beneficial to managers. Blessed to work at the University of Texas, Austin, where I learned from Gautam Ahuja, Johnny Butler, Curba Lampart, and Muir McPherson, people who know how to rise above small-minded colleagues. And blessed now to be at the Leeds School at the University of Colorado, Boulder, where Dennis Ahlburg and David Balkin have given me the space and support that I needed to write this book. And where Markus Fitza, Amanda Harris, and Charlie Kelly have provided much-needed research assistance and due diligence.

Many people in the academic and business communities have contributed to this book; alas, I cannot name them all here. Much of my intellectual debt goes to Nobel Laureate Daniel Kahneman and to Amos Tversky, who was also in line for the Nobel Prize before his untimely passing. They are the founding fathers of behavioral decision theory, the theory that shows how people actually make choices and decisions, including overconfident ones. Fellow researchers Max Bazerman, Dipankar Chakrabarti, Jane Dutton, Syd Finkelstein, Dale Griffin, Anil Gupta, Chip Heath,

David Hsu, Rakesh Khurana, Jim March, Tim Pollock, Dean Shepherd, Barry Staw, Bob Sutton, Richard Thaler, Leaf VanBoven, Jim Westphal, Sheila Widnall, and Brian Uzzi graciously helped by reading earlier drafts of the book, providing e-mailed comments, and otherwise fielding queries and offering opinions. Colleagues at Stanford University's Technology Venture Program, Tom Byers, Kathy Eisenhardt, and Bob Sutton generously hosted my research with Silicon Valley executives.

A number of people contributed to this project by reading portions of this book, including Jim Collins, Diane Coutu, Philip Dignan, Danny Green, Don Hayward, Randy Komisar, and Sandy Warner. Scores of other executives generously gave their time in the interviews that help to bring this book to life—you know who you are and you deserve my thanks! And thanks to my father-in-law and resident radiologist, Tom Stucker, who was always on hand for a second, candid opinion.

Working with my publishing team has been a delight! Jim Collins introduced me to my agent, John Willig, who successfully placed our proposal to publish this book in the right hands. Those hands first belonged to Michael Cunningham at Kaplan, who embraced this effort from the outset, before Jennifer Farthing, Jack Kiburz, and Maureen McMahon took over. Michael introduced a charming and diligent editor in Lorna Gentry to this project.

Thank you to Christina, Don, and Googs for your eternal and unwavering love. Above all, thanks to the loves of my life: my dear wife, Kristin, and our boys, Maxwell Don and Lucas Tom. What a joy it is to share my life with you!

Contents

Introduction

Hubris may be humanity's cardinal sin. The hubris of leaders of state has shaped defining events of past centuries. In 1764 and 1765, British Prime Minister George Grenville overestimated his ability to tax the American colonies, and underestimated the potential for the Americans to revolt, leading to the American Revolution. In 1812, Emperor Napoleon Bonaparte's false confidence in his ability to conquer the Russian heartland led to France's disastrous Russian invasion. And, in 1939, Adolf Hitler invaded Poland.

The hubris of business leaders is stamped on commercial failure, from Parmalat, Swissair, and Vivendi in Europe, to Enron and WorldCom in the United States, and the National Kidney Foundation in Singapore. Very often, hubris is the handiwork of egotistical and reckless leaders of business and state. We hear about the downfall of these individuals on almost a daily basis and you will probably have no trouble conjuring your favorite example of an executive whose excessive ego and stubborn pride has resulted in financial and professional disaster.

For now, put that person out of your mind. Because he or she will distract you from the more present and pressing reality: Hubris is so deeply ingrained in our culture that it is a latent force within each of us. See hubris in the losses that we investors take as we overestimate our ability to make winning deals and trades. Watch hubris in the damage that we do to our health by trying to "play doctor" by diagnosing our own illnesses and when real doctors join forces with pharmaceutical companies in overestimating the benefits of their treatments. Listen to the hubris of rookie executives who join our companies fresh out of university, only to exaggerate how far their inflated grades will carry them—and our business.

Hubris helps to explain why executives make decisions that are bound to fail. Consider, for example, that mergers and acquisitions are at near-record levels, even though seasoned CEOs know that most of those deals fail. In a similar vein, well over 500,000 new ventures are started each year in the United States, and up to two thirds of them will fail. Yet, when entrepreneurs are asked about their own ventures, 81 percent of them believe there is at least a 70 percent chance that their ventures will succeed.[1] Joe Roth, who has run movie production at 20th Century Fox, Disney, and Revolution studios, notes that movie houses release a disproportionate number of movies in May, especially around Memorial Day in the United States, even though their executives know that there are not enough moviegoers to support that many simultaneous film releases. Almost invariably, executives who make these deals believe that they are the exceptions who will beat the odds of failure when, on balance, logic dictates that they cannot.

Hubris originates with our need to be highly confident and our propensity for turning that confidence into overconfidence. So long as crystal balls remain elusive, we're going to be wrong on some judgments that matter most, including those that involve at least some leap of faith and trust, such as taking a job, choosing a partner, or investing in a major project. And, if we are going to be wrong by being underconfident or overconfident, we *should* err on the side of overconfidence. As we will see time and again in this book, we must be highly confident to win in business and life, even if that makes us more susceptible to overconfidence.

Overconfidence is not uncommon, nor need it be damaging. We can act with the best intentions and data and still overestimate next year's sales, our promotion and pay prospects, or the returns from our ventures, projects, and investments. The optimism bred by such overestimation can help spur us on to greater achievements. Overconfidence, as an integral part of the discovery process, is also instrumental to scientific and economic progress. Picture, for instance, Thomas Edison testing over 10,000 combinations of materials before perfecting the lightbulb. Throughout the testing process, Edison remained supremely confident; believing a breakthrough would come earlier than it did. "I have not failed," he said at the time. "I've just found 10,000 ways that won't work." [2]

THE FOUR SOURCES OF HUBRIS

If extraordinary confidence is grounded in the best available data, it is *authentic,* and a positive force for advancement. It is when our confidence is false, when we are confident for the wrong reasons, that two serious problems arise. First, we are more susceptible to being overconfident than if our confidence were authentic. Second, such overconfidence is more likely to translate into actions and decisions that will damage us and others. Hubris refers to the damaging consequences that arise from the decisions and actions that reflect false confidence and the resulting overconfidence. As you'll learn in this book, I have determined that there are four sources of false confidence:

1. *Getting too full of ourselves.* Excessive pride leads to a contrived view of who we are and an inflated view of our achievements and capabilities, one that often depends on external approval and validation.
2. *Getting in our own way.* Our pride can lead us to tackle single-handedly decisions or actions that should be made by or in conjunction with trusted advisors or *foils.*
3. *Kidding ourselves about our situation.* We indulge in false confidence when we fail to see, seek, share, and use full and balanced feedback to gain a more grounded assessment of our situation. We need accurate, pertinent, timely, and clear

feedback, whether positive or negative, to ground our
knowledge about what's going on around us.

4. *Discounting the need to manage tomorrow today.* Because we
may not know whether we're acting with false confidence,
we need to *manage the consequences of our decisions ahead of
time.* This is a question of playing out, rather than planning
out, the consequences of our decisions. Whereas experi-
menting and probing allow us to see the consequences of
our decisions firsthand, planning can increase our confidence without increasing our ability to complete the tasks
at hand.

False confidence is to hubris what bad cholesterol is to heart
disease. Just as the cure for heart disease is to reduce bad cholesterol rather than all cholesterol, the cure for hubris is to fight the
sources of false confidence, rather than to reduce confidence
altogether.

A fundamental and unheralded challenge for any executive
and leader, therefore, is to identify and manage such sources. It is
a matter that I've examined as an executive and researcher over
the past 20 years, from the time that I first felt and saw hubris as a
young investment banker. Based on this research, I have written
*Ego Check: Why Executive Hubris Is Wrecking Careers and Companies
and How to Avoid the Trap* to help you learn how to remain highly
confident—both personally and professionally—without falling
victim to the false confidence that produces overconfident decisions and actions that fuel hubris.

DO CHECK YOUR EGO—
JUST DON'T LEAVE IT AT THE DOOR!

Now be prepared for a jolt: Preventing hubris from damaging
your career and life means rejecting the conventional wisdom of
"checking your ego at the door."

When taken seriously, this cliché implies that we should somehow abandon our ego, and leave it behind as we enter the workplace. But dialing back our confidence is impractical and problematic, because every executive requires tremendous confidence. In fact, some fabulously successful corporate leaders have a level of confidence that seems overdone, even when it is not. Southwest Airlines founder Herb Kelleher chuckles loud and long when discussing his early introduction to the prohibitively unprofitable and competitive U.S. domestic airline industry. "Everybody in Texas would tell me that they thought I was nuts trying to start Southwest Airlines . . . . There probably weren't ten people in the state who would have given a plug nickel for our chances of making a dollar," says Kelleher.[3] Lou Gerstner also must have seemed ridiculously overconfident when he decided to become CEO of IBM in 1993. Remembering those days, Gerstner notes, "The odds were no better than one in five that IBM could be saved, and that I should never take the position."[4] Believing that he could beat those odds, however, he breathed new life into a firm that was on its knees.

Telling executives like Kelleher and Gerstner to check their egos at the door is like telling a kangaroo to walk backwards—the kangaroo will not listen, and, even if it could, the advice cannot work. And yet we are frequently told that successful executives have certain egos and personalities. Take, for instance, management guru Jim Collins, who describes "Level 5" leadership as the highest level of executive capability in his book, *Good to Great.* Collins believes that such leaders possess "a compelling modesty," "a quiet calm, determination," and a bias to being "self-effacing and understated."

Though appealing and widely adopted, Collins's guidance clashes with the logic and evidence that successful leaders can also be proud, charismatic, and extroverted. Former General Electric CEO Jack Welch recently described the best advice he ever received, which came right after he joined GE's board of directors:

It was 1979 or 1980. . . . I had just gone to my first or second
board meeting, and at a party for the directors afterwards, Paul
Austin, the former chairman of Coke, came up to me. . . . He
must have noticed my starched shirt and how quiet I was in the
meeting. . . . He said to me, "Jack, don't forget who you are and
how you got here." I gave him an embarrassed "Thanks." But I
knew what he meant. . . . Next meeting, I think I spoke up a bit.[5]

Don't think the need to confidently be ourselves applies only
to businesspeople, either. Consider the wisdom that has been
passed down to us over the ages from successful individuals in all
walks of life[6]:

- Pablo Picasso wrote: "He can who thinks he can, and he
  can't who thinks he can't. This is an inexorable, indisput-
  able law."
- Marie Curie, the Polish-French scientist who won two Nobel
  Prizes, said: "Life is not easy for any of us. But what of that?
  We must have perseverance and above all confidence in ourselves. We must believe that we are gifted for something and
  that this thing must be attained."
- Swami Vivekananda, the 19th-century Hindu spiritual
  leader, cautioned his followers, "If you think about disaster,
  you will get it. Brood about death and you hasten your
  demise. Think positively and masterfully, with confidence
  and faith, and life becomes more secure, more fraught with
  action, richer in achievement and experience."
- Johann Wolfgang von Goethe, the 18th-century German
  poet, novelist, playwright, and philosopher, said about confidence: "Whatever you can do, or believe you can, begin it.
  Boldness has genius, power, and magic in it."

Highly confident individuals, whatever their occupation or disposition, win because they know and appreciate themselves.
Checking one's ego at the door is entirely the wrong way to think

about managing overconfidence and hubris because it drives a wedge between who we are and how we are supposed to act.

Instead, the key is to check our decisions and actions, ahead of time, to determine whether they reflect authentic or false confidence.

IT'S ALL IN THE RESEARCH

Beginning with my doctoral studies at Columbia University, I have conducted studies of overconfidence and hubris amongst hundreds of CEOs, entrepreneurs, and other executives. In seeking to understand the nature and effects of hubris, I have done over 200 interviews with managers, all the way from CEOs of Fortune 500 firms to front line executives at new ventures in the United States, Europe, and Australia. I have reviewed countless news stories, and I have studied well-researched reports of the famous executives whom you will read about here.

My scholarship reflects a body of logic and evidence, called *behavioral decision theory,* that explains and predicts how overconfidence arises and what it can give rise to. Proponents of behavioral decision theory include Nobel Laureate Daniel Kahneman, as well as the man whom Warren Buffett most trusts—Berkshire Hathaway's second in command, Charlie Munger. "Smart, hard-working people aren't exempt from professional disasters from overconfidence," says Munger. "Often they just go around in the more difficult voyages they choose, relying on their self-appraisals that they have superior talents and methods."[7]

My work with behavioral decision theory shapes the structure and content of this book. What you are about to read has been built upon the foundations of that theory, and reflects the interviews, studies, and reports that form my research base. Bringing this book to life, however, are the many stories you'll read of highly confident executives, those who have triumphed over and those who have succumbed to hubris.

HOW THIS BOOK HELPS YOU BECOME
A BETTER DECISION MAKER

Ego Check reveals the sources of false confidence and explores specific approaches for managing them. We begin in Chapter 1 by examining a framework for distinguishing authentic from false confidence, and exploring the incredible stakes involved in unchecked hubris. The stories of talented but doomed mountain-guide Rob Hall and ex-American International Group CEO Hank Greenberg help illustrate just how costly our pride can be when it takes us over the line that separates bold decision making from foolish bravado.

Chapter 2 explores the roots of hubris, and how it has come to dominate so many aspects of our personal and professional lives. By understanding the ways that false confidence guides our most important decisions—those affecting our wealth, health, and education—we gain a richer understanding of how deeply ingrained false confidence is in our culture.

Chapter 3 uses the case histories of Apple Computer's Steve Jobs and John Sculley to explore the evidence and impact of excessive pride in executive decision making. The chapter frames these classic examples of excessive pride in the executive workplace with specific insights and approaches for managing this primary driver of hubris. Given the potency of excessive pride, we'll dedicate more attention to this driver of hubris than the others.

Chapter 4 elaborates on another source of hubris, a failure to get the right help in decision making. That chapter discusses the importance of cultivating the assistance of trusted advisors—or foils—in the decision-making process. From Carly Fiorina's brilliant rise and tragic fall as CEO of Hewlett-Packard, to the fabulous successes of financial powerhouse Warren Buffett of Berkshire Hathaway and of eBay CEO Meg Whitman, we learn more about the power of decentralized decision making, and the dangers of "going it alone."

There are few more disastrous components of decision making than a failure to get—and act upon—feedback. Chapter 5 elaborates this source of overconfidence and how it can be better managed, and examines how Merck's refusal to embrace negative feedback resulted in a series of costly missteps in its handling of the release and recall of its blockbuster drug, Vioxx.

Chapter 6 provides an approach for tackling the difficult task of managing the potential consequences of hubris. If we're unsure whether false confidence affects our decisions, we may want to be ready for such consequences, just in case. The chapter presents a framework for consequence-management, and compares the approaches of Scaled Composites and NASA, two cutting-edge space exploration organizations, in making decisions grounded in a full knowledge of their worst possible outcome.

Chapters 7 and 8 provide in-depth case studies that synthesize the frameworks and concepts presented in the previous chapters. Chapter 7 examines the case of Jean Marie Messier, former CEO of the French giant, Vivendi. The story of Messier provides a some-times startling look at an executive who rose rapidly to power, and just as rapidly fell from grace through a series of bad decisions that ended in his ouster from the company he had helped build. Chapter 8 outlines the experiences of Michael Dell, of Dell Inc., who learned to keep his ego in check the hard way. Dell's insights on decision making and leadership reflect his learning from a series of mistakes that threatened the life of the firm he founded, and notwithstanding recent stumbles the firm was voted by America's CEOs as *Fortune* magazine's most admired corporation for 2005.

The lesson of these remarkable stories is that we must become more aware of the importance of heedfully managing our confidence. As this book demonstrates, hubris can wreck careers, companies, and even lives. My hope is that the stories you read about and the frameworks and concepts that you learn here will help you make decisions and take actions that will allow you to enjoy the benefits of a healthy ego without succumbing to the dangerous excesses of executive hubris.

1

The High Stakes of Hubris

"We know that second terms have historically been marred by hubris and by scandal."

DAVID GERGEN (referring to the fine line that can separate successful from unsuccessful Democratic and Republican presidents)

Succeeding in our professional and personal lives requires tremendous confidence. Our natural desire to be highly confident, however, leaves us at risk of becoming overconfident, which may be the most pervasive, robust, and important error of judgment that we make. And, as I'll further elaborate, such overconfidence is not necessarily problematic: it is when false confidence drives overconfidence that we become susceptible to hubris.

A fundamental challenge for every executive, therefore, is to stay highly confident without falling victim to the false sources of confidence that lead to overconfident decisions and acts of hubris. These sources, as outlined in the introduction to this book, are getting too full of ourselves, getting in our own way, kidding ourselves about our situation, and failing to manage tomorrow today.

This chapter more closely examines the distinction between authentic and false sources of confidence through two very different case studies. We'll begin with the case of Rob Hall, whose world-class mountaineering and leadership skills helped make him a highly successful entrepreneur. We'll see how his tremendous self-confidence gave way to an overconfident decision during an ascent of Mount Everest that ended in disaster. Then we'll turn to the rise and fall of Hank Greenberg, a supremely confident leader who built the world's most successful insurance business, the AIG group, only to become a victim of his own success.

From these case studies we'll see that we can stop hubris in its tracks by recognizing and managing the false sources of confidence ahead of time. Understanding how hubris can wreck careers, companies and even lives may motivate us to manage those sources, ahead of deciding and acting. Dealing with the aftermath can be a chilling alternative, as we'll now see.

A DEADLY LESSON IN HUBRIS: THE CASE OF ROB HALL

Climbing treacherous mountains requires careful judgment. Here in Boulder, Colorado, at the foothills of the Rocky Mountains, there is a saying that people who climb difficult mountains are "mountaineers," those who successfully descend them are "survivors," and professional survivors are eligible to be "guides." Highly confident guides can make a good living, but overconfident ones can jeopardize lives.

The fine line between confidence and reckless bravado must be carefully managed, as Rob Hall's experience will testify. With his meticulous safety standards, imposing leadership skills, and prodigious stamina, Hall was the leading guide of his time—a legend among guides. But, on the afternoon of May 11, 1996, near the summit of Mount Everest at over 29,000 feet, he made decisions that would cost him his life. He was 35 years of age. His climbing experience shines light on this entirely avoidable tragedy.

Hall discovered his calling as a mountaineer while growing up as the youngest of nine children in a Catholic family in Christchurch, New Zealand. From an early age, he embraced the challenge of finding and climbing new routes to the top of his country's highest peaks, and then started doing that in other countries. At 19, he climbed Ama Dablam in Nepal at over 18,000 feet. After that, he spent three summer seasons in Antarctica as a guide and rescue team leader for the American and New Zealand Antarctic programs, where he was honored by the U.S. Navy for rescuing a lost bulldozer operator. Ten years on, in 1990, he scaled the "Seven Summits"—the highest points on each continent—in a record-breaking seven months.

Blessed with a tall and wiry physique, Hall literally towered over his colleagues, clients, and friends. With his long, straight face framed by a bushy black beard, he cast the impression of an Abraham Lincoln–like statesman. Fiercely resolute and uncompromising, he exuded confidence and leadership. Behind the commanding and intense presence, though, friends knew him as a gentle man with a boyish smile who was living his dream as a professional climber. Buoyed by his achievements, Hall and countryman, Gary Ball, formed the first commercial operation, named Adventure Consultants, to take clients to the world's highest peaks. Before long, they enlisted a buddy, Guy Cotter, as a fellow guide.

By 1992, the firm was charging clients up to $35,000 for Everest expeditions. It was a heady year: On one day, the team successfully helped lead an unprecedented 13 climbers to the summit of Everest and down again. News headlines of that feat hailed Hall and Adventure Consultants as the team that could conquer Everest—for the right price. They had transformed Everest from a trophy destination for elite mountaineers to an adventure for those with the right money, nerve, and stamina. From 1990 to 1995, Hall took pride in his perfect expedition record, as he helped 39 climbers to the top of Everest and back. By 1996, Hall's Everest expedition fees had escalated to $65,000 per client. Adventure Consultants won clients by setting new standards for professionalism and safety. Hall made the rules and religiously enforced them.

No rule mattered more to him than "turnaround time." Because Everest is notorious for its worsening afternoon storms, this rule says that climbers must start descending the mountain no later than 2 PM, regardless of where they stand. Enforcing that rule in 1995, Hall made Seattle Postal worker, Doug Hansen, turn around just 300 vertical feet from the summit, even after Hansen had dedicated years of savings and training to make it to the top. With his 100 percent success rate ruined and Hansen's hopes dashed, Hall redoubled his commitment to seeing Hansen reach the summit and offered him a substantial discount to join the upcoming 1996 expedition.

Preparation for that expedition was organized with Hall's drill-sergeant precision, which reflected his intense personality and immense experience. From the outset of the climb, the team enjoyed the good fortune of fine weather, which made it easier to reach the staging camps along the way to the top. Crawling out of his tent on the last of these camps in the early hours of May 11, Hall saw that conditions warranted a summit attempt that day.

At that time, he could not have imagined the nightmare that would engulf his team later that day. In particular, traffic near the summit came to a standstill because ropes were not installed on time. Hall was further held back because Doug Hansen was sick and couldn't climb at his usual pace. Climbers were falling behind in getting up the mountain. As a result, they were especially vulnerable when unusually limited visibility, gale force winds, and frigid temperatures set in that afternoon.

Like other business leaders, Hall was well paid to exercise superb judgment under exacting conditions. No decision mattered more than whether to let Hansen and the others keep climbing after the turnaround time. In spite of the deteriorating conditions, Hall decided to break his own safety rule and let Hansen continue to climb the mountain as late as 3 PM. Hall and Hansen did reach the summit that day in a pyrrhic victory, but shortly afterward, they found themselves hopelessly stuck in a white-out with Hansen too weak to move. Rather than leave Hansen to die alone near the summit, Hall chose to remain with him.

Tragically, they died together in a frozen hell. Why did this disaster take place? Why would Hall break the turnaround rule by letting Hansen continue to climb so late? Was he overconfident that Hansen would safely get to the summit in spite of the horrendous conditions, the lateness of the hour, and Hansen's rapidly deteriorating condition? Reports suggest that Hall was mentally competent until much later in the day, so what better explanation is there? Although we can't know the answer to these questions with certainty, we can hypothesize that Hall's overconfidence in his (and his client's) capabilities led him to break the turnaround rule, in what became a fatal act of hubris.

Consider that, in 1995, Hall posted an advertisement in *Outside Magazine* for his Everest expeditions bragging of "100% Success! Send for our free color brochure." Hall was broadcasting that his safe and successful climbing experience would safeguard his clients on Everest. In truth, there are no guarantees: Nearly one in every ten people who have made known attempts to summit Mt. Everest have died in the process. Success breeds overconfidence and complacency, however, so let's examine Hall's decisions in light of the sources of confidence we touched on previously.

One client on the 1996 expedition, Jon Krakauer, reported in his book *Into Thin Air* that Hall told him at the base of the mountain that his approach had ". . . worked 39 times so far, pal, and a few of the blokes who summitted with me were nearly as pathetic as you."[1] So was Hall's overconfidence motivated by his belief that he had Everest's measure? Did his success on prior summit attempts make him feel omnipotent—that, somehow, he could meet any challenge that the mountain could present? Or did he feel that he had something to prove after bad weather prevented Hansen and others from reaching the peak in 1995, ruining his claims to a 100 percent success rate? With strong competitors emerging, he could no longer claim to be the undisputed "king of the hill." If the answer to any of these questions is "yes," Hall's overconfidence may have been driven by *excessive pride*—he may have become too full of himself.

There is also the question of whether Hall got in his own way by *failing to get the right help,* given the prevailing conditions. Before the climb, Hall told clients, "My word will be absolute law, beyond appeal. If you don't like a particular decision I make, I'd be happy to discuss it with you afterward, not while we're up on the hill."[2] Few people were as qualified to make life and death decisions on Everest as Hall. But, given the pressures, was he the right person to make dispassionate decisions there and then? And did he underestimate the need to have Guy Cotter or another associate alongside him to take charge should he falter? As we will see in case studies throughout this book, people with exceptional judgment can fail when they make decisions in the wrong time and place, and miss the insights and advice of qualified advisors.

Even if he was the right person to enforce the turnaround time, was he kidding himself about the situation he was facing by failing to *ground his judgment in the feedback* about the deteriorating weather conditions and Hansen's sluggishness? Another primary source of overconfidence is a failure to see, seek, use, and share salient feedback. After a series of unforeseen delays, Hansen and other clients had labored dangerously at extreme altitude. Was Hall sufficiently motivated to act on the adverse feedback of the worsening weather? Or was he simply hell bent on summiting Everest regardless of that feedback?

A final question we must ask when seeking to understand why Hall decided to continue climbing after 2 PM that day concerns the distinction between bravery and courage. To be brave is to jump in heedlessly without adequately considering the risks and consequences. To be courageous is to act with full consideration of the known risks. Disregarding the turnaround time was, literally, a decision that Hall could not live with. Did he underestimate the consequences of breaking the turnaround rule or, did he overestimate his ability to deal with the consequences of doing so? Was he brave rather than courageous, *discounting the importance of managing the consequences of his decisions and actions ahead of time?*

We cannot know how many, if any, of these sources of false confidence shaped Hall's judgment that day. And even when they are in play—for Hall or anyone else—they will not necessarily induce overconfidence and hubris, just as bad cholesterol does not guarantee heart disease. Nevertheless, *any* of these factors places us at the mercy of the false confidence that induces hubris; and Hall was susceptible to *each* one on May 11, 1996.

A FRAMEWORK FOR MANAGING HUBRIS WHILE REMAINING HIGHLY CONFIDENT

Hall's case highlights the razor-thin line that separates highly confident decisions and those that are imbued with false confidence and hubris. On the one hand, we must stay highly confident to succeed in business. Exceptionally confident executives can be and are justifiably proud of what they've achieved.

On the other hand, even the most successful business leader is susceptible to hubris. *Forbes* magazine recently named Henry Ford as the most influential business leader of all time. In *The People's Tycoon,* historian and Ford biographer Steven Watts concludes that, "like many uneducated people who become fabulously successful, he [Ford] was utterly confident in his view of the world and never appreciated what he did not know."[3] Watts goes on to elaborate how Ford became infected by a false confidence that almost destroyed him, his family, and his company. No one is immune to false confidence, so all of us must learn to assess the quality of our decisions and the motivations behind them.

THE HALLMARKS OF CONFIDENCE, OVERCONFIDENCE, AND HUBRIS

As a first step in assessing our own decisions, recall the distinctions between confident and overconfident judgment, and hubris as follows:

- *Confident judgment* reflects our belief about who we are, what we can do, and what we know and can predict. Confidence can be built on either false or authentic platforms.
- *Overconfident judgment* arises when we overestimate what we can do, who we are, what we know, and what we can predict. It's an everyday mistake to be overconfident about our abilities. When overconfidence reflects authentic confidence, it need not be costly.
- *Hubris* arises when false confidence makes us overconfident with damaging consequences.

Hall's experience reinforces the distinction between being highly confident and becoming an overconfident victim of hubris. An accomplished mountaineer, Hall was highly qualified to make critical decisions during the 1996 expedition and proceeded with every confidence. And yet, it is an article of faith among Nepalese or Sherpa guides that *conditions* on this revered mountain dictate mortal decisions and outcomes. Hall defied that wisdom by deciding to let Hansen climb long after the previously determined turnaround time, and despite the weather conditions.

Perhaps that was when he crossed the potentially deadly line where overconfidence turns to hubris. The problem was not that Hall was a supremely confident mountaineer and decision maker. The problem was that he overreached his human limits on a major decision.

Although most everyday decisions call for confidence in judgment, to identify the drivers of the false confidence that produce hubris, we should take a moment to examine the forces at work in our decisions. Stop to reflect on an important decision that you are contemplating. Ask yourself these questions:

- Why am I doing this? Am I motivated by the intrinsic joy I take from the work or my need for certain outcomes? Do I get pleasure out of deciding or seeing the decision work? Who am I trying to impress, if anyone? Am I acting out of a grounded or a contrived view of my capabilities and achievements?
- Am I getting the right input into this decision? Do I have someone whom I can trust to tell me when I am wrong? Am I the very best person to be making this call?
- Am I seeing, seeking, using, and sharing material feedback?
- Have I clarified the conditions in which I could be wrong, and have I tried to experience the worst thing that could happen if I am wrong? Do I know, right now, what I would do if I were wrong? What would it take in time and money to put loss-mitigating action into place?

APPLYING THE EGO CHECK FRAMEWORK TO OUR DECISIONS

Coming to terms with these kinds of questions is essential if we are to rise to the professional and personal challenge of staying highly confident without making the entirely avoidable judgment that yields hubris. These questions directly address the four components of the framework of a sound decision-making process presented earlier in this book. That framework tells us that we must:

1. *Not get too full of ourselves.* We need to gain pleasure from our work and real capabilities, rather than reveling in our decisions. The locus or source of our pride must come from our appreciation for doing good work, rather than

the need for a specific outcome or for approval and validation. This driver of confidence is featured in Chapter 3.

2. *Not get in our own way.* Having—and listening to—a trusted advisor or foil is crucial if we want to stop our pride from leading us to overreach on actions and decisions that are beyond our capabilities. Learn more about the importance of delegating and conferring with trusted advisors in Chapter 4.

3. *Not kid ourselves about our situation.* We must see, seek, use, and share salient feedback to establish what is going on around us. Chapter 5 further explores this issue.

4. *Not manage tomorrow today with false bravado.* Living through the potential consequences of our decisions *before they happen* is the equivalent of testing the waters, rather than plunging in with both feet. Planning alone won't work; we must take the experiments and probes needed to experience the consequences of overconfidence. In Chapter 6, we learn more about the importance of living through the consequences of our decisions ahead of time.

Of course, false confidence and hubris cannot *fully* explain Hall's demise, nor is it the sole reason why people self-destruct in the workplace. But the lesson suggested by Hall's experience is that false confidence can easily enter into our decisions and influence our judgment. To avoid that outcome, we should assess our decisions ahead of time within the four-part "ego check" framework of sound decision making, which is illustrated in Figure 1.1.

Note again that taking *any* of these four pathways leads us toward hubris, and that, by checking our ego, we can heedfully and simply avoid those pathways *ahead of time.* Note also that false confidence does not ensure that we will be overconfident victims of hubris; it only increases the likelihood of such outcomes. Note further that the ceaseless presence of these pathways ensures that we are all susceptible to hubris at any time.

FIGURE 1.1 *Framework for Understanding the Drivers of False Overconfidence and Hubris*

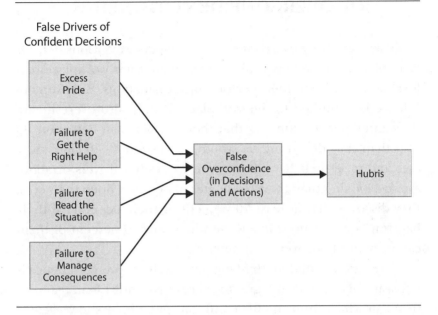

In fact, paradoxically, more successful people are most at risk. With greater success, our belief in our capabilities can more quickly outpace our ability to deliver. Ironically, however, we feel safest from the effects of hubris at precisely the moment when the risk is greatest. As you'll learn later in this book, extraordinarily successful businesspeople, from Warren Buffett to Michael Dell to Jack Welch, have succumbed to—and recovered from—hubris at one time or another. The solution to remaining highly confident without giving way to hubris, as cognitive psychologists demonstrate in study after study, is to improve the thinking that goes into our judgment. *Hubris is not the result of a defective personality; it is the result of bad judgment.*

So the key is to carefully assess the confidence that goes into our judgment, rather than to mindlessly curb our confidence. That's because confidence breeds success and success breeds confidence, both in business and life.

ACKNOWLEDGING THE DUAL NATURE
OF OVERCONFIDENT THINKING

That's also why overconfidence is all-pervasive. Consider, for example, that people typically overestimate their workplace performance relative to their performance evaluations. But overconfidence isn't limited to the workplace. People also overestimate their intelligence, thinking that they will perform better on IQ tests than they do. In my classroom, I tell students to close their eyes and raise their hand if they are, say, better drivers or above average looking than their classmates. When they open their eyes, they discover that at least 70 percent of their peers have their hands up on questions like these when only 50 percent of them can be better than average in their class.

The highly confident thinking that results in overconfidence is pervasive because it's integral to success. No individual, team, or firm can win without highly confident people, as showcased in sports. "It's mostly confidence," says baseball slugger David Ortiz of the Boston Red Sox. "If you go up there thinking you might not get it done, you're out already. I know I'm going to hit you."[4] Competitors sense our confidence. Padraig Harrington, the top Irish golfer, describes the challenge of competing with Tiger Woods: "Tiger was unbeatable because he probably believed that he was unbeatable."[5]

Selling is another setting where confidence determines success. Research into the psychology of persuasion shows that salespeople who "know" that they will win new accounts treat potential customers as actual ones by getting to know them better and otherwise investing in them. In turn, customers respond with consistent behavior, especially placing orders. Studies of tens of thousands of auto and life insurance salespeople shows that they sell more products and last longer in their jobs as they become more confident about sales prospects. Or, as a leading Cisco Systems account manager told me: "Unless you go into a sales pitch 100 percent confident that you'll win the business, you'll lose it to someone who is." (And, by the way, you also need a loss-mitigation or backup plan just in case, as seen further in Chapter 6.)

No wonder that overconfidence defines the terms by which executives compete in some industries. At least that's the view of Oracle's CEO and software billionaire, Larry Ellison:

> The entire history of the IT industry has been one of over-promising and underdelivering. Software executives routinely say that a product is going to be ready on a certain date, and then it turns out to be literally years late. It's happened at Microsoft. It's happened at Oracle . . . . Most senior software executives don't tell out-and-out lies about their products or their businesses. But optimism and exaggeration, those are the standard rules of engagement for combat in this industry.[6]

On the one hand, false confidence has hurt software firms. On the other hand, more highly confident executives are better able to enact the self-fulfilling prophecy that says: Conceiving a great future and becoming convinced that it will happen helps to make it happen. Partners who are in "no doubt" that their marriage will succeed, may be better able to overcome marital difficulties that do arise, and so are more likely to stay married. Some psychologists make a living out of the fact that smokers are more likely to give up smoking when they believe that they can.

Inventors and managers exemplify how confidence enables the mind to conquer matter. Look for highly confident executives and you will also find successful communicators and salespeople, those with the persistence, persuasiveness, and passion to make great things happen. They can be exciting to work with, because they give the impression that they know what they're doing and have the courage to change and effect change. Jack Welch's confidence visibly grew as he morphed from being a cost cutter or "Neutron Jack" to a coach and mentor of executive talent. Today, that self-confidence is ingrained as a core value at GE, spurring executives to think and act simply, boldly, and decisively.

Being highly confident is not always beneficial. In his book, *Jack—Straight from the Gut,* Welch refers to the dark side of confidence as the "razor's edge" on which executives get "too full of themselves" and fall victim to hubris.[7] Ellison refers to his confidence in taking on strategic innovations: "I always feel good when everyone says I'm nuts because it's a sign that we're trying to do something . . . truly new and different. On the other hand, when people say you're nuts, you just might be nuts . . . ."[8]

These concerns have some basis in history. Over 3,000 years ago, the Greek prophets warned us that hubris was and always would be our cardinal sin. Excessive pride, among other things, afflicted some of the leading protagonists of Greek mythology:

- Icarus and his father Daedalus found themselves stranded on the island of Crete and hounded by their archenemy, King Minos. Their only escape was to the Greek mainland, which lay 68 miles across the Mediterranean. Daedalus, using his brilliant architectural and engineering skills, made wings of feathers and wax so his son could fly to safety. Although Daedalus cautioned Icarus not to fly too high lest the sun melt the wax, Icarus, thrilled with the power of flight, ignored his father's warning, flew too close to the sun, and perished. Today, the Icarus Paradox, a subject of intense business interest, is synonymous with executives who exaggerate the reach of their strengths. In his autobiography, Michael Dell notes, "It's been said that a strength when used to excess becomes a weakness. Was that ever true for us."[9]

- Narcissus was widely adored for his great beauty. Drinking at a fountain, he saw his reflection in the water for the first time, and instantly became infatuated with his own bright eyes, golden locks, and rose-like lips. As he got closer to his reflection, it became more blurred, forcing him to withdraw from it. When, devastated by unrequited love, Narcissus wept into the water, he further blurred his image and compounded his misery. Today, narcissists are known for their self-obsession, a preoccupation that drives them to egotistical and gratuitous behavior. Narcissistic leadership is a major topic of management thought.

- In Sophocles' play, *Oedipus Rex*, Oedipus is left as an orphan in the wilderness, without knowing the identity of his parents. As he matures and prospers, he is warned by the prophets that he will inadvertently kill his father and marry his mother. Later, Oedipus became a great ruler, the King of Thebes, with the power to disregard the prophets' warning—which he did. As predicted, he unwittingly killed his father and married his mother. Traumatized by his arrogance and fate, he ripped out his eyes in grief. Hubris underscores what Freudian psychologists call the "Oedipus complex"—the male child's unconscious desire for the exclusive love of his mother, and the possible transfer of the love object to another person or entity, whether in one's work or personal life.

Although these stories have been with us for centuries, their lessons remain fresh. Still, we don't have to look to the ancient Greeks for stories that help us visualize the dangers of falling victim to hubris. More immediate are the many stories that tell of the American dream of rising from rags to riches. For every story such as Henry Ford's, in which an individual's incredible success evolves from the confidence to overcome all the odds, remember the less-often-told tales of how hubris can turn that dream into a nightmare—as in the story of Enron's Ken Lay.

Take one of the most successful executives of the 20th century, Maurice "Hank" Greenberg, who built the world's largest insurance firm, the American International Group, from scratch. In many respects, his rise and fall is a case study of how a highly confident executive can become infected by the false confidence that breeds overconfidence and hubris.

FALSE CONFIDENCE AT THE AMERICAN INTERNATIONAL GROUP: THE CASE OF HANK GREENBERG

On Wall Street, walk a block northeast from the steps of the New York Stock Exchange to 70 Pine Street, and glance up to see a limestone-clad, gothic-like tower crowned in white, like a snow-capped mountain. On the tower's summit stands an open-air platform, along with an enclosed glass observatory that offers one of the area's finest views of downtown Manhattan. This glorious building is the headquarters of the American International Group (AIG), a company whose success stands as testimony to the awesome power of one uncompromising executive.

That man is Hank Greenberg, whose ability, drive, and confidence built AIG into a great and lasting firm. Born in 1925 as the son of a New York City candy store owner, Greenberg left home early to sign up for service in World War II. At 19, he served as a ranger on the beaches of Normandy on D-Day, and then helped to liberate Dachau from the Nazis. Later he saw frontline combat as a captain in the Korean War, during which he received the Bronze star for bravery. Greenberg joined AIG in 1960 and became its second ever CEO in 1967.

For nearly 40 years, Greenberg ruled AIG like a battle-hardened field commander. Famous for relentlessly harassing his managers about their approach to managing risks, he took no prisoners. With his hands-on, detail-oriented, and obsessive leadership style, Greenberg determined who rose and fell on his corporate ladder. With an unfailing zest for care and control, he deployed over 100 internal auditors and scores of in-house lawyers to search for and eliminate anything that was remotely out of place, including questionable insurance claims and colleagues.

Greenberg's leadership style paid handsome dividends to shareholders and selected subordinates, supporters, and sycophants. When Greenberg joined the firm, AIG's market value was about $300 million; it is now over $150 *billion*. AIG is the world's second largest financial conglomerate with a diversified commercial, institutional, and individual customer base in 130 countries; it is a firm that was and remains "built to last." Today, Greenberg owns over $2 billion in AIG stock. He was named Chief Executive Officer of the Year by CEO magazine in 2003, and serves as a director of the esteemed Council on Foreign Relations.

With these achievements in hand, Greenberg could have left AIG on his terms and at his chosen time as a deserving hero. Instead, in early 2005, at the age of 79, he was asked to resign by the directors whom he had handpicked. New CEO Martin Sullivan, who loyally served Greenberg for decades, has virtually ceased all contact with him. Like a player in a Greek tragedy, Greenberg's once-stellar reputation is badly tarnished, if not irreparably ruined.

Following extensive investigations, New York State Attorney General Elliott Spitzer alleges that AIG in general, and Greenberg in particular, engaged in wide-ranging corporate misconduct. On May 26, 2005, Spitzer and New York State Superintendent of Insurance Howard Mills filed civil charges alleging that Greenberg:

- "Routinely and persistently resorted to deception and fraud in an apparent effort to improve the company's financial results."
- "Personally proposed and negotiated" a "sham" transaction with General Reinsurance Corp. whereby AIG paid a Berkshire Hathaway division $5 million to take $500 million of loss reserves and, at the same time, immunized that division from the risks of those reserves.
- Concealed losses from insurance underwriting through offshore shell companies, mischaracterized income from the purchase of life insurance policies, and repeatedly lied to state insurance regulators about its ties to offshore companies.
- Hid underwriting losses from an auto warranty unit by transferring the losses to an offshore entity that it secretly controlled, and papered over losses in a Brazilian subsidiary by linking the losses to a Taiwanese subsidiary.

■ Fraudulently reduced the firm's tax liability. (Spitzer withdrew these last three charges in September 2006.)

AIG accepts that it overstated earnings by $3.9 billion under
Greenberg's tenure. Directors authorized the payment of a $1.6 bil-
lion settlement, at the time the largest single penalty ever paid by a
company to regulators. Terms of the settlement reveal the nature
and extent of wrongdoing: $800 million goes to investors who were
defrauded by false financial statements, $375 million goes to AIG
policyholders harmed by bid-rigging activities, $344 million goes to
states for AIG's underpayment of workers' compensation taxes
between 1986 and 1995, and $100 million goes to the Securities and
Exchange Commission and the State of New York as penalties
assessed against the firm.

If Greenberg is a corporate crook, it is not in the "garden variety" mold of a Bernie Ebbers of WorldCom or Dennis Kozlowski of
Tyco or Calisto Tanzi of Parmalat. For starters, Greenberg has not
been convicted of a crime. In fact, he is challenging the allegations
against him and remains "confident he will prevail." Moreover,
this man's Herculean efforts transformed AIG from an also-ran to
the world's leading commercial insurer, consistently producing
outsized returns for loyal shareholders.

At a minimum, however, Greenberg failed to stop concerted
efforts to manipulate the firm's earnings and, therefore, its stock
price. If Greenberg was oblivious to AIG's gross misconduct, that
lack of oversight would be at odds with his zest for control and
detail. An expert mechanic knows when his own car acts up. So
why did this happen? What may have driven Greenberg to believe
that he could get away with being above the rules that apply to the
rest of us?

Spitzer proposes an explanation for Greenberg's flawed
behavior: Since a one-dollar movement in AIG's stock price is
worth $65 million to Greenberg, he speculates that Greenberg got
greedy by trying to manipulate AIG's share price. While $65 mil-
lion is a fortune, it is also a drop in the ocean of Greenberg's fab-

ulous wealth. Perhaps more telling, there is no evidence that he sold shares ahead of actions that could affect the firm's share price. If greed was the driving motive, Greenberg must have been confident that his actions would pass basic standards of legal, social, and commercial conduct. Executives who use questionable means to pursue greed often do so with the false confidence that they will get away with it.

We must also be open to the possibility that Greenberg's downfall happened because his supreme confidence gave way to hubris. Let's return to the earlier framework and consider evidence that Greenberg's alleged decisions regarding the statement of his firm's earnings, the purchase of his firm's shares, sham insurance transactions and management of the firm's taxes, were driven by false sources of confidence. Return to the four drivers of the ego check framework:

1. *Did Greenberg get too full of himself? Did excess pride guide his actions and decisions?* Greenberg's pride may have depended on market validation of his performance, as evidenced by his fixation with the firm's share price. Recall that for years the firm had been dressing up its accounts to make them look more attractive than they were, even though the firm was performing spectacularly well without the aggressive accounting. The share price had consistently outperformed the market under Greenberg's tenure until about 2001, when it failed to move significantly upwards. Greenberg responded by buying back shares to support the price. Relevant here are the rules that govern how executives must trade shares in their own firm, rules designed to prevent them from manipulating the share price, including that executives cannot place orders to buy and sell shares ten minutes from closing time. When Kathy Shannon, AIG's deputy general counsel discovered Greenberg's instructions to buy the firm's shares, she tried to have them stopped. Greenberg responded to traders by

shouting in a taped conversation, "I don't give a f— what Kathy Shannon says." [10]

2. *Did Greenberg fail to get out of his own way by getting the right help?* Greenberg groomed his two elder sons, Jeffrey and Evan, to succeed him. Yet he failed to relinquish power, even to his sons, who left the firm to realize their ambitions elsewhere. (Jeffrey became CEO of Marsh and McLennan and Evan left AIG for a major competitor, ACE Limited, where he is now CEO.) Whatever his genius, Greenberg was a 79-year-old CEO who had served the firm for 40 years. Even so, he showed few signs of getting meaningful input on major AIG decisions, let alone giving more power to a successor.

3. *Was Greenberg kidding himself about his situation?* For years, AIG and Greenberg were receiving feedback from analysts and state regulators that the firm's accounting policies were unduly aggressive and opaque. When directors investigated allegations of fraud within AIG, Greenberg rebuffed them, dismissively asserting "This is my business judgment!" [11] Did Greenberg needlessly disregard the information that the firm was getting from accountants, analysts, directors, and regulators?

4. *Did Greenberg bravely rather than courageously manage the consequences of his decisions and actions ahead of time?* *Fortune* magazine reports that in the early 1990s, AIG had "for years been improperly booking premiums received for workers' compensation insurance. If true, this meant that the insurance company was cheating state governments out of tens of millions of dollars used to pay benefits to injured workers." Former legal counsel, Michael Joye, concluded that AIG's behavior was "permeated with illegality." [12] Regarding illegal accounting, Joye's handwritten notes say that he was told by an AIG associate, "You should be aware that MRG [Greenberg] knows about this and has approved it." Greenberg's response was to try to neutralize Joye by having him investigated. Greenberg accused Spitzer of persecuting him for

"foot faults" (i.e., minor regulatory indiscretions). Incensed, Spitzer warned, "Hank Greenberg should be very, very careful talking about foot faults. Too many foot faults, and you can lose the match. But, more importantly, these aren't just foot faults." Note that the bill that AIG will pay for these faults is close to $2 billion.

Highly successful people like Hank Greenberg and Rob Hall can reach a point where they believe that that they're invincible or untouchable. That's the point at which hubris will strike, and Greenberg may have been right at its very edge toward the end of his tenure. Henry Kissinger, U.S. Secretary of State from 1973 to 1977, counts Greenberg as a close personal friend and laments Greenberg's downfall as a "terrible human tragedy." Kissinger admits that he could imagine Greenberg going to the "edge of what was permissible," but not deliberately crossing over that line.[13] The reality is that as false confidence takes us closer to the edge and emboldens us to stay there, we teeter closer to the brink of hubris.

SUMMARY

By now you know, this book is not just about the downfall of two exceptionally talented leaders in Hank Greenberg and Rob Hall. Notwithstanding the devastation that Greenberg and other celebrity CEOs can leave in their wake, they are just the poster children who remind us how damaging hubris can be.

Countless executives have been needlessly damaged by false confidence, and in studying those cases, I've come to understand that hubris is systematically embedded in our most important decisions. As we learn in the next chapter, many of the decisions most at risk for resulting in hubris concern how we manage our wealth, health, and education.

Before exploring those issues, however, let's first recap the key points from this chapter:

- We must unleash our confidence. Highly confident people and executives are more successful than their less-confident colleagues. But when we are confident for the wrong reasons, we have the false confidence that gives rise to hubris. The line that separates being highly confident from succumbing to hubris is razor thin and can be crossed in an instant, without us even knowing it.
- *Overconfident* judgment arises when we overestimate what we can do, who we are, what we know, and what we can predict. Such judgment has authentic and false foundations, and the latter serves as the platform for hubris.
- *Hubris* arises when false confidence produces overconfident decisions and actions that cost us and our businesses.
- Four sources of false confidence can impact our decisions and actions and lead to the damaging results of hubris: getting too full of ourselves, getting in our own way, kidding ourselves about our situation, and failing to manage the consequences of our decisions.
- Managing confidence is a critical and unheralded challenge for us all—both inside and outside the workplace. A key to staying highly confident is to appreciate and manage the false sources of confidence that produce hubris.

Now, we'll trace the roots of those decisions to factors that are endemic to society, as a springboard for examining the deeper impact of false confidence and hubris in business, from the largest to the smallest of firms.

2

A Culture of
False Confidence

HOW WE MANAGE OUR
MOST CRITICAL DECISIONS

*"[Motivating people is] deception in the sense that you pump yourself up and
put a better face on things than you start off feeling. But after a while if you act
confident, you become confident. So the deception becomes less of a deception"*

ANDY GROVE, FORMER CEO OF INTEL

Andy Grove provides insight into why executive hubris is so pervasive. We can scrutinize his insight into deception by considering
the prevalence of overconfidence in the decisions we make regarding our most critical resources, those involving our wealth, health,
and education.

As we'll see in this chapter, studies show that entrepreneurs fail
when they underestimate the difficulty of starting successful ventures, which in turn leads them to raise insufficient capital and
overinvest their limited resources too early in the life of their ventures. Many investors consistently overestimate their ability to gain
sizeable returns from owning individual stocks. As already noted,
many of us diagnose and treat our illnesses when we should seek
professional care. At the same time, we are aware that many doctors overprescribe medications when they should, instead, accept
that they simply don't have the answer for every medical problem.
My fellow professors and I tend to exaggerate our teaching ability.
And, when we give our students inflated grades, the students

believe that they have a better mastery of their subject and field than they do.

In this chapter we explore the evidence that false confidence is endemic to how we manage our wealth, health, and education, and through that exploration, gain a clearer picture of how hubris infiltrates the executive decision-making process. A good place to start exploring the dynamics of false confidence is in the creation and management of new ventures by entrepreneurs—a major driver of prosperity in our economies. Ironically, the same confidence that drives individuals to start daring new ventures is also that which can grow into false confidence, a transformation that ultimately damages the businesses they've worked so hard to build. Dean Kamen, inventor of the Segway Human Transporter, is a case in point.

FALSE CONFIDENCE IN MANAGING NEW VENTURES: DEAN KAMEN AND THE SEGWAY

Dean Kamen embodies the notion that behind every successful entrepreneur is a flagrant disregard for convention and consensus. Hailed as an "inventor's inventor," his stellar record includes developing medical devices that have improved and saved countless lives. The fruits of his prodigious capabilities and work ethic are many, including an island—with its own lighthouse—off the coast of Connecticut. He also owns a 32,000-square-foot house in New Hampshire, adorned with London taxis, a helicopter, a landmark windmill, and turbines.

First Inventions: Designing Products for the Ill and Disabled

Kamen has never been satisfied with what he's got. Always impatient and restless, he prefers to challenge and question rather than follow instructions. As a schoolboy, it astounded him that anyone could work on banal homework assignments when the alternatives included reading and studying Albert Einstein, Isaac Newton, and other great minds of science. To him, textbook problems were useless excuses for not working on real, self-directed projects to improve things. Easily bored by teachers, he recalled, "I would sit there trying to think about what they said. And I would fixate on something. So, when they'd ask me a question, I wasn't paying attention because I was thinking about something else. So I'd be accused of daydreaming." [1]

Whether because or in spite of his "attention deficits," Kamen's mind drifted to unusual projects. Before graduating from high school, he had installed control systems for sound and light shows in Manhattan (including the Hayden Planetarium and the Museum of the City of New York) and automated Manhattan's famous Times Square ball-drop on New Year's Eve. After school, Kamen enrolled at Worcester Polytechnic Institute in Massachusetts to study Electric Engineering, where he was once again a chronic underachiever. Failing to gain enough credits within five years to stay in college, Kamen settled for being a college dropout, joining the ranks of Michael Dell and Bill Gates.

What would he do? College engineering projects were obviously too abstract to make a difference. And sound and light projects were not going to change the world. So, Kamen began to work on technologies for disabled and sick people. To this day, the medical devices he developed serve as lasting tributes to his creativity and compassion.

By the early 1970s, Kamen learned from his brother, then in medical school, that doctors lacked controlled ways to administer regular doses of drugs to patients. Patients needed constant monitoring and frequent hospitalization for a host of treatments—insulin for diabetics, blood for hemophiliacs, morphine for those with severe pain, and so on. Patients who could not or would not get to a hospital, especially the poor, faced the bleakest prognosis.

All of that led him to work, with painstaking care and precision, on a portable infusion pump. After years of frustratingly slow development, the product was endorsed by the National Institutes of Health and featured in an article in the *New England Journal of Medicine,* the gold standard for medical research. Kamen became wealthy when Baxter, the international health care company, bought the product in 1982. Today, Baxter sells Kamen's portable infusion pump in large volumes under the Auto-Syringe label.

Another Kamen invention took root when he saw a disabled person struggle hopelessly to get his wheelchair over a sidewalk curb. Troubled by that predicament, he and his team at DEKA (yes, a play on his name) invented a chair to climb stairs and traverse uneven terrain with four-wheel-drive technology. After years of product development, the team built a self-balancing chair that helps riders negotiate stairs. To promote the chair, Kamen took it to a Paris Metro station and proudly rode it to the restaurant level of the Eiffel Tower.

Still, Kamen was bothered that the chair's riders had to crane their necks to talk to standing people, and so he redesigned it to stand up on its hind wheels, much like a horse rears up. Now sold as a centerpiece of Johnson & Johnson's Independence Technology division, the iBOT chairs give disabled riders more control over their movement.

A third important invention resulted from DEKA's search for improved battery power for the iBOT. Research led the team to an energy source based on a 19th-century technique called the Stirling engine by which a piston distills warmer, contaminated water in one chamber into colder and cleaner water in another chamber. Pending products based on this technology can save countless lives in developing countries (watch DEKA's Web site—*dekaresearch.com*—for progress on this and other extraordinary inventions). Kamen is moved by the knowledge that

> ...in some places the average amount of time per day spent looking for water that's safe for their kids by women is four hours. And they carry this stuff, which weighs 62 pounds per

cubic foot, four or five miles. And if it didn't turn out to be the right stuff, or they put their hands in it and contaminated it, they spend the next day or two burying the babies.[2]

From Inventor to Entrepreneur: The Segway Moves Kamen into Business Management

For all those achievements, Kamen's most ambitious project to date is the Segway Human Transporter—a self-balancing, two-wheel-scooter that riders operate while standing. At first glance, it seems like a natural extension of the iBOT with its dynamic stabilization technology for balance and versatility. Faster than walking and much less expensive to own and operate than a car, the Segway could substantially reduce urban congestion and air pollution. It operates at the equivalent of 450 miles per gallon of fuel, making its energy efficiency at least ten times greater than that of a nonhybrid car. In an interview for a 2001 *Time* magazine story called "Reinventing the Wheel," Kamen professed that the Segway would "be to the car what the car was to the horse and buggy." [3]

On closer inspection, the Segway differs materially from Kamen's earlier projects. Recall that his earlier medical inventions were a means for helping needy people. Before the Segway, he told the U.S. broadcast network NBC, "I don't work on a project unless I believe that it will dramatically improve life for a bunch of people." By contrast, the Segway has the features and price tag of a luxury item. Some critics even condemn it as a safety threat to pedestrians in congested areas, labeling it the Sports Utility Vehicle of the sidewalk. In San Francisco, it is banned from sidewalks. Pro-walking groups have denounced it as an unhealthy and inconvenient substitute for walking, given that it weighs 70 pounds and is prohibitively heavy to carry by foot.

Another telling difference is that Kamen set up a new company for the Segway. For his earlier ventures, he licensed or sold technology to major health care companies, including Johnson & Johnson and Baxter, firms that then assumed control over production, marketing, sales, and distribution. Standing astride a Segway before a crowd of budding entrepreneurs at the Harvard Business School, Kamen revealed his ambitions:

> The reason why we uncharacteristically decided to build a whole company around this thing wasn't because I thought in the end we can make a lot more money—because we will; we'll see—but because I really couldn't see spending years of my life developing something which would turn out to be a scooter. People know I get offended when this thing is referred to as a scooter.[4]

Expecting explosive demand, he built a 75,000-square-foot factory near his home and office in Manchester, New Hampshire, that is capable of making at least 40,000 units a month.

As CEO of the Segway, Kamen's role had shifted from that of inventor to that of general manager. It was new territory. Whereas he had previously worked with engineers who loved his manic personality, mesmerizing talent, and workaholic ethos, now he also had to manage functional managers with very different skills, aspirations, and expectations. Kamen and his engineers had looked down their noses at functional managers and their lack of technical expertise. Now, Kamen had to make judgment calls on functional matters ranging from production requirements to public relations, and these were decisions for which he lacked basic experience and training. His decision-making rule seemed to be that if the product was brilliant, everything else would take care of itself. After all, getting business functions right is hardly rocket science, relative to designing breakthrough, self-balancing technologies. Right?

Regarding the Segway's safety on sidewalks, for instance, Kamen took the position that "if they ban them because they're too fast, we'll go slower and say we're not like that. And if they don't ban them, great. *Either way, we can't lose.*"[5] Did that logic blind him to the prospect that the Segway could be banned from sidewalks *regardless* of its speed? If so, did that also mean his firm was ill prepared to lobby regulators and take other actions to counter the opposition?

Kamen the general manager also had to forecast and manage demand in order to establish manufacturing capacity, manage inventory, and build an appropriate sales force. Large clients for his previous inventions had based sales forecasts on the number of sick and disabled users in targeted markets. This time, Kamen took control of forecasting demand—for a radically new product that was opening up a totally new market. Lacking marketing skills (and a healthy respect for those who had them), Kamen dismissed market research—including test marketing and field projects with trial customers that could reveal unexpected outcomes—with unassailable confidence. Perhaps it was self-evident to him that police forces would buy Segways to help officers issue parking tickets, postal offices would provide them to mail carriers, delivery companies would use them to deliver parcels in congested areas, and online distribution companies would use them to pick warehouse items. When pressed, Kamen relied on these assumptions to forecast that the Segway would sell between 50,000 to 100,000 units at $3,000 apiece in the product's first year. Based on these forecasts, he invested hundreds of millions of dollars in infrastructure to support the projected demand, including a state-of-the-art manufacturing facility.

By all appearances, this was Kamen's time in the limelight, and the Segway would be his passport to celebrity. *Wired* magazine labeled him a "breakout artist," CBS's *60 Minutes* called him the "Next Big Thing," and he had even appeared in *Vanity Fair,* rubbing shoulders with Hollywood stars. On ABC's *Good Morning America,* Kamen invited his audience to liken his work to the Wright brothers' invention of the aircraft. Now he could bask in the warm glow of believing his own glorious press.

Being a celebrity entrepreneur had its benefits. With some of America's preeminent financiers—First Boston on Wall Street and Kleiner Perkins Caufield and Byers (KPCB) on Sand Hill Road in

Silicon Valley—beating a path to his door, Kamen could play one off against the other. Thanks to introductions from John Doerr, the lead partner at KPCB, Kamen now rubbed shoulders with the likes of Amazon's Jeff Bezos and Apple's Steve Jobs. Jobs told him that the Segway was the most amazing piece of technology since the personal computer, and he validated Kamen's judgment that the Segway would sell itself: "I don't worry about the big idea because if enough people see the machine, you won't have to convince them to architect cities around it. People are smart and it'll happen. That's the story of the PC." [6]

Bezos was also ebullient, although he did make an offhand mention of one potential problem facing the Segway: "You have a product so revolutionary, you'll have no problem selling it. The question is, are people going to be allowed to use it?" [7]

Doerr is presently in the twilight of a brilliant investing career. Having funded some of the great technology businesses of recent times, including Amazon and Google, he deflects ventures with limited potential, even if they can generate attractive percentage returns. Now he looks for entrepreneurs with revolutionary visions and capabilities—and Dean Kamen fit the profile. In fact, Doerr told Kamen that the Segway would reach $1 billion in sales faster than any company before it, which would value the Segway at tens of billions of dollars.

Exploring the Limits of the Segway's Success

At least some of this confidence has been justified: At this writing, the Segway has beaten the odds of venture failure. It is a remarkable, almost miraculous engineering feat, a tribute to Kamen's prodigious ability, confidence, and energy. The Segway earned Kamen the Lemelson–Massachusetts Institute of Technology prize, arguably the most prestigious worldwide award for inventors. Today, policeman use it to reinforce security, European yuppies ride it in congested cities, wealthy golfers cart their clubs on it, and Disney executives ride it around theme parks.

Yet these limited applications also highlight the Segway's failure to meet expectations. Needless to say, it will not do to the car what the car did to the horse and buggy. Early sales remain anemic as people resist paying the $5,000 price tag, even while energy prices soared. Sales to larger accounts—the U.S. Postal Office, Federal Express, and universities—have been slow. In its first year, the firm's largest customer was Disney, which bought fewer than 50 units for its theme parks and cruise ships. The New Hampshire facility operates below capacity, a hollow reminder of Kamen's grandiose expectations and unwillingness to take advice. Although the Segway remains one of Doerr and KPCB's largest single investments, you won't find it mentioned on KPCB's Web site alongside other featured "portfolio companies."

In fact, in September 2003, the Segway was forced into a product recall with its Web site reporting that "under certain operating conditions, particularly when the batteries are near the end of charge, some Segway HTs may not deliver enough power, allowing the rider to fall. This can happen if the rider speeds up abruptly, encounters an obstacle, or continues to ride after receiving a low-battery alert."[8] The good news was that the recall only affected 6,000 transporters; the bad news was that the firm was supposed to have shipped up to 100,000. Then in August 2006, Kamen told *Time* magazine that he would sell 6 million Segways, reasoning that this was only 0.1 percent of the world's population. Weeks later, the firm announced another recall for all 23,600 Segways that have been sold.

Did Kamen's excessive pride result in false confidence that hurt the Segway? Did his commitment to leaving a footnote in history cloud the judgment needed to make the Segway a market success? We must wonder why Kamen gets offended when outsiders call the Segway a "scooter" or "golf caddie," especially if that needlessly stopped salespeople from targeting the product at those customer groups. We can also ask whether Kamen's need for control led to the unnecessary investment in the New Hampshire facility, which has seriously eroded the business's capital base, when out-sourcing was a viable option.

Perhaps Kamen is also unwilling to seek the advice of trusted advisors. He has been unable to build and sustain a strong senior management team. Three highly paid and seasoned CEOs have come and gone in quick succession, amid frustrations at Kamen's need to micromanage—by his need to approve minor expenses and second-guess numerous functional decisions. Until recently, he has been reluctant to pay what talented managers deserve, making it harder to attract and retain them. Delegating does not come easily to him, especially when it comes to getting help to formulate the firm's strategy. And he bristles at paying for out-side help, including professional services firms that he has char-acterized as "pretentious" and "useless."[9]

We can also question whether Kamen has truly considered whether he's the best person to launch and grow the Segway. The skills needed to forge a successful go-to-market strategy and man-agement team are not those needed to create a sophisticated invention. Here, we can compare Kamen's experience with that of one of his heroes, Sir Isaac Newton. By defining the laws of motion, Newton emerged as the most brilliant mathematician and physicist of his time, if not all time. Falsely confident that his genius would translate into other fields, like investing, Newton lost a fortune in a speculative trading company, only later to decry, "I can calculate the movement of the stars, but not the madness of men." Just as Newton's scientific genius didn't guarantee his skills in investing, Kamen's genius, too, has its limitations.

Finally, did Kamen rigorously consider the consequences and implications of his judgment, and did he fully examine the condi-tions in which he could be wrong? I ask because the firm did not respond to growing evidence of regulatory and customer resis-tance to the product. Steve Kemper had deep access to Kamen while he was reporting on the development of the Segway from 1999 to 2001. In his 2003 book, *Code Name Ginger*, Kemper con-cluded that Kamen ". . . can bend reality to fit his vision. If current reality doesn't suit him, he changes it. That's his habit of mind, his gift; yet it can warp into a self-protective flaw." [10]

As we have seen, the answers to these questions can help to determine whether executives exhibit the false sources of confidence that can produce hubris. Managing each of these issues is a balancing act, one that executives often attempt on a high wire without a safety net. On the one hand, Kamen's supreme and unwavering confidence that the Segway would be a revolutionary product helped bring the invention successfully through product development. On the other hand, it may also have given way to false confidence in his management capabilities, helping to explain why the Segway is yet to realize its still fabulous potential.

Much of the Segway's future rides on whether Kamen can better assess his managerial capabilities or get out of the way. Under pressure from investors, it now looks like present CEO James Norrod has greater discretion to run the business. Time has yet to tell whether this change will cause a turnaround in the company's fortunes.

Betting on Success: How Other Entrepreneurs Bank on Beating the Odds

Kamen is just one example of how entrepreneurs' supreme confidence spurs new ventures, and how it also leads to decisions that hurt if not destroy their ventures. It also helps to explain why so many entrepreneurs start new ventures when the odds or base rates of failure are so overwhelmingly high. Data from the U.S. Small Business Administration shows that well over 600,000 new ventures are founded in the United States each year.

In spite of this activity, between two-thirds and three-quarters of all these new ventures fail within five years of starting, depending on the nature and timing of the venture's founding. Given that venture failure carries enormous financial, social, and emotional costs to entrepreneurs and their colleagues and families, why would anyone want to start a venture? When you pose that question to entrepreneurs, they invariably tell you that they can beat those odds.

An earlier mentioned study surveyed 2,994 entrepreneurs by asking them how confident they were in their venture's prospects and found that 81 percent of respondents said the likelihood their ventures would succeed was over 70 percent.[11] Moreover, fully one-third of those entrepreneurs replied that there was zero chance their venture would fail; for them, the likelihood that *their* venture would succeed was the same as the sun rising in the morning.

Overconfident entrepreneurs provide a great service to our economy. With their unwavering persistence, persuasion, and passion, they boldly start and persist with ventures that more conservative executives won't touch. They might fail the first time, but in the process they can develop the relationships and knowledge that help them to subsequently form a more successful venture.

Ironically, however, entrepreneurs' confidence in their ventures contributes to their failure in at least two ways. First, because they exaggerate their own capabilities, they also underestimate the outside resources they need—they don't raise enough capital. And because they believe that they are on to a surefire thing, they spend what little capital they have too quickly. One entrepreneur who spent more than $20 million trying to launch a Web-based business told a Stanford professor, "Looking back on it, my judgment was often terribly wrong . . . I was never in doubt."[12] No wonder leading venture capital firms, like KPCB, reserve the right to replace founders with seasoned managers (the Segway was somewhat different because Kamen's celebrity gave him more influence over financiers).

Kamen's story illustrates the ways that false confidence affects the fate of new ventures. And for those of us who are not entrepreneurs, false confidence affects how we manage our own and our firm's money. So let's next consider how false confidence affects our investment decisions, and what we can do about it.

FALSE CONFIDENCE IN INVESTING

There is considerable evidence that the pattern of overconfidence found in entrepreneurs seems also to extend to personal investing. In particular, people *over*estimate their investing abilities, and at the same time, systematically *under*estimate their need for money, leading to property foreclosures and inadequate retirement savings.

A recent study based on phone interviews with 1,250 workers suggests that most Americans believe that they will retire comfortably, even if they are not saving enough to make that a reality.[13] The 2006 Retirement Confidence Survey conducted by the Employee Benefit Research Institute concluded that roughly one-quarter of all executives say they are "very confident" that they can retire comfortably. The survey also concluded that "22 percent of very confident workers are not currently saving for retirement, 39 percent have less than $50,000 in savings, and 37 percent have not done a retirement needs calculation." False confidence translates into underestimating the amount of money we need for retirement, which materializes as hubris when we do retire.

Concerning such confidence as investors, researchers from the University of California, Berkeley, studied the performance of 66,465 households who held accounts with a large brokerage firm.[14] On average, the investors in this sample bought and sold shares excessively, selling up to 75 percent of their investments in a given year. And those 12,000-plus accounts that traded the most also experienced the worst performance, by underperforming returns from stock market indices by 6.5 percent.

After carefully considering other explanations for these findings, the Berkeley researchers concluded that overconfidence explains excessive trading. Because we overestimate our investing ability, we sense that we have more investing opportunities than we do, and so trade too much. In this study, men and women were both overconfident, but men were more so and achieved lower investment returns (further analysis of these data showed that

men trade 45 percent more than women, incurring greater brokerage costs and giving their investments less time to work out).[15]
Nevertheless, fund managers are still overwhelmingly men.

Faced with the choice between remaining overconfident and
heeding the wisdom of professional investors, we tend to choose
the former. Consider this advice from legendary investors[16]:

- Warren Buffett, CEO of Berkshire Hathaway: ". . . the best
  way to own common stocks is through an index fund."
- Peter Lynch, stellar portfolio manager at Fidelity's flagship
  Magellan Fund: "Most investors would be better off in an
  index fund."
- Charles Schwab, CEO of Charles Schwab & Co.: "Most of the
  mutual fund investments I have are index funds, approxi-
  mately 75 percent."
- Daniel Kahneman, Nobel laureate in economics, was asked:
  "So investors shouldn't delude themselves about beating
  the market?" Says Kahneman: "They're just not going to do
  it. It's just not going to happen."

One might think that portfolio managers of mutual funds who
invest for a living have an unfair advantage (more experience,
information, and so on) that allows them to beat the market. Not
so. Most portfolio managers do not outperform funds that track
market indices, such as the Standard & Poor's 500 and the Nasdaq
100. Figure 2.1 shows the percentage of actively managed mutual
funds that underperformed the S&P 500 since 2001, highlighting
that on balance such funds underperform the index on a one-year
and five-year basis.

A provocative study written up in the *Wall Street Journal* tried to
examine the affects of removing pride from our investing decisions.[17] This study identified two samples of people. One consisted
of people with average IQs whose brains can normally perform
logic and cognitive reasoning. The other was designed to replicate
the first in every respect except that people in this sample had

FIGURE 2.1 *Percent of Large Capitilization Fund That Are Outperformed by the S&P 500 Index, 2001–2005*

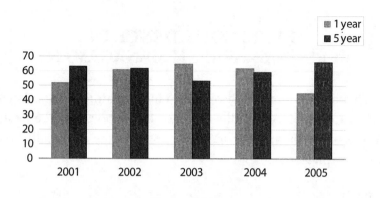

Sources: 2001, Burton Malkiel; 2002–2005, Standard & Poor's

lesions in the section of the brain that controls emotions, including pride. Researchers then asked members of each sample to participate in an investing game, with interesting results. Because members of the second sample were less likely to react emotionally to losses and gains, they were less likely to trade. In the end, this group completed the game with 13 percent more money than people in the first sample.

Don't be unduly alarmed by these results: You don't have to have brain lesions or be emotionally impaired to be a better investor! Results from the study are consistent with the view that people who learn how to manage their pride make better financial decisions than others under certain circumstances. Investing in an index fund or a fund controlled by computer algorithms are obvious ways of removing pride and other emotions from the process of investment.

Overall, most of us seem to think that we're blessed with above average investing skills—which is, of course, mathematically impossible. In that sense, we're not unlike the inhabitants of Garrison Keillor's fictional town, Lake Wobegon, where "all the women are strong, all the men are good-looking, and all the children are above average."

FALSE CONFIDENCE IN PERSONAL HEALTH MANAGEMENT

The same tendency is also evident in our attitudes toward managing our health. And beliefs that we have above-average health and the overestimation of our ability to manage our health have serious implications.

Underestimating Our Health Risks

Many of us believe, for example, that we're less at risk to a range of diseases and negative health outcomes (food poisoning and cancer) than others. For instance, when researchers asked adolescent boys about how confident they are that they can use condoms properly, most boys had a level of confidence that far exceeded their actual knowledge. Another study showed that almost 90 percent of gay men not infected with HIV rate themselves as being at lower risk of becoming infected than other gay men.[18]

All this matters because we are more likely to relinquish bad health habits—smoking, boozing, overeating—when we accept, rather than underestimate, their risks. Moreover, as we grow more confident about our health and health-maintenance capabilities, we will tend to use common wisdom to determine why we are sick and what we should do—to play doctor, in other words. When we get sick, we resist medical help, sensing that the symptoms, ranging from sustained coughs to chest pains, will pass or won't matter. That makes us more reluctant to go to the doctor and otherwise take adequate health precautions. By mistaking chest pain for indigestion, we're less likely to get our hearts checked. By underestimating our vulnerability to cancer, we resist having routine cancer checks. And so on.

False Confidence in Our Ability to Diagnose and Cure Medical Problems

Sore throats are the second most common symptom that we can present to our doctors (after related upper respiratory symptoms of coughs and colds), and their management provides a fascinating case study in the operation of false confidence. Even though sore throats result from a number of causes, including trauma, cancer, and infections, by far the most common cause is infection. Consider the facts surrounding throat infections:

- Infections come in two principal varieties. Viral infections account for between 83 and 95 percent of all adult sore throats, depending on where we live and the time of the year. Bacterial infections that cause strep throat (short for *streptococcal pharyngitis*) essentially account for the rest.
- Generally, doctors cannot diagnose the type of throat infections through a casual analysis in their offices. Instead, they must take a culture from our throats and have this tested in a laboratory to confirm the presence of strep throat.
- Antibiotics—the major treatment for sore throats—can cure bacterial (such as strep throat) but not viral infections.
- Over-the-counter or no-prescription-required throat medicine treats the symptoms of colds and sore throats, but not the underlying infection. Once we finish sucking our throat lozenge, the mild anesthetic in the lozenge wears off and the discomfort usually resumes.
- In up to 90 percent of cases, people with sore throats feel better within two weeks, whether they are treated with antibiotics or not. A saying amongst some physicians is that "throat medicine makes your throat feel better within 2 weeks and doing nothing makes it feel better within 14 days."

We have three broad options for treating sore throats: (1) self-medicate with over-the-counter medicine, (2) visit a doctor, and (3) avoid conventional treatments by doing nothing or using alternative therapies. Though we lack data on the percentage of people that use these treatments, it's clear from the sales of over-the-counter throat medicine and the use of antibiotics for sore throats that millions of people choose the first two options.

Drug companies play on our propensity to spend billions of dollars to self-medicate by spending hundreds of millions of dollars to advertise over-the-counter throat medicines. Buying these drugs does not necessarily help us; there is no strong evidence that such drugs make us better. We often don't know whether they make us more susceptible to unwanted side effects, including increased blood pressure, dizziness, headaches, and rashes. We're unsure about dosage levels that are right for us, and it's unclear when symptoms warrant professional treatment. False confidence may be entering our decision to self-medicate to the extent that we exaggerate our ability to play doctor; we fail to get second, professional opinions; and we lack evidence and experience to update our choices based on our responses to the medicine.

Given these uncertainties, many people turn to the second option of getting professional help. The problem with doing this is that doctors prescribe antibiotics for all manner of sore throats. In fact, one study of 2,244 adults with sore throats in an 11-year period showed that physicians prescribed antibiotics in 73 percent of all cases.[19]

Overprescribing antibiotics would be fine if it cost nothing. But the more that patients use antibiotics, the less effective those antibiotics become. In some very rare cases, adverse reactions to antibiotics are devastating.[20] Economically, the global market for antibiotics is estimated at over $27 billion per annum; and at least some of that is spent unnecessarily on treating viral infections.[21]

Why do doctors overprescribe antibiotics for sore throats? Doctors are busy people and writing prescriptions can seem like a fast fix, reducing the time they must spend in consultation with an individual patient. Another explanation is that doctors don't want to prolong suffering among patients who really do have strep throat. Though rare, strep throat can trigger more serious problems. Finally, prescribing antibiotics does have limited potential to boost patients' confidence in their recovery, which can then promote actual recovery, much like a placebo effect.

Perhaps doctors also just want to give patients what they want, effectively treating patients as customers. Results of a British study of 24 doctors showed that they knew that prescribing antibiotics was the wrong therapy, but did so anyway because they wanted "to maintain a good connection with those patients, and to respect their choices, to please them."[22]

Each of these explanations matters. What they miss is the role that confidence plays in doctors' diagnoses. Psychologists tested for this explanation by examining 114 cases of strep throat that were diagnosed by general physicians. Researchers asked those doctors how confident they were in their diagnosis. Results showed that doctors believed that they had made the right diagnosis on 50 (44 percent of all) cases. Subsequent laboratory analysis, however, revealed that only 25 of these cases (22 percent) were in fact correctly diagnosed. Doctors in this limited sample were twice as confident as they should have been in their diagnoses, prescribing antibiotics at twice the rate that was warranted.[23]

Obviously, overconfidence isn't the only reason doctors prescribe antibiotics for sore throats. The other explanations—cutting consultation time and appeasing patients—could even be more important. Overall, however, if doctors were acting on the best available evidence rather than false confidence, they would tell patients that (1) their sore throats are either viral or bacterial based, (2) the type cannot be determined by a casual throat inspection, and (3) a lab test would establish the right treatment should the symptoms persist.

Unfortunately, doctors' false confidence is not limited to their treatment of sore throats. One study showed that doctors who diagnosed 1,531 patients with pneumonia were 88 percent confident in their diagnosis, when only 20 percent of those patients actually had pneumonia.[24] Another study showed that surgical residents systematically overestimate their surgical skills relative to their performance on standardized medical tests or "boards."[25] In a third study, general physicians overestimated their knowledge about thyroid disorders relative to their performance on a quiz on the topic.[26]

Why are doctors overconfident? More confident professionals do tend to be more persuasive, which gives them more influence over clients and patients. When doctors purport to have all the answers, patients are less likely to question them, and when they express doubt, patients want to know why.

To take an extreme case, one Californian cardiologist, Dr. Chae Hyun Moon, who excessively recommended heart bypass surgery, relied on his supreme confidence to disarm patients' resistance to surgery and requests for second opinions. Boasting about how he built his heart program, he told one concerned 74-year-old patient with no prior history of heart disease, "How dare you get a second opinion!"[27] Another patient, Tom Mitchell, remembers how Moon diagnosed evidence from a routine heart check that was prompted by an emergency appendectomy: "He said, 'See that hanging down right there? That's a widow maker.' And he said, 'That could slough off and you would have a heart attack immediately . . . . You are here. So why don't we take care of it?'"[28] Jay Bradley, a 35-year-old father of three who luckily avoided surgery after a nurse's tip-off, remembers how Moon "put the monitor in front of my face, showed me a little artery on there, and said, 'Well, this is clogged, and this one's the top front of your heart and *there's zero chance of survival.*'"[29] (italics added)

How Doctors Sustain and Extend False Confidence

What sustains this type of practice is a process that psychologists call *cognitive dissonance*. Let's say that a doctor learns that his or her diagnosis or treatment was wrong. At that point, the doctor must decide to accept the mistake and not repeat it, or to justify his or her decisions and actions. The first choice requires that doctors confront their failings. The second, more common choice of justification leads them down the slippery slope to the false confidence that produces hubris. Cognitive dissonance, the process of rationalizing mistakes, ensures that a doctor's false confidence can extend to other areas of his or her practice.

At issue is that many doctors receive limited feedback from peers and patients, which allows them to sustain the errors and effects of false confidence. Psychiatrists, for example, often express complete confidence in their diagnosis of mental illness (e.g., bipolar disorder) when such diagnosis is open to interpretation and cannot easily be proven to be wrong. There is precious little evidence that psychiatrists seek second opinions. And rather than update their diagnoses, they can fall back on limited disclosure of patient treatments and, as a last resort, medical malpractice insurance.

Overall, the manner in which doctors approach symptoms that they are largely unable to cure (the common cold, sore throats, back pain, many forms of cancer, and so on) bears many of the hallmarks of false confidence that infects us with hubris:

- Excessive pride drives doctors to seek and sustain authority over patients by overestimating their own ability to diagnose and treat them.
- Doctors rarely defer to colleagues in their specialty by getting and relying on second opinions from them.
- Doctors often fail to adjust their treatments for evidence at hand, relying instead on their training and personal experience with successful procedures.
- And doctors often fail to help patients understand the potential consequences of their decisions by fully informing them about the risks of taking medicine with highly questionable therapeutic benefits.

Because each of these dynamics is endemic to doctors' interactions with patients, they work to quietly shape a culture of false confidence and hubris. The implications are not trivial: Patients have suffered, and sometimes died, from counterproductive surgeries, and billions of dollars are being spent on unnecessary medicine and procedures that could be directed toward treatments with proven therapeutic benefits.

FALSE CONFIDENCE IN EDUCATION MANAGEMENT

So far this chapter has addressed how overconfidence and hubris are rooted in how we manage ventures, investments, and health. Education is another crucial arena in which overconfidence surfaces: If teachers train students to have false confidence in their subjects, their students could conceivably enter the workforce with such biases.

College students are often overconfident from the outset. In the 1970s, the U.S. College Board surveyed 1 million high school seniors. Students were asked to assess their leadership abilities relative to peers. Results included that (1) 70 percent believed that they had above-average leadership skills, and only 2 percent thought that their leadership skills were below average; (2) 60 percent of the students thought they were above the median in terms of athletic ability, and only 6 percent below; and (3) 60 percent of students thought that they were in the top 10 percent of all students in terms of their ability to get along with others.[30] Don't chalk this up to the false confidence of youth. These findings are compatible with how college professors rate themselves—relative to their peers, 94 percent say they are above-average teachers.[31]

Training Students to Have False Confidence in What They Know

Large classrooms that teach big numbers of students in a limited number of intense sessions are nurseries for false confidence.

With government funding for higher education under pressure, this oversized classroom format is increasingly the norm worldwide. Larger class sizes force teachers to use multiple-choice questionnaires and other mass assessment techniques that encourage students to memorize and quickly regurgitate facts, rather than to apply problem-solving techniques to grasp the underlying concepts. The environment is akin to driving tests and other standardized mass instruction exercises that force students to memorize and quickly reproduce reams of procedures.

While mass training can be effective at helping people to quickly learn and recite new knowledge and skills, the learning does not stick. Worse, such training tends to convince students that they are more competent than they are. When instruction gives students confidence in their skills, but little experience in exercising those skills, the students' confidence will probably outpace their competence.

Grade Inflation and False Confidence in Higher Education

Perhaps a more impactful and telling source of students' false confidence is grade inflation or the tendency for professors to give students a better grade than they deserve. For a variety of reasons, grade inflation is overwhelmingly pervasive in higher education, at least in the United States. A nationwide survey of 80 schools with an undergraduate enrolment of over 1 million students since the mid-1960s shows that grade point averages have been consistently rising across private and public universities (see *www.gradeinflation.com* for a school-by-school breakdown).

Curiously, grade inflation is particularly rife at elite universities. Public awareness of this trend flared in 2001 when Harvard's Dean of Undergraduate Education and History Professor, Susan Pedersen, reported that nearly half of the grades issued the year before were As or A minuses.[32] Only a third of the grades were A or A minus in 1985, and there is no reason to believe that students in the class of 1985 were somehow inferior to those in the class of 2001. Likewise evidence from Northwestern University's McCormick School of Engineering and Applied Sciences shows that 48 percent of grades are A or A minus; and 86 percent of grades are either an A or B.[33] Failing grades are virtually nonexistent at many fine American universities.

The problem with grade inflation is that it gives students an inflated view of what they know and what they can do. This can create an atmosphere in which students expect good grades without much effort. Around the hallways of my college, for example, I sometimes hear students boast, "I didn't do any work but still got a B." Marginal students may be getting college degrees, even advanced ones, when their time and skills may be better served in the workforce. Meanwhile, exemplary students have to struggle to distinguish themselves from the pack and get the jobs that they deserve. Students who are exposed to grade inflation may enter the workforce with a less committed and less resourceful work ethic (and "grade" inflation is also alive and well in performance reviews conducted at the workplace, as we'll see in Chapter 5).

Grade inflation is rampant in part because it promotes a self-perpetuating dynamic between professors and students. Professors who don't engage in grade inflation risk receiving worse evaluations from students than those who do. So rather than become more accountable for their teaching, professors can resort to giving students good grades—I'll scratch your back with a good grade if you scratch mine with a nice teaching evaluation. Harvey Mansfield, a professor of government at Harvard and a longtime critic of grade inflation, writes:

> I have seen my grades dragged gradually higher over the years, while still trailing the rising average. I could not ignore the pressure to meet student expectations that other faculty members have created and maintained, but I did not want just to go along silently.[34]

His solution is to give two sets of grades: One for the registrar and the public record, and another as a private record between him and the student. The implication is that "the private grades, from the course assistants and me, will be less flattering. Those grades will give students a realistic, useful assessment of how well they did and where they stand in relation to others."[35]

I present evidence on grade inflation to highlight how false confidence permeates our educational system. My hope is that students and professors will treat inflated grades for what they are and will work harder to establish more accurate scholastic performance. Moreover, false confidence will continue to thrive amongst those entering the work place so long as colleges and universities persist in offering large class sizes and allowing grade inflation. After all, false confidence that emerges from our education system is also likely to surface in how we manage our wealth and health.

SUMMARY

This chapter has highlighted just a few of the many ways in which our approach to wealth, health, and education causes over-confidence to take root, spread, and calcify throughout our society. Here are some general principles that we've touched on in this chapter:

- Evidence from entrepreneurs, investors, health care workers, and educators suggests that we tend to neglect information about base rates of failure, thinking that we'll succeed on difficult tasks where others fail.
- We use the process of cognitive dissonance to rationalize bad decisions. This process feeds false confidence and makes it more likely that we'll make overconfident decisions in the future.

- Entrepreneurs are generally overconfident about the prospective success of their ventures. Betting that they'll beat the odds, they tend to raise insufficient capital for their ventures and spend it too aggressively, including hubris.
- Investors experience hubris and overconfidence when they trade excessively in shares, fail to invest in index funds that track market performance, and put insufficient money aside for retirement.
- Doctors, like other professionals, make mistakes. When they do, they must resist the tendency to adapt their beliefs to make the mistake more palatable to them. We should expect our health care workers to identify and avoid the actions that produce errors. Doctors can help to avoid such errors by remaining informed about the extent to which they diagnose complaints relative to base rates, and their performance in diagnosing and treating patients relative to peers.
- As patients, we should curb our tendency to "play doctor." When we visit doctors, we should question them about their confidence in their diagnosis and treatment. If doctors make a major diagnosis or recommend a material treatment, especially surgery, we must *always* get a second opinion.
- Grade inflation causes students' confidence to outpace their competence. It demotivates both stronger and weaker students.
- Candid teacher-to-student evaluations are one method for educated people to attain better judgment about their competencies. Through better and more meaningful feedback, we can better match our confidence in our abilities to our true abilities.

Each of these principles touches on the false sources of confidence: letting pride enter our decisions, failing to get out of the way or get the right help, failing to incorporate positive and negative feedback, and failing to incorporate the consequences of our decision in our decisions. The following chapters examine each of these sources in turn, since the more effective we are at managing them, the more authentic our confidence will become, improving our judgment and actions.

3

Getting Too Full
of Ourselves

HOW EXCESSIVE PRIDE
FUELS EXECUTIVE HUBRIS

*"Vanity and pride are different things, though the words are
often used synonymously. A person may be proud without being vain.
Pride relates more to our opinion of ourselves; vanity,
to what we would have others think of us."*

JANE AUSTEN, *Pride and Prejudice*

The previous chapter highlighted a culture of false confidence
and hubris that pervades our approach to managing wealth,
health, and education. When we allow false confidence to guide
our decisions in those critical areas, we are likely to feel its effects
in our professional judgment, as well. Having explored the implications of executive hubris, it's important now to examine its
sources, so that we can better manage it.

And perhaps the most potent source of false confidence is our
pride, which is the focus of this chapter. Pride refers to how we
appreciate and respect ourselves, and excessive pride arises when
we purport to be more than we are or someone who we are not. As
Jane Austen flagged, it can get a bad name when it is confused with
other things, including vanity. The saying that "pride comes
before a fall" often refers to people who decide and speak overconfidently only to learn that they're not quite as "right" as they
think they are.

And yet, authentic pride is indispensable in the workplace; it helps us feel good about our work and drives us to excel. To take pride in our work—enabling colleagues through thoughtful feedback, providing value for customers, sharing best practices, and so on—is to appreciate who we are and what we have done, without any need for external confirmation or approval. Authentic pride enables us to appreciate, rejoice in, and even celebrate our achievements and capabilities in meaningful ways. "Our people put a great deal of energy into the things that ultimately become the big accomplishments in our business," says Michael Dell of Dell Inc. "Acknowledging their achievements reinforces the value that they bring to our company and emphasizes how much we appreciate their efforts."[1]

Quite simply, firms that don't instill a sense of pride in their people cannot get the best out of them. Our pride serves as an internal compass that tells us when and whether we are realizing our potential; and, when managed well, pride is a powerful source of competitive advantage. The danger is that authentic pride—based on real achievements and emotions—can quickly degenerate into excessive pride. Excessive pride, which reflects an exaggerated notion of our strengths and capabilities, is the first of four sources of false confidence, and one that we'll examine in detail here.

In particular, this chapter elaborates on how the pride of Apple Computer's key leaders, Steve Jobs and John Sculley, shaped the fortunes (and misfortunes) of that firm. First, let's take a closer look at the different forms of pride we all feel, so we can better recognize excessive pride at work in ourselves and others.

UNDERSTANDING THE SOURCES AND NATURE OF EXCESSIVE PRIDE

The type of pride that we experience gets shaped by two main drivers. The first is the extent to which we are extrinsically motivated by the outcomes of our work (impressing others, getting rich, gaining power, and so forth) versus intrinsically motivated by the merit and processes of the work itself. The second is the extent to which the data we use to appreciate ourselves is objective or self-serving. This means that two principal forces result in *excessive* pride:

1. We can unduly tie our sense of self to the outcomes of our work, especially other people's expectations of us—giving our pride what we'll call an *extrinsic locus of control.*
2. We can develop excessive pride by basing our own sense of satisfaction on *self-serving data*—in effect, interpreting data to feel better about ourselves.

We all receive pleasure and pain from how others perceive and respond to us. When taken too far, however, that tendency gives others control over our pride. Playing to others' aspirations and expectations makes us characters in their play. Before long we become inauthentic, rudderless, and self-destructive. Picture the junior manager who is so committed to pleasing his boss that he loses touch with who he is and what he can contribute. Picture the owner of a company who is so determined to prove that a competitor is wrong that he takes legal action, even when counsel tells him that he cannot win. Or the downfall of a senior manager with an insatiable and self-destructive need for the power, prestige, and perquisites of a celebrity leader.

We can also be fuelled by excessive pride when our appreciation for our achievements and capabilities reflects self-serving data. Very often we interpret our success in one domain to mean that we will be successful in another. In the process of feeling better about ourselves, we tend to overstate what we have done and what we can do. One overstatement leads to another, driving us toward a false sense of pride. Picture newly hired junior executives who performed so well at college that think they have all the answers at your firm; or the football player who places himself

FIGURE 3.1 *Differentiating between Pride and Overweening Pride*

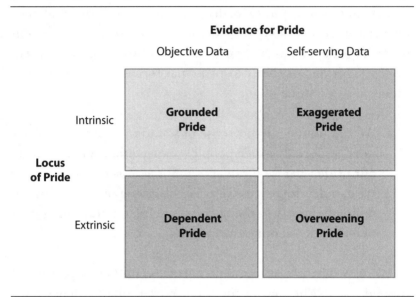

Evidence for Pride

Objective Data   Self-serving Data

	Grounded Pride	Exaggerated Pride
Intrinsic		

Locus of Pride

	Dependent Pride	Overweening Pride
Extrinsic		

above his team, and gets shown the door for his arrogance and lack of teamwork.

Figure 3.1 shows how these factors can differentiate authentic pride from the three types of excessive pride—exaggerated, dependent, and overweening. The vertical axis of this matrix represents the locus of our pride, which is determined by the extent to which our pride derives from internal or external assessments of our capabilities and achievements. The horizontal axis represents the evidence about our work and performance that supports our pride—in other words, whether that pride is authentically grounded in objective data or based on self-serving data.

Obviously, our objective should be to have and convey *grounded pride,* to intrinsically appreciate ourselves and colleagues based on the best available evidence of what we are doing. One form of excessive pride, *dependent pride,* arises when our pride depends on future outcomes rather than present work, including how we want others to perceive us. *Exaggerated pride,* arises when we have an intrinsic locus of pride, but base that pride on self-serving data about our performance, say, because we believe what we want to rather than what the facts tell us. *Overweening pride,* the expressway to hubris, arises when our sense of pride is driven by potential outcomes, including how we want others to perceive us, and is supported by self-serving data about our performance. Hitler, Mussolini, Napoleon, Nero, and Stalin all coveted grandiose empires that would serve as everlasting monuments to their greatness. Fixated on unsustainable ambitions, they each became delusional about the state of their empires and leadership.

Business has seen more than its fair share of overweening pride. As we'll see in Chapter 7, Jean-Marie Messier of Vivendi in France made a series of destructive acquisitions after becoming delusional about the state of his business and the strength of his management. Bernie Ebbers, former CEO of the major telecommunications services firm, WorldCom, knowingly overstated his firm's financial position to sustain his empire. Jeff Skilling of Enron is a notorious example of the dangerous effects of overweening pride.

Unfortunately, overweening pride exercises an almost gravitational pull on people who rise to positions of power. In my research, I've seen how quickly executives move from authentic pride to overweening pride, and we'll see further evidence of the destructive power of overweening pride at the end of this chapter.

For now, let's look at how the dynamics behind the different forms of pride have played out for Steve Jobs and John Sculley— two leaders who have been most influential in shaping the fortunes of Apple Computer.

APPLE COMPUTER, INC.:
A CASE STUDY OF EXCESSIVE PRIDE

Riding the success of the iPod, Apple is presently enjoying unprecedented success with a market value of nearly $50 billion. It's easy to forget that it hasn't always been that way. Witness the

FIGURE 3.2 *Apple Share Price Performance, 1985 to June 2006*

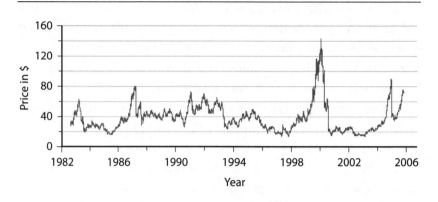

Source: Center for Research in Security Prices

rollercoaster ride that is the firm's share price performance since 1980, as shown in Figure 3.2.

Steve Jobs, current CEO of the company, also was CEO until 1985, when he was fired. Another one-time Apple CEO, John Sculley, oversaw the successful development of the Mac from 1985 to 1990, and then continued to run the company until he was fired in 1993. Jobs returned to lead the firm in 1997, rejuvenating the Mac and launching the iPod. To better understand the role of excessive pride in the wildly varying successes of Apple, recall Steve Jobs's part in this incredible story.

Steve Jobs and the Limits of His Genius

Born in 1955, Jobs is a genius at developing and integrating the critical elements that comprise a successful computer and electronics firm. He has an uncanny ability to know what retail customers covet ahead of time; he has exquisite taste for the design of those products; he knows how to assemble the technology and motivate the team to bring hit products to market; and his charisma and resourcefulness help make him exceptionally persuasive. When Jobs has found the right time and place to unleash that genius, he has been spectacularly successful. When he has allowed his excessive pride to overtake his genius, however, he has experienced unmitigated failure.

Jobs's critics contend that his cofounder at Apple, the electronics wizard Steve Wozniak ("Woz"), really got Apple started. They point out that Jobs has never been able to build world-class hardware or write "mission critical" software. Fresh out of college, Jobs got a start at the video games company, Atari, only after exaggerating his work at Hewlett-Packard—which was to insert screws on an assembly line.[2] These critics also contend that Jobs failed to make a favorable impression at Atari, and enjoyed some headway there only after passing off Woz's work as his. They say that Jobs's only technical contribution to Apple's first commercial computer was the shape of its case.

Judging by these accounts, there is never any middle ground with Jobs: You either love his charisma and creativity or you hate his arrogance, impatience, and petulance. Jobs will call you a "bozo" or "cool," depending on your flair and technical talent. Either way, working with him means tolerating his impulsive shouting matches, his obnoxious and controlling (if not abusive) treatment of some colleagues and suppliers, and his tendency to rush to judgment.

All of that criticism may well be true, but it also misses the point by a very wide mark. Apart from his own prodigious ambition and talent, Jobs started Apple with nothing more than Woz's schematics—rudimentary designs for a simple circuit board for very basic computing. At the time, Jobs was 20 years old and had zero funding for his new business. In fact, Larry Ellison, who counts Jobs as his best friend, talks about a dinner party at which Intel's celebrated CEO, Andy Grove, called Jobs the "inventor of the personal computer industry."

Jobs and Woz were in the right place at the right time. Woz's fraternity was the Homebrew Computer Club, based in the Bay Area of California, where nerds rejoiced in discussing the arcane technical details of computing. Where Woz saw a chance to gleefully share schematics with fellow enthusiasts, Jobs saw dollar signs.

"Steve was the one who thought we could make money," recalls Woz. "I was the one who designed the computer. I was the one who had attended the Homebrew meetings and I had written the software, but Steve is the one who had the idea that we could sell the schematics."[3]

As the nerds strutted and vented at the Homebrew meetings, Jobs looked around for customers. Fortunately, the crowd included retailer Paul Terrell, who told Jobs that there was a market for assembled computers, but not the rough circuit boards that Jobs wanted to sell him. Blindingly persuasive, Jobs talked Terrell into buying 50 nonexistent Apple computers in a deal that was worth up to $30,000. Stunned by the magnitude of the deal, Woz recalls that "nothing in subsequent years was so great or unexpected."[4]

That deal was "great" because Jobs leveraged it to recruit other stakeholders. Somehow he persuaded one of Woz's Hewlett-Packard contacts to lend the pair money and convinced suppliers to extend 30 days' credit on $15,000 worth of parts. In 1976, Jobs famously turned his parents' garage into a low-budget assembly line and delivered Terrell his 50 Apple 1 machines—which, by the way, still needed a case, power supply, monitor, and keyboard. Incredibly, Terrell paid in full, even though the machines fell short of his original specifications.

Seizing the moment, Jobs enlisted more customers and suppliers, including a technology marketing guru, Regis McKenna; a wealthy financier, Mike Markkula; and a seasoned president, Michael Scott. Apple was on its way. The Apple 2, first launched in 1977, overcame many of the limitations of its predecessor to dominate the personal computer market. By 1981, the firm employed over 2,000 people, and held an initial public offering of shares that valued the company at over $2 billion. By 1983, the Apple 2 had an installed base of 1 million units, and Jobs and Woz were wealthy beyond their dreams.

By then, Steve Jobs was synonymous with Apple. He was its evangelist and superstar with the youthful, movie-star face of the personal computer industry, one that would twice adorn the cover of *Time* magazine.[5]

Not satisfied with the success of Apple 2, Jobs found another creative genius at Apple in Jef Raskin, and proceeded to hijack Raskin's pet project, the Macintosh. Wanting to protect the Mac team from Apple's other projects and burgeoning bureaucracy, Jobs set up a separate unit for developers. Committed to making the Mac the firm's flagship product, he gathered some of Apple's best people in the Mac development team and motivated them with tight deadlines and timely charisma. Better yet, Jobs famously found Xerox's graphical user interface and recognized its potential immediately. Sensing the interface's potential, Jobs insisted on putting it on the Mac with a mouse for ease of use, in spite of internal resistance.

With Jobs's forceful leadership and technology vision, the Mac was set to be another blockbuster hit. This time, though, Jobs's pride would block its progress and lead to his dismissal from the company that he built. To all appearances, the success of the Apple 2 had gone to Jobs's 25-year-old head, clouding his judgment in developing the Mac.

Jobs Loses First Rounds in a Bout of Overweening Pride

Jobs was, after all, Silicon Valley's Prince of Personal Computing, a crown that he needed to sustain with an unbeatable new product. With a growing sense of invincibility, Jobs contemptuously dismissed competitors in the personal computing market, including IBM and Microsoft. In the early 1980s, leading software developers, including Bill Gates, were falling over themselves to build applications for the Apple 2, which was considered to be the industry standard.

As far as Jobs was concerned, Gates was just another geek programmer with oversized glasses and a bad haircut—more a laughing stock than a serious competitor. Apple began supplying

Microsoft with the intellectual property that supported the graphical user interface software. When Microsoft kept asking for more
information, Jobs became suspicious and angry, and then went
ballistic at Gates. Summoning Gates from Seattle to Apple's offices
in Silicon Valley, Jobs confronted him with the allegation that he
was stealing Apple's secrets and demanded an explanation. In a
sign of things to come, Gates told Jobs that he saw things differ-
ently: "Well, Steve, I think there's more than one way of looking at
it. I think it's more like we both had this rich neighbor named
Xerox and I broke into his house to steal the TV set only to find
that you had already stolen it."[6]

Still underestimating Gates, Jobs struck a deal whereby
Microsoft could ship mouse-based software a year after the Mac
was launched. Subsequently, Apple filed a copyright lawsuit to
stop Microsoft from shipping such software, only for the presid-
ing judge to rule that Apple had given Microsoft a perpetual
license for the mouse-based interface. Microsoft may have been
able to develop its graphical user interface without Apple, but at
the same time, Jobs and Apple had unwittingly helped Microsoft
develop the most valuable franchise in the history of com-
merce—Windows.[7]

Although this matter would affect the course of the personal
computer industry, it was no more than a side issue within Apple
at that time. At center stage was the challenge of realizing Jobs's
overhyped expectations for the Mac. Consider that he predicted 5
million Macs would be sold within two years of the expected
launch date of May 1983. In the event, the Mac launched in January of 1984, and by September of 1985, the firm had shipped only
about 500,000 units.[8]

Jobs incorrectly believed that the Mac's form would triumph
over its limited functionality. To make the Mac more elegant, he
designed it as a closed box without expansion slots. That meant
that it could not be upgraded with memory and software applications; however, it included desktop publishing capabilities—the
graphics and other applications that enabled users to print flyers,

brochures, and newsletters. Making matters worse, Jobs over-looked the need to get developers the training, software, and other tools for writing much-needed applications that would increase demand for the Mac. Finally, the computer was hopelessly underpowered for more advanced applications. Developers and customers dismissed it as a toy.

Problems with the Mac exposed growing concerns about Jobs's judgment and controlling leadership style. Ignoring the negative feedback coming from the marketplace, Jobs continued to regard himself as the leading light of Silicon Valley and retained an unshakable belief that he was indispensable to the Mac. After all, Jobs *was* Apple. With friends like Mike Markkula on Apple's board of directors, it was inconceivable to him that he could be fired, which he was in 1985.

EXECUTIVE EGO
IN THE APPLE PARKING LOT

In his entertaining book of Apple anecdotes, *Revolution in the Valley,* software wizard and Jobs-admirer Andy Hertzfeld recounts many stories that epitomize how Jobs's exaggerated pride surfaced at Apple. In one such account, Hertzfeld writes that Apple executive Jean-Louis Gassée, who had just transferred from Paris to the firm's Cupertino, California, offices, was walking toward the building one day when Jobs whipped his silver Mercedes into the parking lot and parked it in a space reserved for the handicapped. According to Hertzfeld, "As Steve walked past him brusquely, Jean-Louis was heard to declare, to no one in particular, 'Oh, I never realized those spaces were for the *emotionally* handicapped!'" [9]

Overstating his ability, Jobs fell victim to exaggerated pride, and then to overweening pride as he desperately sought approval from Silicon Valley's leaders. Like a protagonist in a Greek tragedy, Jobs's early success blinded him to the prospect of failure. In 2005, while giving the commencement speech to Stanford University's graduating class, he relived the surprise and pain of being fired by Apple's board. "How can you get fired from a company you started?" Jobs asked rhetorically. Jobs went on to tell the class that Apple hired someone to help him run the company, and that eventually the two clashed. ". . . our visions of the future began to diverge and eventually we had a falling out," Jobs said. "When we did, our board of directors sided with him. So, at 30 I was out. And very publicly out. What had been the focus of my entire adult life was gone, and it was devastating." [10] Of course, that "someone" was the man whom Jobs had handpicked and courted to become Apple's CEO—John Sculley.

Sculley Lands at Apple

Place yourself in the shoes of an ambitious and energetic young executive who has just graduated with an MBA from the Wharton School at the University of Pennsylvania. While many of your classmates select conventional careers in management consulting and investment banking, you opt for a career in marketing. You join a preeminent global consumer products company and quickly acquire an enviable reputation for translating your detailed knowledge about customers and competitors into analytically driven marketing skills.

Among other achievements, you help to transform an unprofitable international division into a highly profitable one, you design marketing campaigns that have since become textbook best practices, and you win market share from your arch competitor who owns one of the world's best-known brands. At 30, you become your company's youngest ever marketing vice president, at 34 you are lauded on the cover of *BusinessWeek* as a marketing whiz, and at 37 you are promoted to president of the company. You are probably next in line to become CEO.[11] The year is 1983, and you are John Sculley at PepsiCo.

Meanwhile, across the country, Silicon Valley and Apple are grabbing the headlines. Along with Gerry Roche of the premier head-hunting firm Heidrick and Struggles, Steve Jobs has been wooing you to become Apple's CEO. "Think of Silicon Valley as Florence in the Renaissance," says Roche. "It's the place where anybody who is excited about doing something to change the world wants to be."[12]

Fabulously charismatic and charming, Jobs disarms you with his legendary flattery, saying that you are one of the few people whom he could *possibly* learn from and work *for*. On a chilly Manhattan afternoon, you and he are chatting on the balcony of his Upper West Side Penthouse apartment. You are smitten by him. As only he can, Jobs poses a legendary question that stops you in your tracks: "Do you want to spend the rest of your life selling sugared water or do you want a chance to change the world?"[13]

Though Jobs may have considered the question of "chance" to be merely rhetorical, it was not. According to Roche, fewer than one out of five CEOs who move into a different industry succeed; and these odds lengthen considerably when the move is into the volatile technology industry.[14] For one thing, the new role required different skills. Soda drinks and snack foods have long shelf lives and quick inventory turnover, which allow them to be sold at high volumes into established retailers. By contrast, personal computers must be sold in lower volumes at higher prices with significant after-sales support. Near-continuous product development is critical just to stay competitive.

For another thing, Sculley would be entering an entirely different culture. Whereas he respected authority, Apple's irreverent wizards questioned it. Whereas Pepsi was run out of a stately corporate headquarters, Apple's headquarters looked more like a run-down university campus. Sculley excelled at formal meetings; Apple's get-togethers were like free-form rap sessions, complete with their own rock star. And, like many other superstars, Jobs had a reputation for being stubborn, uncompromising, and iconoclastic. Sculley could only have speculated about whether and how the two would get along. Finally, Sculley also knew that if he went to Apple and failed, he would burn his bridges back to Pepsi and corporate America.

If you were Sculley, what would you have done? When I present this scenario to executives, some see an irresistible opportunity, even when they know the outcome! Others say they would avoid it at all costs.

So it was that Jobs's famous question continued to eat at Sculley until Apple made the pie sweet enough for him to take the job in 1983. Initially, the decision looked propitious. At first, Jobs and Sculley got along fabulously. Sculley fondly recalls that he had "forged a friendship with a person I would come to think of as a friend, a younger brother, and even a teacher."[15] They became close professionally and socially, even buying the same model Mercedes and beaming in unison for the press. Jobs hosted a dinner party for Sculley, at which Sculley declared, "Apple has one leader, Steve and me." Sculley believed that he could make Jobs the "Henry Ford of the computer age," a reference to Ford's transformation of cars from "an expensive curiosity for the wealthy into a commodity for the masses."

Sculley Stumbles on Excessive Pride

Sculley's perception of the relationship was, "Sometimes, I felt as if I was watching Steve playing me in a movie. The similarities were uncanny, and they were behind the amazing symbiosis we developed."[16]

An alternative hypothesis was that Sculley was trying to play Jobs. Far from his East Coast roots, Sculley says that he began to see "technology through Steve's eyes," becoming dependent on Jobs's insights and validation. As a result, Sculley allowed Jobs's role to expand well beyond the Mac division, leaving Sculley to face the reality that "I had given Steve greater power than he had ever had and I had created a monster." Beholden to the monster, Sculley had lost touch with Apple's position in the marketplace—and his own job security. Having overestimated the strength of his personal and professional relationship with Jobs, Sculley became increasingly vulnerable to Jobs politically.

By the time Sculley surfaced for air, the Apple 2 was well past its shelf life, the Mac was an early bust, Jobs was lobbying to fire Sculley, and the firm was in a tailspin toward bankruptcy. Unaware of the extent of Apple's problems, Sculley had overconfidently borrowed $3 million to buy Apple's shares when they were trading at inflated prices. Now, with the stock price collapsing, Sculley was right on the brink of personal bankruptcy and professional ruin.[17]

It was a crisis that would bring out the best in him. Getting a grip on reality, Sculley made Apple's board of directors choose between him and Jobs. After they chose him, he diagnosed the Mac's problems and fixed them with a combination of product improvements and brilliant marketing. The Mac had its glory years under Sculley's leadership, returning Apple to its preeminent position in personal computing in the late 1980s. At first, Sculley's pride, his sense of achievement and satisfaction at Apple, was dependent on Jobs's view of him and the firm. After Jobs's departure from the company, Sculley used the realities of the Mac's limitations, his broken relationship with Jobs, and his superb marketing skills to ground his pride.

Overestimating Skills and Underestimating the Market

Sculley's marketing savvy helped him pull Apple from its slump in the mid-1980s. But although Sculley was brilliant at realizing the potential of a great product, he had neither the experience nor the talent for conceiving and developing breakthrough personal computers. And, rather than accept that limitation, and work around it by delegating those functions to trusted advisors,

Sculley wanted to fill the void that Jobs had left by becoming a technology visionary in his own right. Did a combination of excessive pride and invalid internal data place Sculley on a flight path from overweening pride to hubris?

Like Jobs, Sculley viewed Apple as a hardware company and so failed to unleash its world-class capabilities in operating systems, laser printing, and desktop publishing. By 1989, it was becoming obvious that Intel owned the industry standard processor for developing hardware and software applications. Nevertheless, Sculley inexplicably kept the Mac on Motorola's processors. As Intel's sales increased, developers were more motivated to produce applications for Intel-based machines, which further increased sales of Intel's processors, creating what was for Apple a vicious cycle.

Sculley's most conspicuous move was to bet the firm on a personal digital assistant (PDA) called the Newton. Sculley saw the Newton as a long-awaited chance to free himself and the firm from Jobs's legacy, and an opportunity to stamp his mark as a technology guru and visionary. Sculley reportedly projected that the PDA market could hit $3 trillion in sales within ten years, but in truth, the product launch was a disaster. Apple consultant Tim Bajarin laments the botched implementation of the Newton, calling it " . . . an astronomical miscalculation . . . . This went on to become a multi-billion-dollar market, and Apple had a chance to be the leader."[18]

Sculley now accepts that the "Newton was too ambitious technically, it was probably too open-ended, and it didn't try to anticipate what its applications would be."[19] Not only did he and the Newton team overestimate the demand for handwriting recognition capabilities, they couldn't get them to work anyway. Beyond technology problems, however, the Newton's marketing program was offtrack, as well. Newton project leader, Larry Tesler, had collected market research that showed that the best applications were for police, fire departments, and medical clinics. Rather than focus on those key customer groups, Sculley ambitiously sought a much broader launch. Ken Wirt, then the Newton's marketing vice president, recalls how the ". . . vision got bigger and bigger . . . . And, yet, the product was barely functional. I remember the night before it shipped . . . we were sitting on the floor patching the operating system."[20] At $699, the Newton was overpriced, its design was too bulky, and it was difficult to connect to a desktop computer.

Sculley did not have the stuff of a technology guru; and his seemingly insatiable desire to become one contributed to the Newton's death. Roche had warned him years earlier that very few leaders of more established East Coast businesses succeed as CEO of highly volatile technology companies. Nevertheless, Sculley anointed himself the firm's chief technology officer, which disgusted and demotivated Apple's developers and managers and prompted Andy Hertzfeld to call him "a total poseur." Jean-Louis Gassée, who ran Apple's French operation before Sculley promoted him to vice president for product development, noted that "he had this absolute passionate need to put his name on things," especially the Newton.[21]

Riding the wave of the Mac's success, Sculley had earlier pontificated in an interview with *Playboy* magazine, "In the next 20 years . . . the Soviets will land a manned mission on Mars." In the same interview, he also predicted that ". . . the value of the Japanese stock exchange will exceed the value of all the American stock exchanges."[22] Sculley not only had an unearthly view of his capabilities as a high technology and global business visionary, but he also took pains to impress that view on the marketplace. In turns, he had moved from grounded pride, to dependent pride, then to exaggerated pride, and finally to overweening pride.

With the Newton a disaster, the Mac losing increasing ground to IBM-compatible personal computers, and hundreds of millions of dollars of research and development funding down the drain, Sculley lost credibility within Apple. The board fired him in 1993.

After leaving Apple, Sculley became the CEO of a small technology firm, Spectrum Information Technologies, only to discover that Spectrum's executives had deceived him about the firm's technology and finances. Four months later, Sculley quit and sued

Spectrum's president, regretting ". . . a terribly embarrassing situation . . . . I ended up with a bunch of bad characters."[23]

Did Sculley's pride hurt him and the firm? Perhaps by "seeing technology through Steve's eyes," he unsustainably placed control of his identity and accomplishments at the firm with Jobs. Conceivably by overestimating his capabilities as a technology executive— the firm's chief technology officer—he seemed to underestimate the challenges of translating research and development into successful new products. And, by viewing and trusting himself as a technology CEO, Sculley evidently failed to perform basic due diligence before signing on with Spectrum.

Jobs's NeXT Lesson in Overweening Pride

Meanwhile, following his acrimonious departure from Apple, Jobs set out to prove to the Silicon Valley elite that he belonged. Rather than run away (as he had briefly considered doing), he created NeXT Computer, Inc., in 1985, if only to show the Valley and Apple's bozo directors. It was a disastrous venture that was in large part started to feed Jobs's pride. Over the course of ten years, the firm would burn more than $250 million in capital in the process of unprofitably selling about 50,000 computers.[24]

One story unkindly illustrates Jobs's overweening pride at NeXT. With the firm failing, Jobs staked its future on a new product, the NeXTstation. The only problem was that the computer system needed a killer application in the movie player, which in turn needed a reliable video chip. Unfortunately, the chip was not ready for the product's launch. Instead of scrapping the launch or launching without the movie player, Jobs staged a hoax, using the computer as a terminal that broadcast content from a laser disk player that was hidden backstage.[25]

Increasingly, Jobs became delusional about NeXT's profitability and prospects, imbued with an overweening pride that led to many of the same mistakes that he had made with the Mac.

After his very public firing at Apple and equally public failure at NeXT, Jobs seemed like a tragic figure—a quintessential victim of excessive pride and hubris. Kicking himself for being hoodwinked by Jobs's bewildering charm, *New York Times* columnist Joseph Nocera wrote, "The real tragedy of Jobs, I think, is that . . . no one bought into the myth of Steve Jobs more than Jobs."[26] Writing Jobs off as a failure, though, is a mistake—one that grossly underestimates both his genius and his ability to reconnect with it.

Jobs Grounds His Pride and Leverages His Talents

In a remarkable twist of fate, Apple bought NeXT in 1997 for its operating system, with the intention of using it for future generations of the Mac. With that sale, Jobs found himself back at Apple as a consultant and then as "interim CEO." Duly humbled, this time Jobs intended to prove that he had learned from his mistakes.

Now Jobs pursued an emerging concept that could again be the kernel of a great business, namely, that listeners should be able to ". . . buy high-quality audio tracks via the Internet and load them directly into iTunes [Apple's online jukebox] instead of going to the store to buy the CDs to rip [copy]."[27]

Rather than throw money at a large, expensive team of hired guns, Jobs gave a few hand-picked people the space and inspiration to thrive under tight deadlines. In particular, he entrusted the project to a young hardware engineer, Tony Fadell, who had always wanted to develop a small, hard-disk-based music player, but could not get funded.

Now Jobs worried about the product rather than the glory. Rather than build the hardware and software from scratch as at NeXT, Fadell collaborated with another company, PortalPlayer, which had completed up to 80 percent of the needed technology. Rather than work on a state-of-the-art product as at NeXT, Jobs sought a "good enough" product that could be continuously upgraded. That meant that the project would not have to wait for next generation applications, including movie players, cell phones, and PDA integration capabilities, that were slowing competitors.

The objective was simplicity in design, use, and underlying technology. With that approach, the firm could also use off-the-shelf components so as not to wait for next generation parts that were under development. Getting out of his own way, Jobs left hardware development to Fadell, who continues to set hardware direction as leader of the iPod division, and software development to his long-standing colleague, Avie Tevanian.

Along with Apple's design chief, Jonathan Ive, Jobs's own focus was much more on the device's shape, feel, and design, rather than its underlying technology. Ben Knauss was PortalPlayer's primary liaison manager with Apple. After the first iPod prototypes were built, Knauss noted that, in Apple meetings, ". . . Steve would be horribly offended he couldn't get to the song he wanted in less than three pushes of a button. We'd get orders: 'Steve doesn't think it's loud enough, the sharps aren't sharp enough, or the menu's not coming up fast enough.' Every day there were comments from Steve saying where it needed to be."[28]

Learning from his mistakes at Mac and NeXT, Jobs refused to let the iPod's form triumph over function, when customers said that the product needed both. Rather than skimp on memory, the first iPod had a 5 gigabyte hard drive, and 32 megabytes of memory—more than most PDAs. Furthermore, Jobs has not let his contempt for Gates prevent iTunes from running on Windows platforms. If Jobs's pride had unduly interfered, he might have had the iPod run exclusively for the Mac's operating system, which would increase Mac sales and shut Windows and Microsoft out. But that would be bad business for the iPod, given Windows's huge installed base—at least for now!

This time Jobs could also leverage his genius for networking and persuading by signing up musicians and music companies as content providers for the iTunes Music Store. Rather than brush aside musicians' fears about piracy, Apple invested heavily in firewall software to prevent music from being pirated from iPods and the iTunes Music Store.

As of this writing, Apple has sold over 1 billion songs on its iTunes site and over 50 million iPods. Jobs once announced that "Apple has invented a whole new category of digital music player that lets you put your entire music collection in your pocket and listen to it wherever you go."[29] The statement claims no more and no less than what he and the iPod team have achieved; it conveys the grounded pride that Jobs can take from the success of the iPod (and the decision-making process Jobs used to develop it).

After a cancer scare, Jobs is back, unleashing his precious genius and putting Apple on a roll that, admittedly, cannot last forever. He has demonstrated that he can lead in good times, and now the question remains whether he has the skills to manage a struggling company. If that scenario plays out, Jobs may again be vulnerable to exaggerated pride.

How Excessive Pride Gave Jobs and Sculley False Confidence

Jobs and Sculley provide a wealth of information and experiences that can help us to better appreciate and learn from the pitfalls of excessive pride. Here are the milestones of Apple's saga of executive hubris:

- Jobs showed ample evidence of grounded pride after he returned to Apple in 1997. Before then, he used his work on "insanely great" products to gain fame and fortune. Now, Jobs cares more about the intrinsic merit of those products. In spite of the success of the iPod, he now shuns personal publicity, making himself available to the media and public to promote the firm's products. Consider also that Jobs sought control over all aspects of the Mac's product development and manufacturing. More keenly aware of his limitations, he now focuses on his strengths in codesigning

products and building and motivating product development teams. Jobs acted from a position of authentic pride
when he launched the iPod. By getting the right help from
expert technology developers and by acknowledging and
avoiding his past mistakes, Jobs could concentrate his own
talents where they'd reap the most reward. By a similar
token, Sculley's marketing initiatives to revive the Mac,
based on a careful assessment of the best available data,
demonstrated the same type of authentic pride.

- Sculley, however, also offered a classic example of the bad
decisions and leadership that can result from dependent
pride—when we rely on external validation. Sculley allowed
himself to believe that he had a symbiotic link with Jobs, and
as a result became "lost" in Jobs's leadership style and
approach to decision making. By relying on that validation,
Sculley became disconnected with his personality and
strengths, and sabotaged his own ability to succeed.

- Although a brilliant strategist in some areas, Jobs failed mis-
erably at his initial development of the Mac, overestimating
his technical capabilities and power within the firm. By failing to acknowledge and respond to the feedback of technical advisors and the marketplace, Jobs invested too heavily
in developing a machine with elegant form, rather than
excellent functionality. And, by failing to truly play out the
consequences of this crucial product launch, he was unable
to predict, let alone avoid, his own ultimate dismissal from
the company he had helped create.

- Both Sculley and Jobs offer classic illustrations of the dangers of overweening pride in the workplace. By apparently
ignoring the pathway to hubris that ended in his fall from
grace at Apple, Jobs repeated the errors of excessive pride at
NeXT. Once again, he relied too heavily on his own gut,
rather than get the right help or seek external feedback in
making product decisions. The result was more elegant,
sleek equipment that didn't offer the right functionality for

FIGURE 3.3 *Jobs's and Sculley's Pride While Leading Apple*

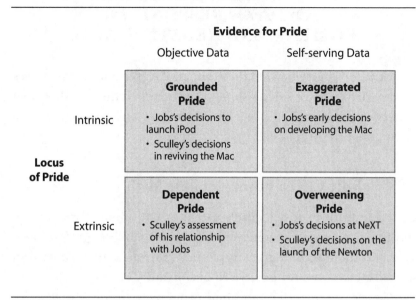

the company's customers. Sculley failed to acknowledge and rely on his true strengths as a marketer, and "bought" into the belief that he was a technological visionary. Ignoring other, more factual external data, Sculley failed to understand the true demands and opportunities of the marketplace when he spearheaded the development and release of the Newton, and turned what could have been an incredibly profitable product launch into an unmitigated and costly failure.

Figure 3.3 further places Jobs's and Sculley's experiences within the framework of pride seen earlier in this chapter.

INVALID DATA:
HOW CEOs RESPOND TO
POSITIVE AND NEGATIVE DATA

Now, let's move beyond the context of Apple and its executives to more broadly consider systematic evidence of the links between excessive pride and hubris. An interesting and important case study concerns other celebrity executives.

Celebrity CEOs: Buying into the Myth

Pride leads us to selectively use information, because positive information about our achievements and capabilities gives us pleasure and the opposite gives us pain. The result is that we tend to get a distorted view of how we're performing.

Consider our well-established propensity to think that we're more responsible for successful performance—whether it is at the team, project, or firm level—than we really are. Pretend that you find yourself in the boardroom and that you are now being congratulated for driving a winning project. Later you are on the front cover of a major business magazine, acclaimed for delivering remarkable firm performance. Will you ignore, reject, or accept the acclaim? Studies show that we overwhelmingly choose the last of the three options, simply because that best supports a positive self-impression—it makes us feel better about ourselves.

We need to be careful, though, because in doing so, we almost invariably overestimate our ability to influence success. Unless you are a solo act, the success of your project or business obviously depends on a host of other factors and people—being in the right place at the right time, building a great team, having the right partners, and so on. That's why some firms, including the investment bank Goldman Sachs, actively work to keep their rainmakers under wraps.

Strong corporate performance results from a complex mix of factors that include, but are not limited to, the skills of the CEO.

Attributing the success of an entire corporation to a single individual provides a simple explanation, however, and one that "plays well" with both the popular press and the public.

The problem is that overblown claims of CEO contribution can have disastrous effects on the individuals and companies at the center of the story. Daniel Vasella, CEO since 1996 of the major Swiss pharmaceutical firm Novartis, explained in an article for *Fortune* magazine the vicious cycle of believing one's own press. While acknowledging that the popular press is prone to exaggerate the strengths and weaknesses of any celebrity CEO, he warns that people are too willing to accept what they read. The real danger presents itself when the CEO indulges in that belief—leading to what Vasella characterizes as a "celebration leading to belief, leading to distortion." Vasella goes on to note, "Then it becomes difficult if not impossible to change the course you and your company are on. . . . You must make the targets—must keep delivering record results at whatever cost to continue the celebration."[30]

Executives who enjoy the warm glow of being celebrated risk getting addicted to the actions that made them celebrities. This can work well for a while, but it also stops executives and their firms from changing with the times. Not surprisingly, there is strong evidence that performance at firms with "celebrity" CEOs steadily declines for three years after their CEOs become glorified.[31]

Cover stories that demonize once-celebrated leaders highlight this phenomenon around the world, from Beijing to Paris. Take Europe. If you are Dutch, you may vividly recall the cover stories of Cees van der Hoeven leading the globalization of the supermarket chain, Ahold. If you are French, you will recall how Jean-Marie Messier was hailed as a genius at the media and telecommunications conglomerate, Vivendi. If you are Italian, you may better remember how Luciano Moggi was once revered at Juventus and how Calisto Tanzi was glorified for leading Parmalat. And in Switzerland, Philippe Bruggisser was once glorified for his strategy of buying minority stakes in European airlines.

In the Asian Pacific region, Chinese managers may relate better to Liu Jinbao's fall from grace as the CEO of the Bank of China. Japanese executives will recall their fallen business heroes, Hiroo Mizushima of Sogo or Yoshiaki Tsutsumi of Seibu. Down Under, John Elliott, the former boss of Fosters Brewing was once touted as a potential prime minister and is now one of a growing list of disgraced CEOs.

Meanwhile, those living in America may be able to visualize several celebrity CEOs who have fallen from grace, including "power brokers" Jeff Skilling of Enron, "Insurance Wizard" Hank Greenberg of AIG, the "Queen of Decorum" Martha Stewart, "Chainsaw" Al Dunlap of Scott Paper/Sunbeam, Denis Kozlowski of Tyco, Bernie Ebbers of WorldCom, and John Rigas of Adelphia Communications.

The common denominator for *each* of these once-powerful executives was that they graced the front covers of major business magazines in vainglorious ways. Another shared trait was a tendency to gravitate toward overweening pride, which occupies the fourth quadrant of the matrix we saw earlier in this chapter. Celebrity CEOs often are *dangerous* because in believing their own press, they sense that they are invincible and omnipotent, which encourages them to push the boundaries of what they and their firms can and should do. Taken to an extreme, this tendency extends to criminal activity. Because cognitive dissonance makes it so difficult for them to backtrack, industry leaders can get increasingly confident until, almost invariably, they unravel.

The Dangers of Denial about One's Failings

By the same token, when CEOs fail to respond to negative feedback and other adverse data about themselves, they also form a distorted view of their performance, leading to exaggerated pride. Singapore's National Kidney Foundation is an unlikely setting to see this destructive process in action.

The island-state of Singapore is a pristine metropolis. Its patriarch, Lee Kwan Yew, is draconian about good citizenship. Drug smugglers face the death sentence. Certain film and television shows are censored, home satellite TV antennae are banned, and some books, magazines, and even popular songs are outlawed. Fines are levied for spitting in the streets or failing to flush public toilets. Until 2004, the government even had a 12-year ban on chewing gum on the grounds that its waste contaminates public places (today, users can only buy it in pharmacies by submitting their identification card numbers; and illegal gum dealers face up to two years of jail time and $5,000 in fines). Meanwhile, mistakes among senior executives and government officials can go undisclosed given that the country's dominant newspaper, *The Straits Times,* has close government and business ties.

Within Singapore, the National Kidney Foundation (NKF) epitomized exemplary citizenship. More than that, it has been heralded beyond Singapore as a model of "social entrepreneurship," showing other organizations how to simultaneously serve financial and social objectives. The NKF was established to aid patients with kidney failure by helping them to get a kidney transplant or by providing medicine and dialysis to ease their suffering. Susan Long, the *Straits Times* journalist who broke the story, describes how the NKF was set up to raise capital to support dialysis rather than send patients home with morphine to die. As a charity organization, the NKF aggressively and innovatively seeks public funds to make that happen.

That helps explain why Singaporeans were shocked and angry when Long raised questions about the behavior of the foundation and its CEO, TT Durai. She cited evidence that Durai used NKF money to install lavish fittings (gold-plated taps and pricey German toilet bowls) in the bathroom of his private office, to fly first class (Durai denied that he was flying first class when evidence proved that he was), and to receive a salary of 600,000 Singapore dollars (US $350,000). Much more damaging was evidence that the NKF exaggerated the number of patients that it had helped, supposedly to support fundraising (an allegation that was later confirmed by an independent report by the accountants, KPMG).

Of course, no one had better, firsthand information about each of these issues than Durai. Rather than come clean, however, he overconfidently had NKF file a lawsuit, alleging that the *Straits Times* article had defamed the NKF. This final nail in the coffin drew further attention to Durai's decisions and forced him to withdraw the legal action. By that time, however, Singaporeans had become outraged at how the NKF was using its funds. In protest, tens of thousands of donors terminated their monthly contributions to NKF, and popular opinion forced Durai to resign.

Powerful executives, like Durai and Jeff Skilling of Enron fame, often insist on getting candid and extensive feedback about themselves and their situation (see Chapter 5 for more on the latter). Problems arise, as we'll see again in Chapter 5, when out of exaggerated pride they don't like what they see, read, and hear. And, if they don't shoot the messengers, they often shoot themselves in the foot by letting their pride get in the way of receiving and openly dealing with negative feedback. It's an issue that has also hurt celebrity European executives, helping to explain the demise of van der Hoeven, Messier, and Bruggiser. Through exaggerated pride, these leaders rejected and ignored negative feedback about themselves and their businesses—a process of executive hubris we will see again in Chapter 6.

Guided by Pride: A Link between Executive Hubris and Higher Premiums Paid in Mergers and Acquisitions

Consider how exaggerated pride also surfaces in the decisions that CEOs make regarding how to grow their firms. Few decisions are more important than those concerning whether to acquire another business and how much to pay for it.

Figure 3.4 shows the number of mergers and acquisitions (M&A) in the United States and globally since 1970. The raw num-

FIGURE 3.4 *Number of U.S. and U.S. Cross-Border Mergers and Acquisitions, 1970–2005*

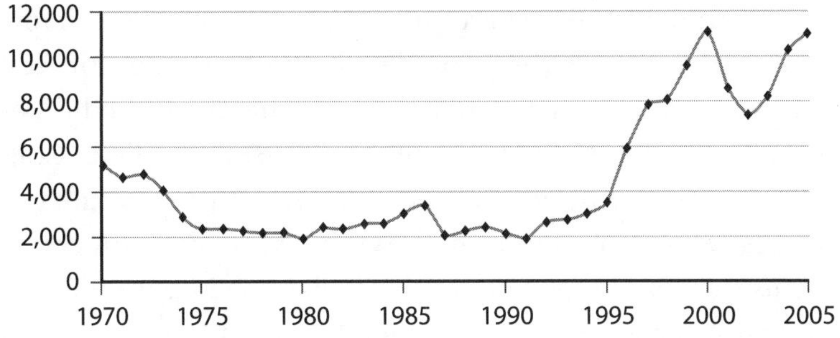

Source: Mergerstat.com

ber of M&As in the United States in 2005 was 11,013, as recorded by Mergerstat, with a dollar value of over $1.2 trillion.

The principal advisors to acquiring firms are investment bankers who monitor acquisition premiums—what acquiring managers pay above the target firm's preexisting share price. On any deal, bankers collect data on premiums that indicate the fairness of the offer that they are working on, relative to comparable deals.

Reflecting on the size of premiums, the famed investor Warren Buffett quipped, "Apparently many managers were overexposed in impressionable childhood years to the story in which the imprisoned handsome prince is released from a toad's body by a kiss from a beautiful princess. Consequently, they are certain their managerial kiss will do wonders for the profitability of Company T(arget)."[32]

Witness the courtship between Steve Case, former CEO of America Online (AOL) and Gerald Levin, former CEO of Time Warner, which was passionately consummated when they announced the merger of their companies on January 10, 2000. Before the announcement, Time Warner shares traded at $65. Case was so confident in the deal that AOL offered Time Warner shareholders $110 for their shares, effectively saying that Time Warner would be worth 70 percent more because of the marriage.

On paper this valued the merged group at over $350 billion, a deal hightly touted by some leading Wall Street analysts.

So it was that AOL's share price and market value collapsed, meaning that Levin grossly overestimated the value of AOL's "Internet economy" assets. That might not have mattered if Levin had used a standard "collar" to protect his shareholders. Collars allow either party to void the deal if the share price of the other party falls below a predetermined level. Levin justified his decision not to use a collar as follows: "With a collar, the implication is that you are not really sure and you need this kind of protection. *I wanted to make a statement that I believe in it.*"[33] Unfortunately for Time Warner shareholders, this statement effectively cost them tens of billions of dollars.

Not using "collars" and paying high premiums in such deals could be justified if the premiums could at least be recovered. But, just as overpaying for our house erodes our returns from it, paying higher premiums usually undermines acquisition returns. Basically, premiums reflect acquiring managers' judgment about how much more an acquired business would be worth under their control, as seen in the AOL/Time Warner deal. Concerned about the size of acquisition premiums, investors generally sell the acquiring company's shares when they learn about the deal, often significantly reducing the share price in the short term and the long term.[34]

Why would acquiring managers pay such acquisition premiums for deals that generally hurt their shareholders? I became interested in this puzzle after working as an investment banker and developing a suspicion about the conventional wisdom surrounding these deals.

One theory was that acquiring managers did not have enough skin in the game—they lacked sufficient ownership in their companies to worry enough about premiums. Yet the results showed that acquiring CEOs with greater stock ownership were also paying high premiums, presumably because they were certain about the merits of their acquisitions. What's more, CEOs who paid higher premiums also seemed as closely monitored by institutional investors and a vigilant board of directors as other CEOs. Another theory was that acquiring managers pay more when there are stronger synergies or ways that the two businesses can benefit each other.

While plausible, none of these explanations recognize that acquisitions fail when acquiring managers pay too much for them, regardless of the merits of the motive for doing the deal. Another hypothesis is that overconfident managers who exaggerate their acquiring capabilities would pay higher premiums, as Buffett predicted. Intrigued, my colleague at Columbia University, Don Hambrick, and I scrutinized more than 100 acquisitions to predict the premiums that the acquiring companies would pay. Our results showed that companies led by more "hubristic" CEOs—those with more recent media praise, successful recent performance, and feelings of superiority over subordinates (as reflected by how much they paid themselves relative to the next highest paid executive in their firm)—paid higher premiums.[35] By contrast, acquiring firms with a proven track record, like General Electric (GE), make better deals by removing their CEOs from acquisition pricing. At GE, a notable exception was its acquisition of the investment bank, Kidder Peabody. Describing this deal as his worst mistake, Welch says that he got "too full of myself"—too involved in committing to proceed and how much to pay.[36]

Welch is hardly alone. Most celebrity CEOs believe their own press and therefore become wedded to the actions that produce celebrity.[37] Acquiring CEOs are often driven by ego: They overestimate the value that they can extract from acquisitions by paying excessive premiums.

Paying higher acquisition premiums is just one type of decision-making outcome that is affected by excessive pride; and, in this case, it is usually exaggerated or overweening pride. As we allow pride to enter our decisions, those decisions increasingly reflect our personal biases rather than a rational analysis of the underlying data. What results is false confidence and hubris.

Beyond CEOs: How Compensation Fuels Pride and False Confidence

Executives must have grounded pride. Every firm, therefore, should strive for rigorous debriefs, performance reviews, and tight corporate governance over senior managers to encourage executives to accept and use negative feedback for what it's worth. Unfortunately, however, more often these executives use selective judgment because they get selective feedback, as we'll see again in Chapter 5, which deals with feedback about our situation rather than ourselves.

Welch now gets paid tens of thousands of dollars to conduct seminars in which he motivates large numbers of executives. He has an exercise in which he asks executive audiences, "How many of you work for a company with integrity?" The result is that about 95 percent of hands go up. And then he asks, "How many of you get straight-between-the-eyes honest feedback about your performance?" About 5 percent of hands go up.[38]

This problem (an honest firm that fails to give honest feedback) compounds when performance reviews are sugarcoated or when compensation otherwise does not reflect performance. A similar problem of selective feedback occurs when customer focus groups fail to provide real information about how products stack up against best-in-class competitors.

Pretend that you are overpaid. Perhaps your firm did well, even when you did not, so you've just received a big bonus that you don't feel that you truly deserve. How are you going to react to the bonus? You might choose to ignore it completely—hard to do, given its effect on your bank account. You might choose to downplay the raise, telling yourself that you don't really deserve it but you'll take it anyway, but that's also hard to do if getting paid more makes you feel more deserving and appreciated.

More likely, you'll convince yourself that you deserve the bonus, maybe even convincing yourself that your performance was better than it was. At that moment, your confidence increases, even if your actual performance has not. If you had a grounded self-assessment of your performance before the bonus, you now have a false level of confidence in your performance. This is just one way in which feedback, as conveyed by our compensation system, causes us to get ahead of ourselves, fuelling exaggerated pride.

Jaime Dimon, CEO of JPMorgan Chase, is working through this problem as he tries to integrate three large banking firms with different cultures: JPMorgan, Chase Manhattan Bank, and BancOne. Pay for executives from these different firms varies widely. Some retail banking managers at JPMorgan are paid up to $4 million annually, while counterparts at BancOne are paid up to $400,000 annually. In some cases, the profits managed by the BancOne managers exceeds that managed by their JPMorgan counterparts. Dimon wants to reduce pay for regional bank managers not just to lower costs but also to help reduce potential sources of overconfidence in the higher-paid JPMorgan managers. By fostering false confidence, greater compensation can actually diminish our resourcefulness and productivity.

Consider a similar dynamic in which star executives switch firms. One study of over 1,000 star security analysts shows that analysts who are paid handsomely to switch firms actually become worse judges of securities at their new firm.[39] Part of the reason for these declines in performance is that greater compensation is a form of feedback that gives executives an inflated view of their capabilities at managing the different demands of their new position.[40] The complacency that can result from this sort of ungrounded positive feedback can play out in diminished performance.

In the next chapter we explore an approach to managing our pride, namely by getting the right input in decision making or refusing to decide on matters in which excessive pride is likely to impinge on our judgment. For now let's turn to some governing ideas about identifying, avoiding, and managing excessive pride, ideas that revolve around the locus or source of our pride, the way that we interpret data for self assessment, and the manner in which pride plays out in the workplace.

SUMMARY POINTS FOR AVOIDING AND MANAGING EXCESSIVE PRIDE

The Locus of Pride

Taking every pride in capabilities and achievements makes us happier and more productive. Authentic pride comes from within from the intrinsic joy we take from doing good work well. But, when our pride is dependent on extrinsic rewards including getting approval, it can easily become overweening pride and a fast-track toward hubris. Here are some tips for avoiding this type of exaggerated pride:

- Be understated about sharing successes with colleagues, at least at first. Don't give the impression their approval is needed for your good work.
- Ensure that your decisions are motivated by business rather than personal objectives. Are they in your best interests or in the best interest of the company? If you're taking pride from waging a vendetta, for instance, you're placing your source of pleasure in your ability to inflict pain on another person, placing more control of your pride in their hands.
- Examine the authenticity of your decisions and behaviors. Are you acting inconsistently as you move from one role to another in a bid to impress others? Are you contriving to be someone you are not?
- Avoid spending excessive time on impression management, rather than getting on with the job.
- Discount praise, including celebrity, which is used by others to elicit the behavior that they want, rather than the behavior that is right for you. Make it clear that others are also responsible for performance.
- Avoid treating compensation as the sole objective. When you do, you are more likely to develop a false sense of confidence

when you are overpaid, and potentially a false lack of confidence when you are underpaid.

Interpreting Data for Self-Assessment

Information about the consequences of our decisions and actions is grounded on what we've done, and should be a source of pride. Information about the potential consequences of such decisions is purely speculative, and is, at best, a source of pride in the making. Embellishing and exaggerating information is dangerous and unsustainable because it places our pride on a shaky platform.

Because self-serving data regarding our capabilities leads to exaggerated or overweening pride, keep these points in mind:

- Ignoring or discounting errors signifies that we're overstating information about our capabilities and achievements.
- Often we overattribute our contribution to good performance and underattribute our contribution to bad performance. To stay grounded, we must accept our contribution to both good and bad performance.
- We also suffer from exaggerated pride when we assume that capabilities and achievements in one area can be transferred to another. This is the effect of assuming that our skills in one domain can be leveraged to another, which we've witnessed in Dean Kamen's story as he tried to make the transition from inventor and technologist to general manager.
- Again, try to disconnect your sense of pride from your compensation.

How Pride Plays Out in the Workplace

This chapter looked at the four types of pride—authentic pride, exaggerated pride, dependent pride, and overweening pride—and explored their uses and dangers in the executive workplace.

Pride is a vital emotion in the workplace. It is the pleasure that we take from doing a good job. When we feel better about what we're doing, we're more motivated and productive. Like any other emotional force, however, pride must be carefully managed. Denial, for example, protects us from the hit that our pride takes from adverse data about our capabilities and achievements. But, it also obviously removes us from business realities. Excessive pride results in bad decisions because it distracts us from business objectives. Here are other key points to remember about excessive pride:

- The nature of our pride depends on the quality of evidence that we have about our capabilities and achievements. Is your pride authentic and based on solid, objective data? Or is it contrived and excessive because it is based on self-serving data?

- Embellishing and exaggerating data about our performance is a dangerous game that is exceedingly difficult to backtrack from. Very often, people try to sustain the illusion that the truth is the lie, because being seen to lie undermines their credibility and pride.

- The nature of our pride also depends on the locus from where we get pleasure. Do you take pride from independently experiencing your capabilities and achievements? Or does your pride depend on potential outcomes, including how you want others to perceive you? So be careful if you choose to adopt a role model or try to play a role model. Remember how Sculley became unglued in his early years at Apple by trying to play Jobs.

- *Grounded pride* arises when we intrinsically appreciate ourselves and colleagues based on the best available evidence of what we are doing.

- *Excessive pride* arises when we develop an inflated view of ourselves based on our need for certain outcomes and approval and on our tendency to use self-serving data, rather than facts, to support positive self-impression. Dependent, exaggerated, and overweening pride are the three forms of excessive pride.

- *Dependent pride* arises when our pride depends on future outcomes rather than present work, including how we want others to perceive us. The implication is not to place your sense of pride on outcomes that you can't control

- *Exaggerated pride* arises when we have an intrinsic locus of pride but base that pride on self-serving data about our performance, say, because we believe what we want to rather than what the facts tell us. The implication is to treat data that you receive about yourself as though it were data about someone whom you are impartial about.

- *Overweening pride* arises when our sense of pride is driven by potential outcomes, including how we want others to perceive others, and is supported by self-serving data about our performance. The implication is to have a trusted foil to tell you in a candid and timely manner when, how, and why you are wrong, as in the next chapter.

4

Getting Out
of Our Own Way

HOW FAILING TO GET THE RIGHT
HELP FUELS EXECUTIVE HUBRIS

"I have nothing but confidence in you, and very little of that."
GROUCHO MARX

Groucho Marx's quip, along with Herb Greenberg's experience at AIG, highlights why many executives lack badly needed foils.

While a fool is a setup person, someone we take down to advance our argument or prospects, the *foil* is an ally, someone who helps us win. Whereas an alter ego is someone who is so similar to us as to be virtually another self, the foil has complementary capabilities and ambitions. Unlike a subordinate, who may want to unseat us, the foil works with us on a joint agenda. Equally unlike a confidante, who may selectively tell us what we want to hear, the foil presents the facts as they are and tells us—often in artful ways—when we're confused or misguided. And, where a lackey or a gofer will obediently do our bidding for us, the foil cleverly and sometimes humorously knows how and when to push back.

Foils are people who inform, underscore, enhance, and complement our distinctive strengths. That's why I think every executive, whatever his or her level and position in the firm, should work toward having a number of foils. After all, it's not inconceivable that, on occasion, we will be wrong. Having the right foil, and knowing when to get his or her input in the decision-making process, is a natural way to stop excessive pride from influencing our decisions. Because decision making is a chance for us to stamp our mark on our work, communities, and families, it is also a way to feel better about ourselves. That means we have a bias toward making decisions that belong to others, as illustrated by Dean Kamen's manufacturing and marketing decisions for the Segway or John Sculley's insistence on handwriting software recognition for the Newton's launch.

Even when we are well qualified to make a given decision, our pride can make us do so in the wrong time or at the wrong place or both. Few if any guides were better qualified than Rob Hall to make judgment calls on Mount Everest. Yet with so much riding on a successful summit attempt on May 11, 1996, it was questionable whether he was the right person to enforce the turnaround time rule that day. With his prodigious charisma, Steve Jobs is a maestro at launching new products, and yet, as we learned in the previous chapter, he launched the NeXTstation prematurely, a disastrous decision he made, in part, because he lacked someone who could persuade him to call it off.

All this begs the question: How do we know when we should decide and when we should let go? A simple rule of thumb is that we should get out of the way of decisions that invoke or excessively engage our pride. When we take pride from deciding rather than enjoying the outcomes of decisions (whether we make them or enable someone else to do so), it's time to back off and let the foil decide. Because the art of delegating is integral to keeping our pride in check, it's also a key way to deal with the false confidence that induces hubris.

That's why this chapter deals with using power versus getting it, focusing on five powerful executives at major companies. Three of these executives, Carly Fiorina at Hewlett-Packard, Larry Ellison at Oracle Corporation, and Warren Buffett at Berkshire Hathaway, operate within a centralized decision-making environment. The other two, Sir Martin Sorrell at WPP, and Meg Whitman at eBay, adopt a far more decentralized process.

We'll begin with Fiorina. As CEO of Hewlett-Packard (HP) for six years, Fiorina got caught on the slippery slope that runs from wielding power to becoming a victim of overconfidence and hubris.

GETTING THE RIGHT INPUT WHEN DECISION MAKING IS CENTRALIZED

HP's Carly Fiorina Goes It Alone—and Loses

In 1998, *Fortune* magazine named Fiorina—who was then a relatively obscure president of Lucent's network services division— the most powerful woman in American business, celebrating her as a bold, charismatic, and even glamorous sales woman. (*Fortune* would continue to bestow the title on Fiorina every year until 2004, which is when Meg Whitman of eBay assumed the mantle.)[1]

Within a year of that article's publication, HP's board of directors named Fiorina as the firm's CEO. At the time, Fiorina was 44 and had never been a CEO. She also was the first person to be appointed from outside the firm to lead its unique culture. Supremely proud, Fiorina was charged with overseeing a firm with 145,000 employees in 178 countries.

Six years later, in January 2005, *Fortune*'s Carol Loomis again wrote of Fiorina in a prescient cover story about HP's acquisition of Compaq titled, "Why Carly's Big Bet Is Failing."[2] Among other things, Loomis charged that Fiorina had destroyed value for HP shareholders by buying Compaq; she also wrote that, with the exception of printers, each of HP's businesses was badly underperforming. Within two weeks of that story's publication, HP's board demanded and received Fiorina's resignation. While many factors contributed to her dismissal, board members, colleagues, journalists, and analysts uniformly cite her inability to effectively delegate.

Fiorina's firing masks her auspicious start at HP, where she arrived to turn around a damaged firm. Morale had been hurt by the spin-off of the firm's instruments and measurement business, Agilent, which many regarded as the firm's core business. Without Agilent, HP was held back by its barely profitable personal computer and server businesses. Breathing fresh air into the firm, Fiorina soon committed it to a new strategy based on enterprise computing (integrating business functions with Web-based infrastructure) for large customers. She personally intervened to win major accounts—Amazon.com and Procter & Gamble, among others—which HP may have otherwise lost to its major competitors, EDS and IBM. She revitalized the innovation arm of HP (HP Labs), investing in initiatives such as digital imaging and publishing technology; rewritable DVD software for recording, erasing, and rerecording music and video content; and energy-efficient "smart cooling" for servers.

By far the defining decision of her tenure, however, was to buy Compaq. Successful technology acquisitions, which are predicated on getting the best out of acquired people, are like great marriages: Each party *must* benefit the other and, in the process, contribute to what they believe is a mutually beneficial and worthy cause. Anything less, and one party grows resentful while the other becomes marginalized and alienated. Everything rides on retaining and motivating key people, namely those who can turn present and prospective products into winners in the marketplace.

Given the opportunities these executives have elsewhere, it's tough to buy their loyalty. Nevertheless, HP senior management and their advisors from McKinsey & Co. tried to do just that, offering the "key 200" Compaq executives incentives tied to staying at the firm for two years after the merger. As it turned out, however, the incentives were more like shackles that locked the executives into a search for an exit strategy. Once the two years passed, these key executives bolted for leadership positions at competitors including Dell, EMC, IBM, Nokia, and Oracle.

Fiorina's autocratic style and the merger's questionable performance only hastened the flight. In October 2003, she had 11 direct reports; within 16 months, only 5 remained. Reports within HP circulated that Fiorina was looking for scapegoats and firing unlucky individuals who fit the bill. When asked about the firings, Fiorina expressed regret that she hadn't "done them all faster. Every person that I've asked to leave, whether it's been clear publicly or not, I would have done faster."[3] Sentiments like those jarred with the "respect and compassion" that she purported to have for HP's people, and with the values that are supposedly embedded in the HP way of bringing out the best in its people.

Fiorina's actions and statements increasingly isolated her in the corner office and made her more susceptible to a false sense of confidence in her decisions and actions. After the Compaq merger, the assumption was that Compaq's CEO, Michael Capellas, would be the firm's chief operating officer and could serve as her internal foil. Such an assumption was based on delusions, given that Capellas aspired to be a CEO—and there was obviously only room for one at HP. When he left, Fiorina effectively became the firm's chairman, CEO, president, and COO, even though her strong suits are communications and marketing, not operations. All that made her a powerful figurehead, but her failure to empower people to make key decisions was eroding her circle of influence.

Consequently, fewer people were willing or able to tell her that she was wrong. Subordinates became as concerned with how their initiatives would "play with Carly" as they were about whether the firm needed them. Whether she was unable and unwilling to get the right information about her deteriorating position or whether she ignored it, one of her closest advisors told me that Fiorina remained "supremely confident, even borderline delusional about the actual challenges and the metrics of success." She needed the right help.

At any large firm, the principal source of these data is the chief financial officer; and at HP, that was Bob Wayman. With more than 30 years' experience at the firm, Wayman knew HP inside out and was a natural candidate to serve as a foil, someone who could set and implement the metrics or scorecard to guide the firm's performance and processes. His ability to filter the mountains of data available in a firm HP's size, and his deep appreciation for the firm's heritage, made him invaluable. Yet, Fiorina had Wayman collect votes from institutional investors for the Compaq deal and grew disillusioned as it became clear that Fiorina was relegating his role to that of enforcer and compliance officer, rather than decision maker. By 2003, Wayman talked openly about retiring.

A series of conspicuously unilateral decisions only highlighted Fiorina's detachment from the real needs of the firm and her false sense of confidence. Breaking with company culture and tradition, she purchased a flashy Gulfstream jet for her travel. She insulated herself behind assistants within the executive suite and blamed deteriorating performance on subordinates. And, she used guilt to tell people how much they had let her, the board, and the firm down.

By December 2004, Fiorina was quoted as saying, "I am the CEO of Hewlett-Packard. I love the company. I love the job—and I'm not finished."[4] That confidence had been shared by directors who fiercely supported her during the Compaq deal. But now that those directors had unequivocal evidence of executive departures, Fiorina's failure to delegate, and HP's inadequate financial performance, they had to act. Rather than force her out, directors initially encouraged her to delegate more decision making to Vyomesh "VJ" Joshi (head of printing and personal computing), Ann Livermore (services and enterprise computing), and Shane Robison (chief technology and strategy officer). Fiorina did add personal computers to Joshi's portfolio, but that was not enough delegation to get the help she needed. HP's board would have to make her delegate.

Loomis describes how the issue came to a head at a board meeting on January 24, 2005:

> Some directors felt strongly that the enterprise side of HP, which encompasses servers and storage, should be put under Shane Robison, the company's chief strategy and technology officer. It appears that Fiorina was greatly opposed for at least two reasons. First, Robison, though well thought of at HP, had never run a business. Second, Fiorina is reported to have argued that it was the CEO's prerogative, not the board's, to make decisions about managers. She argued that if Robison did not succeed in the job he was proposed for, she would be blamed.[5]

At the follow-up board meeting on February 7, Fiorina remained unmoved. The board of directors asked Fiorina to leave the meeting, before concluding that she must leave the firm.

Granted, HP's problems were much larger than Fiorina's failure to delegate. Her challenges included overseeing the complex integration of a large merger and a slowdown in technology spending at large clients. I emphasize her autocratic style, however, because it seemed to give her false confidence about her standing in the firm. Sensing that she was impregnable, she overestimated her ability to sway colleagues and board members, and she underestimated the importance of giving more power to senior managers. As her decision making became more autonomous she became more isolated from the firm and its board. And, she went against the HP grain forged by the foil relationship between Bill Hewlett, the "engineer's engineer," and Dave Packard, the hard-nosed businessman.

One unanticipated side effect of Fiorina's firing was to consolidate the power of HP's chairwoman, Patricia Dunn. After Fiorina's departure, Dunn overaggressively investigated possible leaks of information from HP Board members, including spying on fellow Board members in an act of hubris that led to her resignation.

Both Dunn's and Fiorina's cases are reminders that the trick to building and managing power is to increase one's sphere of influence by empowering colleagues, rather than assuming their power. It's a lesson that Hurd has taken to heart as he, Joshi, Livermore, Robison, and Wayman continue today to stage an impressive turnaround at HP.

Finding and Trusting the Right Foils at Oracle

Obviously, not all autocratic managers become victims of the false confidence that induces hubris. As Steve Jobs's experience illustrates, even those whose careers suffer from the effects of hubris can still recover. Larry Ellison, Oracle's founder and CEO since 1977, is a case in point of an autocratic leader who, by and large, has managed to find and work effectively with the *right* foils.

Few executives come close to having the power that Ellison wields as the leader of one of the world's three largest software firms. In many ways, Ellison *is* Oracle: He shapes the firm's strategy; he is the firm's forceful, outspoken, and charismatic evangelist; and he determines who rises and falls on its corporate ladder. His handpicked biographer, Matthew Symonds, characterizes him as "enormously vain, intellectually dominating, and irrepressibly extrovert."[6] What you will read now draws substantially from Symonds's thoroughly researched book *Softwar,* together with my interviews with present and former Oracle executives, including Chairman Jeff Henley.

Ellison's false confidence took Oracle right to the brink of bankruptcy in 1990 and 1991. At that time, his energy and creativity drove rapid growth, but he overlooked the need for the controls and processes that would convert the growth into sustained profits. Believing that the firm's database products would carry the firm, Ellison underestimated the importance of financial and sales controls. Instead, what he relied on was a "five in five" strategy. "I was simply extrapolating the annual doubling of revenues," says Ellison. "We would reach $5 billion in five years. I had absolutely no idea how absurd and naïve the plan was."[7]

Ellison Learns Some of the Rules of Sound Delegation

Focused on his passion for products and technology, Ellison lost sight of the other essential business functions and he had the wrong people in place to carry them out. The firm's CFO, an engineer rather than an accountant, took his eyes off the cash flow. His sales chief hired an ultra-aggressive sales force that rewarded gunslingers for booking sales, rather than collecting receivables. Before long, the firm was making unprofitable sales and faced a cash flow crisis. Some Oracle directors held Ellison responsible and wanted him out

Crisis made Ellison get the right help—and just in time. Four executives stand out: Jeff Henley, the firm's CFO from 1991 to 2004 and chairman of the board since 2004; Ray Lane, the firm's president and COO from 1992 to 2000; Safra Catz, Ellison's chief of staff from 1999 to 2004, and CFO from 2005; and Charles Phillips, who has been responsible for customers and partnerships since 2003. All but Lane remain as major contributors to the firm.

Ellison calls Henley the grown-up who cleaned the firm's financial mess. Over countless decisions and their implementation, Ellison saw in Henley a mature, seasoned, and disciplined decision maker who could be entrusted with the firm's accounting and finances. According to Ellison, Henley rises above other "bean counters" because "he says exactly what he thinks. He's fiercely loyal to the company. He looks out for the interests of our shareholders, employees, and customers. And he's a leader. As they say in the military, it's been an honor to serve with him."[8]

Ellison and Henley share a relationship that is rooted in longstanding personal as well as professional respect. Ellison has a reputation for compulsive and vitriolic outbursts, overly aggressive growth plans, and impatience, which can make him hard to work with. Henley has said of Ellison that he has a "shorter attention span than most" and is "not a guy who wants to grind through the details." Talented executives have come and gone, but not Henley, who tells me that he enjoys "Larry's sense of humor and contrarian thinking." He's not afraid to "go after Larry" because "Larry has a thick enough skin that he won't take offense," *when the time is right.*

As their relationship matured, Henley became more confident that he could mentor Ellison, telling him at one point that "he [Ellison] had created too much competition inside the company. He hadn't pushed teamwork enough, so he had a group of people on his executive team who just hated each other. He also realized that hiring really smart people, very smart, young engineers or whatever, had to be balanced by bringing in people who had some business experience."[9]

In 2004, Henley transitioned from being CFO to chairman of the board, a post that Ellison relinquished for him. Henley confides that an ongoing risk is that Ellison is such a dominant personality that his bias for deciding will suffocate other perspectives on products and customers. Much of the success of Ellison's new decision-making process hinges on Safra Catz, who joined the firm as Ellison's chief of staff in 1999. As the firm's chief operating and chief financial officer, Catz is easily Oracle's second most powerful executive. Not surprisingly, Henley and Ellison call her an effective foil. Having watched Ellison and Catz work together for seven years, Henley describes their relationship as one based on, "Rapport, support, and trust. . . . Because she has his ear more than anyone, she's able to get him what he wants and be straight. . . . She's very smart, analytical, and persuasive with facts."[10]

Ellison calls Catz "my chief confidante and counselor." He says, "She and I share a high-bandwidth communications link. We finish each other's sentences. We come to the same conclusion in the same amount of time. We rarely disagree, but when we do, she's not shy about expressing her opinions. If she thinks I'm wrong, she freezes me with one of her piercing stares and tells me I'm wrong. . . . I can count on her telling me the truth as she sees it." [11]

Catz, a lawyer by training, relies more on logic and facts than personality to drive decisions. That makes it harder for Ellison's personality and will to produce false confidence and hubris. Ellison notes, "In an argument when nobody has any facts—and I've seen a lot of those—the person with the strongest personality wins. But when one person has the facts and the other doesn't, the one with the facts always wins. When both people have the facts, there's no argument." [12] Catz has an uncanny appreciation for where Ellison is coming from, which allows her to frame facts in a constructive, nonthreatening manner. So even though Ellison controls final decisions, Catz shapes the parameters by which they get made and, therefore, the decisions themselves. Then, she sees to it that they get implemented. As a result, it's difficult to overestimate her behind-the-scenes influence at Oracle today.

Differing Views of Ellison's Trusted Advisors

Ray Lane has a different view of the relationship. To him, Catz is Ellison's alter ego and lackey. His vantage point is that of president and COO of Oracle during the 1990s, a position he held before falling out with Catz and Ellison and before leaving the firm. As a former senior Oracle officer who still cares about the firm and has largely reconciled with Ellison, Lane recalls meetings in which "Larry would ask the questions: How much does it cost to do this or that? And she [Catz] would go out and write in the headline first and then fill in the rest from Larry's perspective." [13]

Catz retorts that she's there to "help Larry," and her ability to complete Ellison's sentences certainly suggests that the two are in sync. At issue is the extent to which she can and will get Ellison the candid and often unpleasant feedback that he needs and when it is needed, especially if she is part of the problem.

At this writing, the firm is at a crossroads: Management has not created significant wealth for shareholders since around 2000 (about the time Lane left), and its strategic shift away from building applications toward buying and integrating them has yet to bear fruit. As the spearhead of this campaign, Catz is responsible for acquiring, and more important, integrating, a host of software businesses, including PeopleSoft/JD Edwards, Siebel Systems, Retek, Hotsip, and Sleepycat. Catz's role has taken her out of her comfort zone as a policy maker, to the hands-on demands of integrating acquired technology—one of the more difficult challenges in business.

Now a lead partner at Kleiner Perkins, Lane believes that Catz and Ellison overconfidently paid too much for these acquisitions (a hallmark of executive hubris that we saw in Chapter 2). And he is entitled to his opinion; under his watch, Oracle grew software sales tenfold, making the stock a Wall Street favorite. For that, Ellison made him a billionaire owner of Oracle stock and gave him day-to-day management of the firm, except for technology development (which Ellison retained) and finance (run by Henley). For a brief time, in fact, Ellison was so distracted by sailing that Lane was the firm's *de facto* CEO. But, by the end of the 1990s personal differences destroyed their professional relationship. Ellison recalls that the two did try to become friends but that it didn't work, adding that "Ray's a serious duck hunter. I raise mallards every spring. We couldn't be more different in personality and pastimes."[14]

Based on my research, however, I beg to differ with the idea that the Ellison/Lane relationship suffered from differences in the two men's personalities. Instead, I believe that the relationship suffered professionally more because of their similarities. At first blush, the two do seem to have the complementary strengths— Ellison in technology, Lane in operations—that can make for a great partnership. At a deeper level, however, they both like to exert influence through persuasive personalities, strategy formulation, and deal making. Says Ellison, "Ray manages by force of personality. He wills things to get done . . . . He built the kind of personal relationships that he could rely on when it came time to close a big deal. That made him a fantastic salesman."[15]

Ellison could be talking about himself. Two forceful personalities can disagree or, as a senior Oracle executive told me in confidence, "When two men think they're Jesus, at least one of them must be wrong—and quite possibly both."

Another similarity is that they both saw and continue to see themselves as technology visionaries. Once Ellison decided to get more involved in the firm after his sailing sojourn, only one strategy could prevail amongst two uncompromising leaders. Here are just a few of the disagreements that developed between the two executives:

- Facing fierce competition from the German firm SAP in applications (accounting, customer relationship management, human resources, legal, inventory management, and so on), Ellison believed that Oracle should combine its world-class database software with its own applications suite. He gave his 33-year-old chief of staff, Ron Wohl, the daunting challenge of developing the applications, integrating them with each other, and then combining them with the firm's database software for customers in different markets. Lane believed that Wohl, while talented, was unqualified for the gargantuan role. Lane also contended that Wohl's failure to deliver applications on time hurt customer relationships and made Oracle uncompetitive. Ellison wanted to persevere with Wohl and Lane wanted him fired—yesterday.
- Frustrated about the time taken to develop applications, Lane wanted the firm's powerful sales force to sell "best of breed" applications suites. In this strategy, Oracle would profit by integrating its applications with those from third-

party vendors and compete with SAP while the applications were being developed. But, Lane underestimated the challenges of integrating the different applications, and their upgrades. Increasingly, Ellison grew impatient with the strategy.

- Ellison wanted all Oracle technology platforms to be delivered on the Internet. While Lane supported that, he also wanted to continue to sell the applications on client/server or more distributed platforms hosted by a client's server.

Overlapping skills, competing ambitions and agendas, and a lack of candor and mutual respect made Ellison and Lane incompatible as foils. They became unable to effectively negotiate, much like two high-profile lawyers trying to assert their egos to settle a defamation case. For starters, Ellison underestimated how long it would take to develop required applications, frustrating salespeople and customers. And Lane underestimated how sacrosanct technology development was to Ellison and how hard Ellison would fight to retain control over it.

Ellison knew that he couldn't simply fire Lane overnight because that would be too disruptive to the firm's relationships with customers and its sales force. So Ellison and Catz slowly but surely stripped Lane of responsibility. Barely on talking terms with Catz and Ellison, Lane could only watch, wince, and wait for the right time to leave. Henley recalls how Ellison's pride damaged the relationship:

> . . . once Larry got so deep into Ray's pants, it was clear to everyone that this was not going to last, but it could and should have ended a little better than it did. Ray was actually willing to leave, but he just wanted to do it in his own way . . . . He was a trooper, a team player . . . for years he and Larry were a real strong team. And then it turned. [16]

The broader issue is that highly talented executives like Lane have left Oracle voluntarily or involuntarily to literally create *tens of billions* of dollars of value as founders and leaders of competing firms. Marc Benioff is now chief executive of a sales-force automation company, salesforce.com, Inc. Thomas Siebel, at one time a lead Oracle salesperson, became founder and head of customer relationship management at software rival Siebel Systems, Inc., which Oracle acquired for nearly $6 billion. Craig Conway, another salesperson, became head of human resource management software company PeopleSoft. And Greg Brady founded I2, the supply chain software specialist. And that is far from an exhaustive list of one-time Oracle executives who have taken their talents elsewhere.

Ellison's style is to conquer new land and burn the boats behind him, which is wonderful if you're at the vanguard—and deathly if you're still in the boats. For instance, Ellison describes his decision to fire Geoff Squire, president of the firm's International Operations in the early 1990s, as the "mother" of mistakes. He laments the loss of "perhaps the most talented field executive we've ever had at Oracle."[17] Squire, along with another departed Oracle executive, Gary Bloom, went on to build Veritas, a software company recently acquired by Symantec for $13.5 billion.

Taken together, this evidence suggests that Ellison failed to get the best out of a number of exceptionally talented field executives by not giving them the responsibility they deserved. Instead, his approach has been to crowd out such executives with codependent relationships to run the firm, first with Lane then with Catz. On the other hand, he did resurrect his career and save his company by finding and working with foils in his senior management teams, even if he was acting out of necessity.

HOW SUCCESSFUL COMPANIES STRUCTURE THE EXECUTIVE FOIL RELATIONSHIP

When I look across leading American and European corporations, a number of successful foil relationships come to mind, some of which are listed in Figure 4.1. As this list suggests, CFOs often serve as foils at leading firms. At GE, for example, Keith Sherin's foil relationship with CEO Jeff Immelt reflects 20 years of joint experience initially in the plastic business and then at GE's health imaging business, where Immelt was CEO and Sherin was CFO. Through countless meetings and decisions, Immelt has seen Sherin argue for what's good for the firm, which often diverges from what Immelt wants to hear. Still, as GE director and former chairman of JPMorgan Chase, Sandy Warner, told me, it is a mistake to believe that Sherin is Immelt's only foil—vice chairmen Michael Neal, John Rice, and Bob Wright also play that role in different capacities.

Preventing Power from Begetting Hubris: Evidence from Berkshire Hathaway's Warren Buffett

Obviously having a single foil is never enough—the key to real and lasting success is to have the right relationships with a number of trusted managers. At Oracle, the question is whether Ellison has placed trust and responsibility in enough colleagues, and whether he is prepared to help bring out their best. One person who he might consider learning from in this respect is Warren Buffett, Berkshire Hathaway's CEO. Berkshire Hathaway is a conglomer-

FIGURE 4.1 *Successful Foil Relationships in American and European Corporations*

Company	Senior Executive	Position	Foil	Position
Berkshire Hathaway	Warren Buffett	Chairman	Charlie Munger	Vice-Chairman
British Petroleum	John Browne	CEO	David Allen	Group Managing Director
Dell	Michael Dell	Founder/ Chairman	Kevin Rollins	CEO
eBay	Meg Whitman	CEO	Pierre Omidyar	Founder/ Chairman
			Maynard Webb	COO
GE	Jeffrey Immelt	CEO	Keith Sherin	CFO
Microsoft	Steve Ballmer	CEO	Bill Gates	Founder/ Chairman
Mittal Steel	Lakshmi Mittal	Chairman/CEO	Malay Mukherjee	COO
News Corp	Rupert Murdoch	Chairman/CEO	Peter Chernin	President/COO
Oracle	Larry Ellison	Founder/CEO	Safra Catz (after 2000)	CFO
			Jeff Henley	Chairman
Union Bank of Switzerland	Marcel Ospel	CEO	Peter Wuffli	Chairman
			Marcel Rohner	Deputy CEO
WPP	Martin Sorrell	CEO	Paul Richardson	CFO

ate, headquartered in Omaha, Nebraska, that has diversified holdings, but specializes in property and casualty insurance.

The firm's stellar reputation reflects its sustained exceptional performance. Overall, the firm's gains are 21.5 percent per annum since 1965, versus 10.3 percent for the S&P of the largest 500 U.S. stocks. Berkshire's returns have exceeded the index in all but 6 of the past 40 years. If you invested $1,000 in the firm in 1965, it would be worth about $3 million today, while about $50,000 if you invested in the S&P 500.

More to the point of this chapter, the firm generates over $40 billion of revenue with a staff of what the firm calls "13.8" people who are based at its Omaha headquarters. As the firm's chairman and CEO for 40 years, Buffett is also all-powerful. Once again, journalists have simplistically attributed much of the firm's success to Buffett. And yet Buffett's success would not be possible without the people he works with. Consider some of the ways that he's managed to avoid the problems that beset Fiorina and Ellison by having the right foils to decide which companies to invest in and how they should be managed.

A clear principle that underlies Buffett's approach to investing is that his ego produces bad investments. A case in point was the firm's 1990 investment in USAir, which, like most other airlines, had high fixed costs, strong unions, and commodity pricing. By 1994 Berkshire had lost 75 percent of its USAir investment, leading Buffett to tell the firm's shareholders: "I was neither pushed into the investment nor misled by anyone when making it. Rather this was a case of sloppy analysis, a lapse that may have been caused by the fact that we were buying a senior security or by *hubris*."[18] (italics added)

Although he ultimately sold the USAir stake for a healthy profit, the experience taught him that he was just as vulnerable to false confidence and hubris as the next person. Drawing on this lesson, Buffett knew he needed to work more closely with Vice-Chairman Charlie Munger. The Berkshire community affectionately calls Munger the "abominable no-man" for his eagerness to find holes in Buffett's arguments and proposals. (Howard Buffett, Warren's eldest son, says that his father is the second smartest man he knows—ranking him right after Charlie). It's a trust between the two friends that was forged by their background growing up in Omaha, where Munger worked at the Buffett family grocery store. The two became partners when Buffett was 26.

Both men are fiercely independent thinkers, and insist on assessing investments separately from one another to ensure objectivity. Usually (USAir was an exception), investments are screened and approved by both men, such that Buffett describes all decisions as those that are made by "Charlie and me."

Munger has been a crucial influence on Buffett's investing approach. Whereas Buffett began investing by searching for undervalued companies or "bargains," Munger taught him that paying a fair price for a great company would trump paying a great price for a fair company. A convert to behavioral decision theory, Munger relies on a checklist approach for managing the decision-making biases, especially overconfidence, that make and break deals. Overconfidence ranks high on Munger's list. Buffett trusts that Munger ". . . never lets ego interfere with rationality." As a result, errors are overwhelmingly ones of omission (walking away from good deals) than commission (making bad ones).

Other than having Munger screen deals, Buffett works tirelessly at building trust with owners and leaders of Berkshire's operating companies. He refuses to invest in their businesses unless and until he takes the time needed to feel personally comfortable with their values, integrity, and work ethic. Having made the investment, he then gets out of the way and gives them the freedom to set budgets, capital expenditures, and other operational policies (as when he agreed with RC Willey CEO Bill Child's decision to keep the Utah home furnishings business closed on Sundays, in keeping with Child's Mormon convictions).

Buffett's relationship with Lou Simpson, who helps manage a large Berkshire holding, GEICO insurance, further exemplifies this approach. "You may be surprised to learn that Lou does not necessarily inform me about what he is doing," writes Buffett. "When Charlie and I assign responsibility, we truly hand over the baton—and we give it to Lou just as we do to our operating managers. Therefore, I typically learn of Lou's transactions about ten days after the end of each month. Sometimes, it should be added, I silently disagree with his decisions (but he's usually right)."[19]

No Berkshire annual report is complete without Buffett's lavish praise for operating managers. Shareholders are usually requested to express their gratitude to those managers at Berkshire's annual meetings.

Foils Must Tell Us When to Step Back, Step In, and Step Aside

Trusting foils like Child and Simpson does not mean ignoring them. Exceptions to his hands-off rule arise. When Buffett learns about unethical conduct and mismanagement in the operating companies, he is quick to his feet. In 1991, he moved from Omaha to New York City to become interim chairman of the investment bank, Salomon Brothers, after he learned that senior managers looked the other way when a rogue trader threatened to ruin the large bond trading business. Buffett helped stage a successful turnaround at Salomon Brothers, and the company was later purchased by Citicorp. Buffett is biased against shutting down problematic operations, but will do so when needed. Referring to a troubled reinsurance division of one subsidiary, Gen Re, he writes, "Charlie would have moved swiftly to close down Gen Re Securities—no question about that. I, however, dithered."[20]

Today, Buffett has been so successful for so long that his pride may prevent him from stepping aside when he should. After all, he was born in 1930, and he is six years younger than Munger (we should also note, perhaps, that Viacom's Sumner Redstone was born in 1923, and Rupert Murdoch of NewsCorp was born in 1931). Buffett claims that he has already delegated some investing responsibility to a successor, though he will not say who the successor is and what is being delegated. In his 2005 letter to his shareholders, he rhetorically speculates about

> . . . whether the board will be prepared to make a change if that need should arise not from my death but rather from my decay, particularly if this decay is accompanied by my delusionally thinking that I am reaching new peaks of managerial brilliance . . . . Some managers remain effective well into their 80s— Charlie is a wonder at 82—and others noticeably fade in their 60s. When their abilities ebb, so usually do their powers of self-assessment. Someone else often needs to blow the whistle.[21]

Can Buffett step aside before shareholders (including the philanthropies that are inheriting over $40 billion in value from his shares) get hurt by this *inevitable* decline in his prodigious talents? On the one hand, Buffett knows how hard it is for friends and business associates to tell successful leaders that their time is up. On the other hand, he confidently relays, "We have an outstanding group of directors, and they will always do what's right for shareholders. And while we are on the subject, I feel terrific." [22]

Perhaps he has false confidence in his relationship with his directors, all of whom are his friends. If so, the onus should also be on Buffett to subject himself to more candid self-assessment. Consider this acid test: What would happen to the value of Berkshire shares if Buffett, for one reason or another, ceased to function effectively? If the answer is that Berkshire would be significantly damaged, Buffett should hasten the process of delegating.

It is striking that there are so few leaders who make provisions and space for successors. A refreshing counter-example is Carol Bartz, who built and managed the successful supplier of advanced personal computer design tools, Autodesk, and is now stepping down as the firm's CEO. It is a very unusual case: Bartz is 57, she created spectacular wealth for her firm's shareholders, and says that she "cried my eyes out" upon deciding to step down. Even more remarkable is that her chosen successor is Carl Bass, whom she had *fired* as a troublemaker in 1995 before rehiring him. After putting their differences aside, Bass, as the firm's COO, became Bartz's principal foil. Bartz says, "If you never change your mind about people, you won't have the talent you need." [23] The firm gets to keep Bass and Bartz gets to go out on top.

Each of these cases highlights the central theme of this chapter: Finding and working effectively with the right foils is a critical way of managing one's pride and, therefore, of curbing false confidence and hubris. The right foils know when to tell us when we are wrong, and they enable us to step back, step in, and step aside.

In general, what makes Buffett and Munger effective foils is that they have (1) long-standing personal and professional respect,

(2) complementary perspectives that they express openly and independently, and (3) compatible ambitions and agendas. At a more decentralized level, Buffett also knows what he wants in operating managers and then trusts them to do their jobs. As we've seen in these case studies, working with the right foil diffuses the effects of pride, overconfidence, and hubris in a centralized decision-making environment, whether you are an entry level executive or CEO.

GETTING THE RIGHT HELP WHEN DECISION MAKING IS DECENTRALIZED

So far we've looked at using a foil to get help with our decisions. Another option is to get out of the way, by letting others decide. This is a necessary executive function within any decentralized decision-making process, where decision-making processes and transparent data on executives' performances must substitute for a foil relationship.

Of course, this does not mean that decentralized decision making is a panacea for false confidence and hubris. It can delay decision making, as managers wait for their initiatives to get higher level approval (a problem we explore shortly in a case study about eBay). Unless decisions are made within tight parameters, multiple decision makers may not be in sync. A third problem concerns the law of large numbers: As more people decide, there is a greater likelihood that at least one will be infected by false confidence. WPP is an interesting case study of how decentralized decision making can both check and enable false confidence.

When Executives Trust Too Much: Martin Sorrell and the WPP Group's "Benattigate"

Like Buffett, Sir Martin Sorrell, CEO of the WPP Group, has been fabulously successful by finding the right businesses to invest in and the right managers to run them. A recent experience, however, testifies to the dangers of delegating to someone whose pride affects his or her judgment; and of engaging our pride in dealing with that person.

As background, Sorrell has aggressively worked to turn WPP into the second biggest marketing services group on earth, through hundreds of acquisitions since 1986. Today, the firm employs nearly 100,000 people in over 2,000 offices across 106 countries. WPP is a parent company that owns advertising agencies, including Grey Global, J. Walter Thompson, Ogilvy and Mather, and Young and Rubicon. WPP also owns a number of media buying companies, including Mediaedge:cia and Mind-Share. Each of these subsidiaries essentially operates as an independent company—with help from Sorrell and his small, London-based "center." Each has its own CEO, including highly regarded executives like Shelly Lazarus of Ogilvy and Mather and Ann Fudge of Young and Rubicon.

Sorrell trusts and frequently meets with leaders of the operating companies to learn more about clients, managers, and growth opportunities. To help coordinate and control the subsidiaries, he takes pride in the "center," the unit that helps operating managers by providing a centralized administrative function, freeing such managers for creative and customer work. The center also collects data and intervenes where necessary to clarify financial and business developments. It then serves as a catalyst by facilitating interactions between WPP's global subsidiaries. To create shareholder value, divisions must benefit each other, say, through customer referrals, the integration of services, and exchanges of best practices. Finally, the group acts as a central portal to coordinate services for large, global clients, from "soup" (such as basic research on customers) to "nuts" (such as ad campaigns). Global account managers coordinate services for clients like Ford and Vodafone that literally spend hundreds of millions of dollars with WPP each year.

Sorrell recently appointed country managers to increase the center's value added to the local operations. In theory, country managers serve as the center's eyes and ears, relaying local needs and information to the center and catalyzing synergies and other opportunities within the countries. In practice, country managers mediate foil relationships between Sorrell's senior management team and the operating divisions, and sometimes they overstep their brief by serving more as enforcers than enablers.

Consider the case of Marco Benatti, a Sorrell ally for nearly a decade, who was WPP's Italian country manager from 2002 through 2005. On the surface, Sorrell and Benatti had the ingredients of a strong partnership. Benatti was a fellow entrepreneur with an urbane demeanor who could help WPP with his deep Italian business connections. WPP's performance in Italy strengthened their relationship: In Benatti's time as country manager, Italy's profits grew from US $18 million to $41 million. And there was never any question that Benatti wanted Sorrell's job or could have it.

All of that changed on January 9, 2006, when Sorrell personally flew to Milan to fire Benatti. According to Sorrell, Benatti had overspent his budget by just over half a million euros ($600,000), charging that Benatti was taxing the Italian subsidiaries when he should have been introducing them to clients, getting them to cross-sell services, finding talented local executives, identifying acquisition targets, and so on.

Overspending the budget may be a sideshow given WPP's global revenues of over $8 billion. At center stage is Benatti's involvement in WPP's purchase of an Italian media buying company called Media Club, and Sorrell's visceral reaction to Benatti's choices. In December, Benatti and Sorrell vigorously disputed the earnout amount (additional compensation based on improved financial performance following the acquisition) from Media Club that WPP owed to Benatti: Benatti wanted €8.9 million (US $10.7 million) and Sorrell thought that the right number was closer to €300,000 (US $360,000).

Incensed by Benatti's apparent greed, Sorrell launched an internal inquiry. According to WPP, Benatti partially owns Media

Club and had also been directing WPP business to FullSix, an Italian media company in which he owns a 42 percent stake. Benatti is fighting back by suing WPP for unfair dismissal.

Among other things, this example highlights Sorrell's propensity to attract love/hate relationships. In particular, Sorrell had to decide whether to persuade and even pay Benatti to leave quietly or to pursue him for damages. The former would have kept what European journalists called "Benattigate" at bay and Sorrell's romantic relationship with Benatti's translator and foil, Daniela Weber, out of the public eye. Sorrell chose to fire Benatti and seek restitution. I mention Sorrell's relationship with Weber because it could have colored his ability to manage Benatti's departure.

So it was that instead of leaving quietly, Benatti vividly recalls being fired: "Martin wouldn't even shake my hand; I was in shock. . . . For a moment I thought it might be a joke. But Martin walked me to the elevator and told me to leave the office. I told him that I would at least like to gather my things, but he told me that if I didn't get on the elevator immediately he would call the police."[24]

While Italy contributes less than 3 percent of the firm's profits, the matter has damaged the firm's public relations, client relationships, and management stability in Italy and beyond. Recent interviews that Sorrell has given to explain WPP's record financial performance have degenerated into a discussion of Benattigate. The saga prompted a Morgan Stanley analyst to downgrade WPP, citing "recent issues in Italy, where the country manager has been dismissed and fraud investigations begun." Benatti estimates that Sorrell has spent up to $10 million on corporate detectives from Kroll, forensic accountants from Deloitte, lawyers, public relations companies, and WPP staff to investigate the matter. To justify his decision to WPP shareholders, Sorrell must extract at least that from Benatti, which remains to be seen.

Benattigate continues to make great copy for European journalists and Sorrell's detractors. Sorrell deflects the criticism by insisting that Benattigate is an isolated incident. When asked whether he has learned anything from it, Sorrell responds: "Yes, in future, I have got to be a better judge of character." Clearly, Benatti was incompatible as a foil and this damaged Sorrell's ability to help the firm's Italian operations. Another issue concerns whether Sorrell was the best person to decide and act on a matter in which his pride was so clearly engaged. Sorrell has a reputation for needlessly picking fights. Regarding his foes, a reporter from London's *Sunday Times* recalls, "When he won the hostile takeover of Ogilvy & Mather in 1989, advertising guru David Ogilvy was so incensed that he called him 'that odious little shit.' Chris Ingram, former boss of media-buying group Tempus, said he would rather 'lick an abattoir floor' than work for Sorrell."[25] An alternative for Sorrell is to have Paul Richardson, the firm's finance director, decide and act on matters that invoke Sorrell's pride.

Benattigate highlights the obvious point that decentralized decision making only works with clearly understood and functional foil relationships between the decision makers. Without those relationships, such decision making can be the worst of both worlds, leaving the firm vulnerable to false confidence among senior and line managers. Perhaps Benatti overestimated his importance and influence in Italy; and perhaps Sorrell underestimated the damage that the matter would cause the firm in general, and its Italian operations in particular.

Pride quickly interferes with rational decision making, whether a firm is run by an autocrat or whether decision making is more decentralized. To see a more systematic approach to decentralized decision making, and how it tempers the impact of pride, false confidence, and hubris, consider how Meg Whitman orchestrates decision making at eBay.

Meg Whitman and Decentralized Decision Making at eBay

Whitman has been eBay's CEO since 1998 when the firm was a highly promising online auction company with over 3 million registered users, $16 million in annual sales, and a market value of over $30 million. Under Whitman's watch, the firm has grown to over 180 million registered users, generates more than $4.5 billion in revenues; and has a market value of over $30 billion.

Fortune now calls Whitman the most powerful woman in American business (unseating Carly Fiorina from that title in 2003). Procter & Gamble CEO A.G. Lafley, who appointed Whitman to his board, refers to her as one of the few leaders whose ". . . circle of influence is greater than their circle of control."[26]

Whitman exemplifies how leaders can become more influential and can extract their pride and false confidence from decisions by *selectively* empowering others.

Empowering Decision Makers at All Levels

Whitman regards the firm's founder and chairman, Pierre Omidyar, as a foil. In fact, before taking the eBay job, Whitman says she needed to know that Omidyar was going to remain at the company. "My going-in hypothesis was that Pierre was really smart," recalls Whitman, ". . . as far as I was concerned, we were going to be twins for the foreseeable future."[27]

The relationship between Whitman and Omidyar works because they tackle problems from very different perspectives. Whitman is an analytically driven problem solver with a background in management consulting, whereas Omidyar's familiarity with eBay's community of buyers and sellers helps him gauge how they will respond to management decisions. Mirroring the relationship between Buffett and Munger at Berkshire, Whitman rarely makes major decisions without him. Often, they arrive at the same conclusion from separate perspectives, independently concluding, for example, that the firm should ban the sale of firearms—even if that would predictably anger certain community members.

eBay is setup to be an egalitarian community, in which each community member should be treated with equal courtesy and respect. This philosophy has guided some of Whitman and Omidyar's more difficult decisions, including those to refuse bulk discounts to power sellers (including large retailers like Sears and Home Depot), to crack down on community members who are fraudulent and don't honor trades, and to buy PayPal and Skype to facilitate easier payments and interactions between community members.

In practice, eBay hosts numerous subcommunities of traders in vertical categories that range from consumer electronics to sporting goods to travel services. It's a natural setting to empower category managers—with responsibility for customer segments—to make operating decisions.

Effectively, category managers are entrepreneurs who are responsible for their own retail businesses. Take the case of Azita Qadri who was the head of the Lifestyle Group for eBay in the UK before becoming eBay's Small Business Manager in the UK. As a category manager, Qadri's decision-making responsibilities included developing an annual strategy for her category (given external supply chain analysis and quantitative analysis of category trading data), leading direct sales campaigns to attract targeted sellers, designing cross-category selling campaigns in coordination with the eBay UK Marketing and Site team, and finding and developing (including through education programs) talented people to lead at the firm.

Whitman's relationships with executives like Qadri are impersonal, set more by performance rules and standards than personal interactions. Each category manager must justify the firm's investment in his or her category by referring to their performance on common, just-in-time metrics concerning trading and traffic trends and customer satisfaction. Satisfaction of community members ranges from 10 (most happy) to 1 (utterly disgusted); 7 is about average. While the metric can be used to assess the overall quality of the firm's services, it's more useful at the category level, since satisfaction levels vary widely across categories. What results is a large number of small decentralized decisions at the category level that Whitman is largely unaware of. When those decisions are taken together, and shared for best practices, they explain movements in subcategory and firm traffic and revenues that Whitman and senior managers carefully watch.

A Structured Approach to Defusing False Confidence

At eBay, middle managers are intended to serve as enablers for the category managers. Following GE's model, Whitman rotates executives around the three major divisions—eBay USA; eBay International; and PayPal, the firm's payment services division (an emerging division is the firm's online telephone service, Skype, which eBay acquired for $2.6 billion).

Executive rotation regulates the process by which divisions benefit each other. Moreover, it helps Whitman observe, compare, and advise prospective successors in different roles. That matters because she is on record as saying that ten years is the longest any CEO should serve a firm, which puts her departure at 2008. Finally, it encourages a companywide approach to decision making, because managers who have worked in other divisions are more knowledgeable about how their new division can benefit the others.

With nine years of experience at the major strategy consulting firm, Bain & Co, Whitman's decisions follow a structured problem-solving approach that avoids ad hoc decisions. The background of a number of senior managers reinforces that approach—John Donahoe (president of eBay's marketplace) is a Bain & Co alumnus, and Beth Axelrod (head of HR) and Matt Bannick (head of eBay International) are McKinsey & Co. alumni.

Problem solving at eBay always involves defining and scoping the parameters of the problem so it can be broken down into manageable chunks or subissues; generating hypotheses that guide analysis and data collection; performing the analysis that informs the hypotheses; and synthesizing the results to produce a decision. It is when the results of the analyses are at hand that the decision-making process gets contentious. "We have heated debates," says Whitman. "We reach consensus or I make the decision. If I am wrong, I change it, and I don't take myself too seriously." Of course, once the decision is made, the expectation is that every decision maker supports it until there is strong evidence to revisit it.[28]

Whitman accepts that she can only work effectively with a limited number of foils, perhaps up to five. Her transparent and decentralized decision making underpins what Lafley calls Whitman's growing circle of influence, and provides some guidelines to remove false confidence from her own and others' decisions. To recap:

- Whitman has a small number of foil relationships: Chairman Omidyar helps gauge the reaction of eBay's community to new processes and rules, and COO Maynard Webb helps ensure that the Web site supports mission-critical tasks. Those relationships have lasted nearly as long as Whitman's tenure at eBay.
- Whitman delegates decisions at the subcommunity level to category managers, who gain resources based on standardized and transparent data and rules. It's a process whereby better-performing subcommunities and their managers get more resources and professional opportunities.
- Decisions reflect a structured decision-making process that is based on consensus or, when the decisions get contentious, on Whitman's judgment.

eBay's regimented approach to decision making is one of the company's most impressive qualities. At eBay, the danger is not so much overconfident decision making but bureaucratic creep, in which major decision makers become increasingly removed from the community and market forces.

SUMMARY

The case studies in this chapter teach us much about the consequences of executives who rely on their pride, rather than trusted advisors, to guide their decision making. That makes the willingness (and ability) to cultivate and use foils a hallmark of great leadership. Consider these points from the experiences of the five high-profile CEOs that are featured here:

- Autocrats—those who command employees by telling them what to do and how to do it—are most susceptible to false confidence and hubris. Because they are least likely to get input for their decisions, they lack information that false confidence is driving their decisions and actions.
- Autocrats who work with the right foil or foils, as Larry Ellison's experience suggests, go far toward mitigating their susceptibility to false confidence and hubris.
- The role of the foil is to tell us when we are wrong; and to tell us when to step in, when to step back, and when to step aside.
- Effective foils improve decision making through complementary capabilities and perspectives.
- Effective foils share a common agenda and ambition. The minute that one party feels threatened by the other, the foil relationship unravels, as it did between Ellison and Lane.
- Effective foils also share a level of trust and personal respect that must be built over time. That puts leaders who join your

firm from outside at a disadvantage, unless they join you with foils.

- Because foil relationships must be nurtured and managed, you can weaken the effectiveness of the decision-making process if you have too many foils or rush to have a foil. Some evidence suggests that five may be the maximum number.

- Various decentralized decision-making structures are available to reduce false confidence among top-level decision makers and line managers. At WPP, the center helps to do this; at eBay, Meg Whitman uses category managers for this purpose.

- Structured problem solving provides a regulated approach for taking personal biases (particularly pride) out of decisions. The combination of having the *right decision makers* as well as the right *decision-making approach* always trumps overreliance on one over the other.

We've seen the importance of counting on foils and other trusted advisors to provide us with important feedback about our performance and the quality of our decisions. In the next chapter, we learn the importance of actively seeking out that feedback and acting on it—whether or not we like what we hear.

5

Kidding Ourselves about Our Situation

HOW FAILING TO GROUND JUDGMENT IN FEEDBACK FUELS EXECUTIVE HUBRIS

"Ignorance more frequently begets confidence than does knowledge: it is those who know little, and not those who know much, who so positively assert that this or that problem will never be solved by science." [1]

CHARLES DARWIN

Chapter 3 examined how excessive pride prevents us from knowing ourselves, as self-puffery leads us to unduly impress others and to use self-serving data to assess our performance. In this chapter, we'll study how our assessment of our *situation* determines whether our confidence is built on a false or grounded platform. We'll see how underestimating our situation can lead our confidence in our abilities to outpace what we *can* deliver.

Getting ahead of ourselves seems to be the norm in the workplace, from Hollywood to the building industry to e-commerce companies and sites. Movie studio boss, Joe Roth, was asked why so many major movies are released in the United States on Memorial Day and Independence Day weekends. "Hubris. Hubris," replied Roth. "If you only think about your own business, you think 'I've got a good story department, I've got a good marketing department, we're going to go out and do this.' And you don't think that everybody else is thinking the same way. In a given weekend in a year you'll have five movies open, and there's certainly not enough people [moviegoers] to go around."[2] And yet Roth accepts that he overestimates the prospects of his own movies by underestimating his competitors' movies.

Similarly, one study of over 2,000 engineers at two technology companies showed that between 32 and 42 percent of engineers rate themselves in the top 5 percent of all engineers within their firms because they underestimate the complexity of their projects.[3] Because they exaggerate their ability to deliver on schedule, their firms expensively use "buffer time" to manage late projects (witness Microsoft's delays in launching versions of Windows and Vista).

Many successful firms systematically pay surprisingly large penalties to subsidize managers who use poor judgment in reading their situation, effectively subsidizing executives who get ahead of themselves. Perhaps a better solution is to develop skills for avoiding the problem in the first place.

Heedlessly underestimating the underlying realities of our situation and the ability of competitors to outpoint us is the third source of false confidence that induces hubris, costing us and others. Managing this source—working toward more grounded situation assessment—is the focus of this chapter. As we will now elaborate, the key to developing grounded judgment is to get and use the best available feedback.

GAUGING THE QUALITY OF FEEDBACK AND OUR WILLINGNESS TO ACT ON IT

The nature of the feedback that we get at work can be considered along two dimensions. The first is the quality of feedback we get about our situation: It may be accurate, pertinent, immediate, and frequent (call this strong); or it may be vague, delayed, and infrequent (call this weak). The second dimension is our willingness to act on that feedback: It may be intense—say, if we're dealing with life and death matters as a surgeon; or it may

FIGURE 5.1 *Assessing the Effectiveness of Feedback*

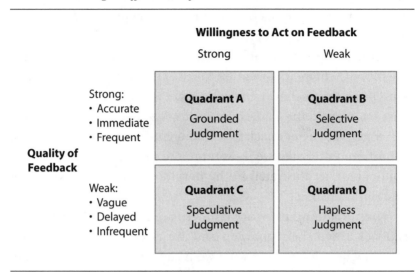

be weak—say, because we do not like, trust, or know the source of the feedback or because our evaluation and pay are not tied to how we gain and use feedback.

The matrix shown in Figure 5.1 summarizes how we can use these two dimensions to assess the value and effectiveness of feedback and the type of judgment resulting from that feedback. You can use this matrix to determine the type of judgment you apply when making different kinds of decisions, noting that you'll find yourself in different quadrants on different decisions.

Many professionals get great feedback and are intensely motivated to use it, as we will see in the case of the professional basketball player, Steve Nash. Here, both high-quality feedback and our strong willingness to act on it result in decisions that are based on *grounded judgment* (Quadrant A in the matrix). Of course, grounded judgment is what every executive must strive for.

At other times, executives may get great feedback, but don't take it to heart or make it an integral part of their decision-making process. When executives ignore or discount feedback, their decisions are based on *selective judgment,* a label that refers to our propensity to make decisions about situations that are based on feedback that pleases us or fits our preconceptions of our situation (Quadrant B in the matrix).

Perhaps the most typical scenario in the workplace is a third category of judgment—what we'll call *speculative judgment* (Quadrant C). In this scenario, executives get weak feedback that they must act on, as is the case on most projects. Because projects take time to complete, feedback from them tends to be vague, delayed, and infrequent. Later, we'll examine the implications of this type of judgment, as illustrated in the development and marketing of prescription drugs.

The remaining category concerns executives who get weak feedback about their situation and are not especially motivated to use it when deciding in what we'll call *hapless judgment* (Quadrant D in the matrix). It's easy to think of this type of decision maker as incompetent when it often refers to capable people who are in the wrong role. A brilliant quantitative analyst, for example, may have a spectacular IQ, and yet may lack the interpersonal skills and emotional intelligence to exercise good judgment as a businessperson, hedge fund investor (remember the collapse of Long Term Capital Management, which was founded by two Nobel prize–winning economists), or dean of a business school. Blissfully ignorant of their limitations, executives make matters worse for themselves, their colleagues, and their organization by being unaware of their weaknesses. Being unskilled and unaware of it through a lack of good feedback and any willingness to act upon feedback produces *hapless judgment.*[4]

I encourage you to treat this matrix seriously and use it in determining the type of judgment underlying your own decisions for three reasons. First, it will help you to predict how and when you will get ahead of yourself and so become more susceptible to the false confidence that breeds hubris. Second, the matrix offers a starting point for more grounded situation assessment. Are you failing to get high-quality feedback or, for whatever reason, are you unwilling to act on it—or a combination of both? Third, this matrix can guide compensation and performance evaluation systems that reward us for getting and using feedback. Leading firms, including GE, treat all executives as though they are in similar situations and therefore receive similar quality feedback, when that clearly isn't always the case. Apart from anything else, that approach discriminates against executives who, for no fault of their own, receive inferior feedback.

DECISION MAKING BASED ON GROUNDED JUDGMENT

So, having grounded judgment means receiving prompt, accurate, and frequent feedback, and being highly motivated to act on it. Professional basketball player Steve Nash offers an excellent illustration of this type of decision making. Nash has succeeded in his field by translating feedback about his situation into superb professional judgment.

America's National Basketball Association (NBA) is the world's richest basketball league with the best players and teams. It is the league that any young player dreams about joining. A Canadian basketball player without an overpowering body, exceptional quickness, and freakish jumping ability simply does not make it to the NBA. Steve Nash, who was the most valuable player (MVP) in the NBA in 2005 and 2006, is the exception.

Nash built his career from nowhere, out of nothing more than drive and guile. The son of a soccer player, Nash naturally gravitated toward soccer and Canada's favorite sport, ice hockey. Growing up in Victoria, British Columbia, he discovered basketball in the eighth grade. Latching on to the game, he epitomized the undersized kid who willed himself to succeed by tirelessly shooting baskets, usually alone. Picture him practicing in the rain or shine, night or day, outside or inside. By watching the ball either swish through the basket or tumble away from it literally millions of times, Nash got and gets clear, immediate, and ongoing feedback on his playing strengths and weaknesses.

After graduating from high school, he and his coach believed that he could play college basketball in the United States, and together they applied to over 20 colleges. Team after team rejected him. "A recruiter would see this average-sized white kid," recalls Nash, "and then he'd have to go back to campus and say 'Hey, I saw this kid from Canada' and before he finished, everyone would say, 'Hey, we got a thousand kids like that.'"[5] The *only* college that would take him was the University of Santa Clara, which is much better known as a nursery for Silicon Valley types than as a springboard for basketball superstars. Driven to learn from his mistakes, Nash kept improving at Santa Clara, and his confidence grew commensurately.

Unlike Nash, other players with more innate talents emerge as early stars in school and college. Propped up by coaches and sycophants, these players typically are supremely confident about their professional prospects from the outset, relying more on talent than hard work and feedback. Instead of reassessing their abilities and confidence, as competitors like Nash catch up with them, they believe that they are sure to succeed at the "next level." No wonder scouts prefer a combination of super talent and work ethic over talent alone.

Nash still draws upon the critical feedback he gets from watching the results of his dribbling, passing, and shooting in practice and games. On any given week, he shoots up to 2,000 baskets. Before each game, he tunes up by shooting balls at various angles and distances from the basket. A *Sports Illustrated* journalist, Jack McCallum, recently caught up with him after a drill to tell Nash that he had seen him shoot 163 baskets. "Any idea how many you made?" asked McCallum. "A hundred thirty," replied Nash, overestimating the number of baskets he had successfully shot by two.[6]

With that guess, Nash perfectly illustrates healthy overconfidence: He slightly overestimated the number of baskets that he successfully shot even if his estimate was based on his best available evidence. More generally, Nash is about 80 percent confident that he will make a basket on any given shot in pregame drills. Ask him what percentage of baskets he'll make during games and he'll give you more detail: Over 40 percent when he is further from the basket (past the three point line) and better than 90 percent from closer range (at the free throw range).

Teammates and coaches trust Nash, because his grounded confidence wins games. Teammate Raja Bell says, "The beauty of Steve holding (rather than shooting) it is that you know he's holding it to help you out . . . he'll always have an answer."[7] If he were overconfident, he'd be taking shots that Bell and others should be taking. If he were underconfident, he'd pass up shots that he should be taking. Nash has what basketball players mean by great shot selection, or "court IQ." His coach at the Phoenix Suns, Mike D'Antoni, gladly accepts Nash's overconfidence as a small price to pay for his superb professional judgment.[8]

Being highly confident and largely right defines great judgment. It's a question of working tirelessly to get into situations where we get the best possible feedback. As a basketball player who makes hundreds of decisions in a game, Nash relies on that judgment as well as his well-practiced skills to be the best in the game.

Of course, you don't have to be a star athlete to have grounded judgment. Many professionals get accurate, prompt, and frequent feedback, and use it to stay competitive—think here of world-class pilots, highly respected surgeons, and top-flight salespeople with tight customer relationships. Lawyers, management consultants, and investment bankers also can fall within this category, to the extent that they get timely feedback after each transaction or engagement, and that feedback might easily affect their compensation and promotion. What distinguishes the quality of their judgment is how they use feedback.

DECISION MAKING BASED ON SELECTIVE JUDGMENT

Quadrant B of the "feedback effectiveness" matrix character-izes the type of judgment we draw on when we get great feedback but are not motivated to act on it. As discussed in Chapter 3, even when we get excellent feedback, pride can interfere with our abil-ity to accept and act on it. Let's face it: Negative feedback is unpleasant to accept, even if our failure to use it hurts us. Have you ever resisted selling shares that have plummeted in value, refusing to accept clear evidence that the investment failed? Have you ever "doubled down" or bought more shares in a firm as its share price fell further? My colleague at the University of Califor-nia, Berkeley, Barry Staw, has conducted numerous studies that demonstrate how and why we escalate our commitment to a failing course of action, rather than walk away from it.[9]

Other examples of discounting salient feedback about our sit-uation abound. Dan Rather was a brilliant newsman and broad-caster for 24 years. In 2004, he resigned prematurely after an incident in which he doggedly refused to accept growing evidence that his reporters had relied on forged documents to describe President Bush's National Guard Service. Overconfident about his sources, Rather made an error of judgment in an act of hubris that blemished an otherwise stellar career.

Rather's example highlights the costs of hearing what we want to hear, of seeking out feedback that supports preferred beliefs. Likewise, accepting praise and rejecting or discounting criticism helps us to feel better about our situation and promotes false confidence.

Optimism as a Tool for Dealing with Relentlessly Negative Feedback

Executives who work at tasks where failure is endemic, includ-ing certain types of selling, publishing, and product development, often ask me how to manage negative feedback that can wear them down. The answer is you need a highly optimistic disposition, and, having that, you need to act on feedback to compete with fellow optimists.

As an illustration of the power of optimism, consider the case of life insurance agents. Frustration and disappointment are ever-present for these agents, who get rejected by at least nine out of every ten potential customers. Prospects are difficult and expensive to find, and even harder to qualify or convert into customers. Customer feedback comes in the form of clear, prompt, frequent, and almost unwavering renditions of the word *no*. Yet, the best life insurance agents can make over $200,000 a year.

University of Pennsylvania psychologist Martin Seligman led a team that studied 15,000 applicants for life insurance sales positions at the Metropolitan Life Insurance Company, a major U.S. insurance firm, to find out (among other things) whether optimists make the best sales agents.[10] Using a questionnaire, researchers measured applicants' optimism and pessimism. They also found a "special force" of 129 agents who demonstrated their lack of knowledge of insurance products by flunking the industry test, but were hired anyway because they were highly optimistic. They then tracked the performance of the successful applicants (the "regular force") and the special force for two years after the questionnaire.

Seligman and his team found that after two years, the most optimistic regular force agents outsold their most pessimistic colleagues by 37 percent, and the special force optimists outsold the pessimists in the regular force by 88 percent.[11] On average, the special force agents remained at MetLife for years longer than their less-optimistic colleagues. Identifying and keeping the right agents has saved the firm a fortune in recruiting and training costs, and obviously results in a more productive sales force. Similar results have also been found in settings like real estate, banking, motor vehicles, and office products.

Seligman shows that optimists tend to be more productive and resilient because they have different attitudes to success and failure than pessimists. For optimists, success is a stable outcome that reinforces their efficacy. Optimists view failure as an isolated event that they can learn from, but which says little if anything about their underlying personality and capabilities. More successful salespeople at new ventures often tell me that "failure is not failure," it is a chance to practice and learn—a stepping stone that brings them closer to success. By contrast, pessimists see success as a one-time event that they cannot control. For them, failure is a sustainable event that speaks to their abilities.

In the spirit of these results, Seligman believes that optimists "have a set of self-serving illusions that enable them to maintain good cheer and health in a universe essentially indifferent to their welfare."[12] His advice is to strive to be ever more optimistic, even if that means selectively using feedback in order to sustain the illusion of optimism.

The problem is that when optimism becomes extreme, it also prevents us from learning from rejection and, therefore, feeds false confidence. Unshakable optimism helps us to move on to the next customer or deal without taking valuable learning from the customer we lost. Executives with optimistic dispositions make better choices when they learn from both positive and negative data—when they can migrate closer toward Quadrant A. For optimists, the trick is not to discount or ignore relentlessly negative feedback about a difficult situation (i.e., stay in Quadrant B), it is to learn from it (i.e., commit to moving toward Quadrant A) and have a loss mitigation plan just in case (see Chapter 6).

DECISION MAKING BASED ON SPECULATIVE JUDGMENT

The third type of judgment that we invariably face is speculative judgment. Here, we're highly motivated to act on feedback, but the available data we receive is weak—the feedback is vague, off point, delayed, and infrequent; that is, judgment must be at least somewhat speculative—we just can't get the information that we need to make a fully informed decision. We don't know what our closest competitor is doing, for example, or we lack reliable data about how customers are responding to a product launch, even as we face pressing decisions about how much to invest in the launch. We get mixed signals from our boss about whether he or she is truly committed to our present initiatives.

To migrate from the speculative judgment of Quadrant C to the grounded judgment of Quadrant A, the trick again is to work on getting the best available data. Although you simply may not be able to get the accurate, frequent, and timely feedback that you need for an entirely grounded decision, you can strive for it. Otherwise, speculative judgment will turn to hapless judgment.

Take drug safety, a matter that can make or break pharmaceutical and biotechnology companies. Rather than search for more safety data, drug companies have been accused of launching drugs prematurely before properly searching for and evaluating safety data. Everything is at stake. Consider that liability for the German drug company Bayer AG from acute renal failure associated with its anticholesterol drugs, which have been withdrawn from the market, may be as high as $3 billion. Liability for Wyeth from valvular heart disease and pulmonary hypertension problems associated with the anti-obesity medicine Redux may be as high as $22 billion. Estimates of the liability for Merck from cardiovascular problems associated with the pain reliever drug Vioxx run as high as $50 billion. When the Irish biotechnology firm Elan removed its multiple sclerosis drug Tysabri from the market, the company lost over 75 percent of its market value.

The story of the massive and costly failure of the drug Vioxx and the corporate culture at Merck in which it was developed showcases how and when speculative judgment degenerates into hapless judgment. We'll begin our review of that case study by humanizing the process within which pharmaceutical companies develop and release of new drugs.

Merck's Management of Vioxx

Hal Barron, the chief medical officer at Genentech, places the average cost of developing a new drug at well over $800 million (similar to the cost of developing a new car). On average, it takes 12 years for a drug to go from the laboratory to the drugstore, and it's a longshot that any individual drug will make it. Fewer than 1 in 1,000 compounds that enter preclinical testing with laboratory and animal studies make it to human testing; and 1 in 9 drugs that are tested in humans gets approved by the U.S. Food and Drug Administration (FDA).

Drug firms can spend up to four years and tens of millions of dollars on preclinical trials. At each step of the drug development and testing process, the firm's chief scientists—such as Baron—must decide whether to proceed to the next step. A green light can *only* be justified by the prospect that a compound will become a blockbuster drug with enough sales to generate very compelling returns on the huge, ongoing investment. With their sights firmly fixed on blockbusters, executives tend to spend more time hoping that compounds will hit the jackpot than worrying that they will be shut down for safety reasons.

Drug developers face some pressure to selectively disclose safety and efficacy information. Data comes in large part from tests that are mandated by regulatory agencies, such as the FDA in the United States and the European Agency for the Evaluation of Medicinal Products. Figure 5.2 lists the U.S. tests, their purposes, the test population, and the average time to completion.

Assessing and managing safety throughout this process is expensive. Emerging safety issues can always stop a drug's development, and such a red light means walking away from a massive financial, organizational, and personal commitment to a project designed to produce immensely worthwhile, even life-giving results. Scientists face enormous pressure to find confirming information that drugs are efficacious, rather than disconfirming evidence that they are unsafe. Moreover, proof that drugs are

FIGURE 5.2 *Time Line for the FDA Pharmaceuticals Testing and Approval Process*

Test	Purpose	Test Population	Average Time
Preclinical testing	Assess safety and biological activity	Lab and animal studies	3–4 years
Phase 1	Determine safety and dosage	20–80 volunteers	1 year
Phase 2	Evaluate effectiveness of drug at different doses and look for side effects	100–300 patient volunteers	2–3 years
Phase 3	Verify effectiveness; monitor adverse reactions from long-term use	1,000–3,000 patient volunteers	3 years

Depending on results, file new drug application with FDA.

Test	Purpose	Test Population	Average Time
FDA	Review process and approve or reject	N/A	1–3 years

Source: Compiled from various sources

unsafe is hard to find. All of that means that rosy scenarios about prospective sales of drugs under development can trump bleak assessments of side effects.

Extended delays between the launch of each phase of the testing process mean that executives get poor feedback about drug prospects. Because safety can only be seen amongst large samples of patients who have used the drugs for years, results from the tests merely indicate or suggest safety levels, but can't actually determine them. Whatever our doctors may tell us, no drug is completely safe: There will always be a trade-off between risk and benefit.

To get the FDA's stamp of approval for any drug is a Herculean feat. That's why news of FDA approval is celebrated by drug companies and their shareholders, even if the approved drug remains therapeutically and commercially unproven, which brings us to Vioxx.

For years, Merck was revered in the business, health, and phil-
anthropic communities. In *Fortune* magazine's annual surveys, the
firm was named by businesspeople as America's most admired
firm *every* year from 1987 to 1993. Between 1995 and 2001, Merck
presented 13 major new drugs for treating conditions that ranged
from asthma to AIDS/HIV for FDA approval. Those drugs were
approved with an average time of 11 months, an unprecedented
time to approval. The firm's drug development record was a glowing tribute to its leaders, especially the Harvard-trained physician,
Edward Scolnick, who ran the firm's laboratories.[13]

Respect for Merck and its leaders also reflected the millions
of dollars of medicines that the firm donates to fight infection in
third-world countries. Merck has been a worldwide leader in corporate philanthropy for years, and there are few better examples
of that than Merck's management of river blindness. The disease
is caused by small parasitic worms that get under the skin through
bites left by black flies that breed close to rivers. Rather than sell
its cure for river blindness—the drug Mectizan—Merck has
donated it since 1987 through the Merck Mectizan Donation Program, the largest medical donation program in history. Over 20
million people in at least eight developing nations have received
the drug.

In spite of its success and philanthropy, however, by 2000,
Merck was seriously underperforming. Shortly afterwards, executives had to cancel drugs for depression (which failed to be effective in clinical trials) and diabetes (which posed a cancer risk),
which they expected to be blockbusters. For investors, patent
expiry on blockbuster drugs loomed larger than the promise of
future ones. Investors mercilessly dumped Merck's shares, driving
the stock price down from $80 in 2001 to $50 in 2004 to about $40
at this writing.

Crisis hit on September 30, 2004, the day that CEO Ray Gilmartin withdrew Vioxx from the market, the $2.5 billion-a-year
drug used by 20 million Americans since May 1999, in response to
information that Vioxx may significantly increase the risk of heart

attacks and strokes, or "cardiovascular events." This announcement alone pushed the firm's stock price to under $30, wiping
over $25 billion from the firm's market capitalization, unleashing
a torrent of lawsuits, and raising ethical questions about management's judgment.

Commentators have had mixed views about Merck's handling
of Vioxx. An editor of the *Wall Street Journal* described Vioxx as just
another unfortunate example of a product that lost a competitive
race for a big market, in this case to Pfizer's Celebrex, which generates over $3 billion in sales a year. The former editor of the highly
prestigious medical journal the *New England Journal of Medicine,*
Dr. Marcia Angell, disagrees. For her, Vioxx was a damning indict-
ment on both Merck and the FDA, as she writes in a letter to the
editor of the *Wall Street Journal*:

> The fact that Vioxx probably increased the risk of heart
> attacks and strokes was known for three years, but Merck
> downplayed it and did not undertake studies to settle the mat-
> ter, while the FDA sat on its hands. . . . As you [*WSJ* editor]
> acknowledged, the risk was confirmed only serendipitously in
> a clinical trial for another purpose. . . . Since COX-2 inhibitors
> like Vioxx are no better than over-the-counter drugs for reliev-
> ing arthritis symptoms, far more expensive, and of only limited
> effectiveness in preventing gastrointestinal complications, it's
> hard to share your enthusiasm for them except as cash cows
> for Pfizer and Merck.[14]

The merits of these arguments should be placed firmly within
the context of the extraordinarily costly, laborious, and risky drug
testing and approval process we saw earlier. That's the environment within which Merck's management gathered feedback to
decide what to do with the drug, and it helps explain how their
false confidence may have lapsed into a culture of executive
hubris.

Underestimating Risks and Overestimating the Power of Marketing

As early as 1997, Merck had seen warning signs that Vioxx might have some unwanted side effects. In an e-mail memo, Dr. Alise Reicin, a Merck scientist, wrote that the "possibility of increased C.V." (cardiovascular events associated with Vioxx) were of "great concern."[15] Further, in 1998, a team led by Garret Fitzgerald, a professor at the University of Pennsylvania, was able to show that Cox-2 inhibitors in general interfere with enzymes that are thought to ward off cardiovascular disease. Fitzgerald immediately notified Merck and other major drug companies of these findings, and about their implications for the increased risk of heart attack and stroke.

Nevertheless, Merck executives were jubilant when the FDA approved Vioxx in May 1999, after merely nine months of review. In its 1999 annual report, Merck told its shareholders that the drug was its "biggest, fastest, and best launch ever." Scolnick said that Vioxx's "major advantage over Celebrex [Pfizer's competing drug] is its duration of action." He noted that since Merck's patents on two leading drugs were about to expire, Vioxx was set "to fill the void" as a "once-a-day pill."[16] Scolnick, who oversaw a $2.5 billion research and development budget in 2002, went on to say, "We know what we have, and we fell pretty confident. Understate and overperform—that's how I was brought up in science."[17]

In spite of Scolnick's confidence, Merck and its competitors lacked and continue to lack compelling evidence that Cox-2 inhibitors provide significantly more relief for arthritis pain than naproxen and aspirin. Management focused instead on Vioxx's ability to relieve the potentially serious stomach problems that Cox-1 inhibitors can trigger, even though many people take Cox-1 inhibitors without experiencing stomach discomfort.[18] That's why Merck's management approved an expensive study, called "VIGOR" (Vioxx Gastrointestinal Outcomes Research), to demonstrate just that.

Dr. Fitzgerald, an authority on Cox-1 inhibitors told me, "The problem with this class of drugs—and it is not just a Vioxx story by any means—is that they were developed for a niche market for a safety indication (in effect, gastrointestinal issues)—not new efficacy. Then they were marketed to the mass of the population and the forecast safety problems emerged but were not offset by superior efficacy."

Although other drugs in this class may share the same weaknesses, at issue here is whether Merck's senior management, including Scolnick and Gilmartin, were kidding themselves on at least two crucial matters: Did they believe that the drug was more potent than it was, underestimating its safety risks and overestimating its ability to overcome stomach problems common to Cox-1 inhibitors? And did they believe that they could impose a questionable drug on millions of middle-aged and elderly people with everyday pain through aggressive marketing that targeted patients and doctors?

Turning to the latter, one industry research firm, Verispan, estimates that Merck spent over $500 million on direct-to-consumer marketing for Vioxx.[19] During prime-time television, millions of Americans viewed former Olympic and ice skating champions rejoice in how happy the drug makes them in middle age. The objective of any consumer drug campaign is to promise actual and potential consumer benefits, so that customers will then "talk to their doctors" about these drugs. It's a practice by which patients pressure doctors into prescribing advertised drugs, including those that lack therapeutic benefits.

Nevertheless, Merck's sales force aggressively sought to persuade doctors to prescribe Vioxx. In particular, 3,000 salespeople were recruited to promote Vioxx to doctors with $2,000 in incentives for meeting sales targets. Each representative was given detailed instructions on how to curry favor with doctors, all the way from shaking their hands (no longer than three seconds) to eating bread at dinner (small, bite-sized pieces).

Certain doctors were targeted for special treatment. Miami, Florida, rheumatologist Dr. Roy Altman was given $25,000 to run his own "clinical trial." Dr. Robert Ettlinger, a rheumatologist in Tacoma, Washington, was also singled out as someone who should get money for "panel speeches, meetings, and clinical trials." Dr. Max Hamburger, a New York rheumatologist, led a consortium of physicians who were "high-volume prescribers and huge adopters of Celebrex," according to another Merck memo. That prompted Merck to join Pfizer in sponsoring Hamburger's retreats at which doctors discussed guidelines for prescribing arthritis medicine.[20] Each doctor insists that Merck has not influenced their prescription-writing practices or otherwise bought their favors, but research suggests that staying impartial toward providers of these favors is problematic if not impossible.

From Speculative to Hapless Judgment at Merck: Failing to Act on Feedback about Vioxx

Needless to say, Merck salespeople were encouraged to downplay any potential to cause heart attacks and strokes. In 2000, the firm actually issued a "cardiovascular card" to help salespeople respond to doctors' safety queries.[21] Included was information that Vioxx was 8 to 11 times safer than comparable drugs, which is an estimate that has subsequently been questioned.

Excluded was evidence from Merck's own VIGOR study that Vioxx could cause heart attacks. Although intended to demonstrate that Vioxx created fewer stomach problems than its rival, Celebrex, the study revealed that that the risk of "cardiovascular events" for subjects taking Vioxx are 1 in 200, versus 1 in 1,000 for subjects on naproxen.

The crucial results of this study, partly authored by Merck executives, were published in the *New England Journal of Medicine* in November 2000 in an article that emphasized Vioxx's stomach or gastrointestinal benefits; but, the discussion of cardiovascular events was downplayed and minimized even though the "prevention of one complicated gastrointestinal event was offset by the occurrence of one serious (i.e., potentially fatal) cardiovascular event," according to later analysis by the present editor of the *New England Journal of Medicine,* Dr. Gregory Curfman.[22]

In examining the results, Scolnick wrote that the cardiovascular risks were "clearly there" and that they were a "shame."[23] Later he confessed to being in "minor agony" over Vioxx's potential to cause heart attacks and strokes.[24]

2001 brought more bad news about Vioxx. In August, Cleveland Clinic scientists published results of their own study, which showed that Vioxx increases the risk of heart attack. Then Chairman of Cardiology at the Cleveland Clinic, Dr. Eric Topol, a strident critic of Cox-2 inhibitors, claims that Merck failed to listen to his resulting concerns. In September, the FDA ordered Merck to notify doctors about Vioxx's safety risks and to change its label to reflect those risks.[25] Scolnick then told senior Merck managers in an October 2001 e-mail, "Be assured, we will not accept this label."[26] When regulators asked Merck for more safety information, Scolnick called them "bastards" and, later, "devious."[27] Merck waited until April 2002 to change the label to acknowledge the risks.

The following year, Merck released an internal memo saying that "upper management" was canceling its proposed study of the cardiovascular risks of Vioxx for unknown reasons. But in October of 2003, Merck did fund a study that it later reported in the medical journal *Circulation,* which showed that Vioxx poses a 39 percent greater risk of heart attack than Celebrex. In August of 2004, Kaiser Permanente, in collaboration with the FDA, reported that policy holders on 50 mg of Vioxx had much higher risk of cardiovascular events. The following month, Merck scientists learned the results of the "APPROVe" (Adenomatous Polyp Prevention On Vioxx) study, which they commissioned and designed to see whether Vioxx could prevent polyps from growing in the colon: results showed that 25 mg of Vioxx (the minimum dose) significantly increases the risk of heart attack compared to a placebo for patients who take it for at least 18 months.

Finally, in January 2005, David Graham, associate director for science at the FDA's office of drug safety, published an article in the medical journal *Lancet* saying that Vioxx may have caused up to 140,000 excess cases of serious coronary heart disease in the U.S. by the time it was withdrawn from the market.[28] Merck dismissed the claim as speculation.

A Long and Painful Lesson in Executive Hubris

What matters is that Merck executives chose to sell the product until September 30, 2004. Aside from the huge sales that were at stake, the false confidence may also have reflected a culture of insularity and hubris at Merck's pristine, wooded headquarters in Whitehouse Station, New Jersey. Scolnick, for example, seemed to become increasingly irascible as he approached retirement. According to Eve Slater, formerly Merck's vice president of clinical and regulatory development and a 19-year veteran of Merck labs:

> Ed [Scolnick] alienated many researchers by becoming more abusive in meetings, playing favorites, and making succession choices that didn't make sense to people. The result was, people were afraid to tell him where the problems were. There was suddenly this emperor's-new-clothes mentality.[29]

When the time came to withdraw the drug, Gilmartin described the decision as "easy" and "ethical."[30] The alternative, he said, would have been to go to the FDA "and have the prescribing information for the product updated with these new findings," which some of his advisors apparently recommended. Perhaps that's why there was a one-week delay between when Scolnick's successor, Dr. Peter Kim, learned about the results of the APPROVe study and when Gilmartin recalled Vioxx

Kim still considered returning the product to the market as late as February 2005, even in the face of impending lawsuits.[31] His justification was that if all Cox-2 inhibitors are potentially harmful, Vioxx's risk should be assessed relative to those posed by competitors. Perhaps Merck's scientists and marketers believed that doctors would prescribe it, in spite of the risks to patients' lives and doctors' medical malpractice insurance.

In May 2005, Richard Clark replaced Gilmartin as the firm's CEO, after Gilmartin received $38 million of compensation in 2004, comprising salary, bonus, and the sale of Merck shares.[32] Facing nearly 10,000 Vioxx lawsuits, Clark needed a legal strategy. As of this writing, this strategy includes taking every case to trial with a legal budget of $1 billion. The initial legal defense, which the firm has subsequently reviewed, was that the firm did not know about Vioxx's heart attack risks until September 2004. Accounts of the trial revealed that Merck lawyers alienated the jury by not clearly relaying the scientific evidence and by questioning plaintiffs about whether their loved ones would have had a heart attack even without Vioxx.

Various factors underscore Clark's confidence that Merck will prevail in court. Amongst other things, he has declined to establish a liability fund. He claims that Vioxx is not a pressing priority and that he spends about an "hour a week" on the matter.[33]

That may not be enough. In May 2001, Robert Ernst, a 59-year-old Texas triathlete who had been taking Vioxx, died suddenly in his sleep. Jurors decided that Vioxx contributed to his death and awarded his widow $253 million in damages (that award is under appeal and is sure to be lessened, given the Texas damage caps).[34] In explaining their decision, one juror cited Reicin's 1997 memo as evidence about when the firm first knew about the drug's risks. Another juror complained about not knowing "what the heck they were talking about," referring to Merck's efforts to explain the science behind Vioxx. A third wondered why Merck's senior executives were not present at the trial, raising questions about their arrogance.

It should also be emphasized that Merck has appealed the decision, and has subsequently won comparable cases. Still, in another case on April 5, 2006, a New Jersey jury awarded John McDarby, who suffered a heart attack, $3 million, with his wife receiving another $1.5 million for loss of "society and services of her husband." Moreover, the jury awarded the couple a further $9 million in punitive damages because Merck's failure to disclose safety concerns in selling the drug showed a "wanton and willful disregard of another's rights."

With many more legal cases pending, Vioxx is an ongoing financial and public relations nightmare for the firm. Once the world's leading pharmaceutical company and the envy of the industry, Merck now faces greater challenges in hiring the best scientists and, therefore, developing blockbuster drugs.

Attaining feedback on drug safety and efficacy is enormously challenging. But, the Vioxx affair raises questions about the manner in which Merck's executives, from Gilmartin, Scolnick, and Kim down the ranks, received and used feedback. Did they fail to attend to the adverse information that was before them? Did they refuse to seek and obtain information to definitively establish the cardiovascular risks, as the decision to stop this targeted test in early 2002 would suggest? Did they not break down the information they had from the VIGOR and other studies to establish the true risks? Are these data suggestive or conclusive that Vioxx causes heart attacks? Or should their suggestiveness suffice? If the answer to any of these questions is "yes," a heedless failure to act on the best available feedback of the drug's safety and efficacy produced false confidence.

The *minimum* amount of evidence that Merck had or should have had about such a risk is now a matter of public record. As you consider the time line of events shown in Figure 5.3, place yourself in the shoes of Merck's senior scientists who should have had this information. Ask yourself what you would have done—admittedly with the benefit of hindsight.

In a January 2006 *Harvard Business Review* article, Max Bazerman and Dolly Chugh argue that raising self-awareness is a matter of *seeing, seeking, using,* and *sharing* feedback. Granted, there are

FIGURE 5.3 *Time Line of Critical Events Surrounding Vioxx*

1994	Ray Gilmartin named Merck CEO; Vioxx, Cox-2 inhibitor, discovered.
1997	E-mail from Dr. Alise Reicin, a Merck scientist, notes, "The possibility of increased C.V. (cardiovascular) events (e.g., heart attack) is of great concern and may kill."
1998	University of Pennsylvania professor Garret Fitzgerald notifies Merck and others of his team's findings that Cox-2 inhibitors (including Vioxx) interfere with enzymes thought to ward off cardiovascular disease.
Jan. 1999	Merck launches VIGOR trial.
May 1999	FDA approves Vioxx for marketing.
Mar. 2000	Merck VIGOR trial reveals that Vioxx is four times more likely to cause heart attacks than Naproxen.
Nov. 2000	Merck scientists publish article in the *New England Journal of Medicine (NEJM)* that shows that Vioxx causes fewer stomach problems than Naproxen; a short section underscores its cardiovascular risks.
Aug. 2001	Cleveland Clinic publishes in *JAMA* study results documenting increased risk of heart attack with Vioxx.
Sept. 2001	FDA tells Merck to notify doctors about Vioxx's safety.
Apr. 2002	Merck changes label on Vioxx to acknowledge "possible" heart attack risk.
Oct. 2003	Merck-funded study reports that Vioxx poses a 39 percent greater risk of heart attack than the competing drug, Pfizer's Celebrex.
Aug. 2004	Kaiser Permanente reconsiders covering Vioxx.
Sep. 8, 2004	Vioxx is approved to treat juvenile rheumatoid arthritis.
Sep. 23, 2004	Merck serendipitously learns from outside investigators that people on Vioxx for at least 18 months are twice as likely to have a heart attack than those taking a placebo.
Sep. 30, 2004	Merck withdraws its $2.5 billion Vioxx medicine from the market after 20 million Americans have taken it.
Oct. 1, 2004	Merck share price falls dramatically, wiping over $20 billion from the value of its shares.
May 5, 2005	Richard Clark, longtime Merck manufacturing executive, replaces Gilmartin as CEO.
Aug. 19, 2005	Texas jury finds Merck liable for death of Robert Ernst, awarding his widow $253.5 million in damages; Merck's share price falls another 8 percent, erasing $5 billion from its market value.
Nov. 3, 2005	New Jersey jury finds Merck not liable for injuries to an Idaho man who had a heart attack.
Dec. 2005	Executive editor of *NEJM* accuses Merck of misrepresenting the results of a clinical trial in a November 2000 article.

ongoing questions about whether the present drug discovery and development system can yield accurate and timely feedback to halt unsafe drugs. And yet, did senior Merck managers discount the feedback that they were receiving about Vioxx, gaining false confidence about Vioxx's safety and prospects? Did these highly talented and confident executives who should be intensely motivated to act on feedback about drug safety overlook or discount it? If so, they became infected with hubris, joining the ranks of talented and successful executives who have slipped from the speculative judgment of Quadrant C to the hapless judgment of Quadrant D.

DECISION MAKING BASED ON HAPLESS JUDGMENT

People who get poor quality feedback and are not motivated to act on it tend to fall into three camps: *indifferent, unskilled,* and *delusional.* An interesting recent study showed that some people get ahead of themselves because they suffer a dual burden: They are unskilled and, because of that fact, they are also unaware of their lack of skill.[35] This category can include senior executives who are in the wrong role or over their heads, as well as junior executives who flounder on their first assignment.

Some executives might possess high skill levels in certain areas, while lacking other essential skills for very different types of situations. When I worked in investment banking, a colleague I'll call "Fred" earned a reputation for incisive and thorough analytical skills. He could quickly cut through the most complex business problems. In fact, he attained an unheard of first place in every examination at one of the top universities in Australia before continuing the pattern at one of the world's finest business schools. When he returned, his sharp mind and work ethic were unmatched.

While superb at clinically diagnosing a situation, he had a harder time figuring out what made his colleagues tick. Even though his intellectual intelligence (IQ) was off the charts, his emotional intelligence (EQ) "needed work"; and his IQ was not enough to get the best out of his teams. Like most finance-minded executives that I've worked with, Fred believed that motivation starts and ends with the "carrot and the stick": big bonuses, coupled with a fear of getting fired. With this mind-set, he had trouble relating to the emotions and concerns that others at the firm were displaying, and he tended to have a calculated approach to conflict.[36] Given his superb analytical skills, partners at the firm overlooked Fred's difficult relationships with colleagues. Inevitably, what made his situation untenable was that he was so unaware of the situation facing his colleagues that he had trouble building strong work relationships.

Then there is the category of the delusional executive. Like Hans Christian Andersen's character, the emperor with no clothes, delusional CEOs will rein so long as senior executives lack the craft, courage, and candor to give their bosses hard feedback, and their bosses fail to demand feedback or deny the feedback they receive. This is the defense that Enron's former CEO, Ken Lay, used to claim that Jeff Skilling and other Enron executives kept him in the dark about fraudulent corporate activities.

Denying the Realities of Executives' Situations: The Limitations of Forced Ranking Systems

Every business strives for a "high performance culture." As we've seen, that culture requires that professionals within it demonstrate superb judgment; they must be highly competent and have the confidence to make their abilities count. But how do you build that kind of performance within the organization? Two central themes emerge from this chapter that can answer that question:

1. To operate with essential confidence and grounded judgment, executives need accurate, immediate, frequent, and
   pertinent feedback, and they must act on it.
2. The nature of our work and how we get rewarded for it will
   determine the quality of our feedback and our motivation
   to act on it.

Any performance evaluation system that strives to build a high
performance culture by promoting executives with grounded
judgment should incorporate these realities. Different performance evaluation systems are appropriate for different professional environments, depending on the quality of feedback that's
available to executives.

Yet up to one-third of all major U.S. organizations—among
them American Express, Bausch and Lomb, Cisco, GE, Intel,
Hewlett-Packard, Microsoft, PepsiCo, and 3M—use a one-size-
fits-all system performance evaluation system that is called
"forced ranking," also known as "rank and yank." While these systems differ across firms, they all are based on the premise that
firms must identify the *relative* difference in performance and
potential among executives. Based on certain criteria, executives
are ranked so that the best performers get rewarded and the
worst are fired.

Under Jack Welch, for example, GE followed a 20, 70, 10 system: The top 20 percent of executives got heavily rewarded and
groomed for promotion, the "vital" 70 percent in the middle got
supported and trained to improve, and the bottom 10 percent
were fired. Keith Sherin, GE's CFO, has about 15 executives who
report directly to him: the CFOs of each of GE's major businesses,
as well as the firm's key treasury and risk management officers.
Being ranked in the bottom 10 percent of this category can be a
ticket out the door, even for some highly successful and experienced executives. And the system fosters an overly competitive
environment, especially among those who are close to making the
top 20 and/or the bottom 10.

The Failings of the Forced Ranking System

GE has been a major source of best practices that has been successfully copied globally. Forced ranking is often considered to be one of them. It is not. That's because it somewhat idealistically assumes that all executives operate in Quadrant A, where they get superb feedback that they can readily act on; and if they don't, they'll be ranked lower on the curve.

Each year, for example, Goldman Sachs competes for the best finance-oriented MBA graduates from leading universities like Columbia, Harvard, London Business School, Stanford, and Wharton. From that recruiting process, hundreds of associates enter each of the firm's divisions, including investment banking, the division that provides large corporations with advice on mergers and acquisitions and capital raising transactions.

The firm's associates program is a kind of Olympic training ground for budding Wall Street wizards. Associates find themselves on a relatively level and highly competitive playing field. Central to Goldman's values is that each executive should contribute to clients through high-quality work, to colleagues through high-quality cooperation, and to their professional development by learning how to better serve clients and colleagues.

At its best, the system gives Goldman associates open and honest feedback about where they stand relative to their elite peers. When the system works well, associates get feedback as the firm completes transactions, and that feedback becomes the basis of annual evaluation. With constant feedback, the most competent associates are "calibrated," or have a sound assessment of their abilities. They quickly learn when they do sloppy analysis; they closely witness prospects of less successful friends and peers dim; and they have a long way to go before they can manage client relationships, let alone hit the financial jackpot of making partner.

The problem, of course, is that there is no level playing at Goldman, or any other business for that matter, for a simple reason—no two executives face an identical situation. The vast majority of executives may aspire for Quadrant A judgment, but find themselves operating in the other quadrants, often because their bosses are not adept at giving timely and candid feedback. Before adopting a forced ranking system, managers should answer these questions:

- Is it reasonable and effective to compare executives with one another because their work involves different challenges and contexts?
- Do forced rankings demotivate high-performing executives who are put in a difficult situation or who are compared with other stars?
- Is firing the bottom 10 percent better than retraining them or resetting their expectations?
- Does forced ranking create an environment where someone wins at someone else's expense?
- Is forced ranking the best way to identify the very best and the very worst performers?

The Novations Group surveyed 200 human resource professionals at companies employing more than 2,500 people on the effects of forced rankings. Stanford researchers Jeff Pfeffer and Bob Sutton summarize the results as showing that forced rankings

>...resulted in lower productivity, inequity and skepticism, negative effects on employee engagement, reduced collaboration, and damage and mistrust in leadership. [37]

Instead, performance evaluation systems at firms with talented people must give equal weight to how they *see, seek, use,* and *share* feedback, based on executives' situations. That's why at this writing a number of leading firms, including Microsoft and PepsiCo, are dropping or have dropped forced ranking systems.

If firms want executives to act on feedback, they must tie compensation and performance evaluation systems to it. At many firms, however, the culture of false confidence is infused through these systems. Selective judgment fed by compensation drives a wedge between what executives contribute and what they get paid. And speculative judgment becomes hapless judgment when executives face pressure not to disclose and act on evidence to cease (or start) a course of action. So, while firms may accept that their executives should work toward grounded judgment, their processes and actions often pull those executives toward the hapless judgment of Quadrant D.

SUMMARY

As we have seen in this chapter, false confidence relates to the quality of feedback that we receive and our willingness to act on it. By evaluating those factors, we can use a four-part matrix to determine the type of judgment that results. That matrix includes these quadrants:

1. *Quadrant A.* Our judgment is most *grounded* when we have strong feedback and are highly motivated to act on it. Staying grounded depends on incessantly striving for accurate, immediate, and frequent feedback, and acting appropriately upon that feedback.

2. *Quadrant B.* False confidence arises when we receive excellent feedback and, for whatever reason, are not motivated to act on it. Executives in this category tend to discount negative feedback and focus on positive feedback. Organizational processes, including those that overpay executives, can systematically create and sustain selective judgment. As the life insurance example illustrates, optimism enables executives to prevail and win when they face constant failure and rejection. Among optimists, however, those who act on negative feedback will outperform those who do not.

3. *Quadrant C.* Our judgment is *speculative* when we receive inadequate feedback, even if we're highly motivated to act on it.
4. *Quadrant D.* Our judgment is *hapless* when we're unskilled and unaware of it. This type of judgment can occur even in highly intelligent people.

The trick in managing your judgment and maximizing your decision-making capabilities is to commit to moving toward Quadrant A. Unfortunately, however, many executives slip toward Quadrant D. Where you find yourself in this framework determines the action needed to make that shift.

Here are some other important points we've covered in this chapter:

- The quality of our judgment can move between these categories. As we've seen in this chapter, speculative judgment becomes hapless judgment. By the same token, the quality of our judgment can improve with improved feedback and awareness of the need to act on it.
- Performance evaluation systems are essential for providing executives with adequate, timely, effective feedback. To be effective, they must incorporate the realities of executives' situations.
- Forced ranking performance evaluation systems often don't work because they reflect a one-size-fits-all approach that treats all executives as though they receive equal feedback. Because equality of feedback is rarely the case, these systems are incompatible with encouraging executives to move toward and maintain grounded judgment.

This chapter has highlighted how speculative judgment can degenerate into hapless judgment. For better or worse, speculative judgment is often unavoidable: We're going to have to make decisions based on uncertain future outcomes. Even if we know how our present customers are responding to our products, we can't fully know how prospective ones will respond. Even if we know how effective we are at our present job, we can't fully know how effective we'll be once we're promoted or transferred. The list of variables goes on.

Therefore, the challenge becomes one of defusing problems from speculative judgment by facing the potential consequences of our decisions and actions today—before they have occurred. As the next chapter demonstrates, even when our judgment is well grounded, we've got to be prepared for all potential consequences—to accommodate outcomes that can help or hinder us. After all, there's always a chance that our judgment is driven by false confidence, even if we don't know it at the time.

6

Brave Rather
Than Courageous

HOW FAILING TO MANAGE
TOMORROW TODAY FUELS HUBRIS

"While we are free to choose our actions,
we are not free to choose the consequences of our actions."

STEVEN COVEY, *The 7 Habits of Highly Effective People* [1]

While we may not be able to determine the consequences of our actions, we certainly can manage them—and ahead of time, before those potential consequences become a reality. As you or your colleagues contemplate decisions, you may be unsure whether those decisions are infected by false confidence. So it's important that you prepare for that possibility by managing the consequences of your decisions as you make them—just in case.

Recent events in the United States highlight the importance of establishing what could go wrong and the consequences of underestimating what can go wrong. Perhaps the U.S. administration underestimated international and Iraqi resistance to the invasion of Iraq. General William Wallace, former commander of the main U.S. Army ground force that invaded Iraq, said in 2003 that "the enemy we're fighting against is different from the one we'd war-gamed against."[2] In other words, America's military was not fully prepared to deal with the full range of potential consequences of the decision to invade Iraq.

153

According to President Bush, the Federal Emergency Management Agency (FEMA) underestimated the damage that was caused by Hurricane Katrina and, therefore, failed to implement an effective operation to rescue victims in New Orleans. Former FEMA chief Michael Brown countered that the Bush administration overestimated the agency's ability to manage the tragedy, reflecting an "overconfidence that FEMA had handled September 11, we had handled the California wildfires, we had handled the 2004 hurricanes right in the middle of the presidential elections."[3] The Katrina disaster illustrates how false confidence causes us to overestimate our ability to manage dire consequences.

In a similar vein, the National Aeronautics and Space Administration (NASA) knew about serious problems with both the *Challenger* and *Columbia* shuttles, but launched them anyway. The failures of those missions were costly in lives, and in the reputation and credibility of America's space program.

Granted, it's easy to be clever after the fact. So the trick is to have an approach to anticipating and managing the consequences of unduly confident decisions ahead of time. It's never enough to simply anticipate the consequences of decisions that are potentially imbued with false confidence. Instead, we must *live through* those consequences by playing them out in the field rather than planning them out in the conference room. In reflecting on how he built his empire, the founder of Bloomberg L.P. and the current mayor of the city of New York, Michael Bloomberg, wrote: "While our competitors are still sucking their thumbs trying to make the design perfect, we're already on prototype version no. 5 . . . . It gets back to planning versus acting: We act from day one: others plan how to plan— for months."[4] In essence, we must manage tomorrow's consequences today by acting rather than planning.

This chapter offers a framework and supporting processes for doing exactly that. We'll develop the framework for managing the potential consequences of decision, and then test its application in a context that involves life and death decisions, large investments, and the public's imagination—man's race to explore space.

A FRAMEWORK FOR
CONSEQUENCE MANAGEMENT

Executives who rely on strategic and contingency planning techniques are not truly managing potential consequences. All too often, these techniques use assumptions that make their way into spreadsheets and then form abstract scenarios that are divorced from reality. Recall, for example, the implications of Dean Kamen's brave assumptions about sales of his Segway human transporter, and regulatory opposition to it. Strong evidence (if only from studies of student projects) suggests that planning makes us more confident, but *not* more capable because it softens us to the real challenges that lie ahead.[5]

Even worse, it puts planners in the driver's seat and doers in the trunk. Southwest Airline's founder and chairman, Herb Kelleher, argues, "The meticulous nitpicking that goes on in most strategic planning processes creates a mental straightjacket that becomes disabling in an industry where things change radically from one day to the next." Kellehr say, "We have a plan. It's called doing things."[6] Intensive planning is no way to manage the potential consequences of false confidence.

Instead, managing the potential consequences of important decisions is hard work that must be done by yeomen rather than consultants. An example from my former colleague at the London Business School, Gary Hamel, helps to illustrate. A team at Shell Chemicals, a division of the Royal Dutch Shell group, had a seemingly compelling idea: Why not formulate detergent and fabric softener products at supermarkets, dispense them from bins, and sell them in reusable containers? Customers would get a cheaper product, retailers would get more business, and Shell would get more value from the active ingredients that it sells to detergent makers. A no-brainer, right?[7]

Many teams would proceed by making best-guess assumptions, estimating the net present value of the opportunity, and making the appropriate investment. Not the Shell team. Rather than con-

jure abstract scenarios in conference rooms, they searched for
them in the field. In doing so, they identified very real problems
with the opportunity: Many retail outlets are too small to justify the
investment in dispensing machines and containers; larger retailers
were concerned that the new product would cannibalize sales of
higher margin products; and customers would take some convincing about changing their buying habits and getting comfortable
with product quality. Armed with this information, Shell resisted
the kind of ambitious and expensive product launch that has
marred Kamen's Segway.

Accepting and dealing with potential problems ahead of time
is uncommon because it involves hard and often unpleasant work.
Developing conditions in which we could be wrong, acting them
out, and dealing with their consequences is an exercise of spotlighting the *potential* for our errors and faults. It's also a practice
that can attract unwanted labels—*gatekeeper, naysayer, cynic,* and
even *whistle blower,* among others.

This puts the onus very squarely on leaders to embrace the
consequences, positive and negative, of important organizational
decisions. A framework for rising to this challenge contains three
simple and sequential elements:

1. First, and most obviously, we've got to *establish the full range
   of potential consequences.* We must determine the conditions
   in which we could be wrong to know what could go wrong
   ahead of time.
2. The next stage of the framework is to *be primed—both willing
   and able—to act on adverse knowledge.* As the Vioxx disaster in
   the previous chapter and the *Challenger* and *Columbia* disasters
   outlined above suggest, knowing what can go wrong and
   being prepared to act on those negative consequences are two
   very different things. In fact, they can be like night and day.
3. And, we need to be sure that we're around to fight another
   day; that is, we need a *backup or "loss mitigation" action in
   place—just in case.*

Perhaps executives who we've seen earlier in this book would have avoided hubris by starting with this simple framework. Did mountain-climber Rob Hall, for example, adequately envisage the conditions in which he and Hansen would fail to descend Everest? Did Kamen fail to consider the conditions in which the Segway would not sell at large volumes? Did Carly Fiorina need to more closely examine how she might lose the support of HP's directors in order to understand how she may lose her job? And did Merck executives, including Gilmartin and Scolnick, fail to appreciate when Vioxx would produce heart attacks? This book highlights only a few examples of how executive hubris results from the failure to manage the potentially disastrous outcomes of decisions.

To see the above framework in action, let's contrast the decision-making processes at two of the world's leading aeronautical and space exploration organizations—Scaled Composites (or Scaled) and NASA. At first blush, this seems like an unlikely comparison. At this writing, Scaled operates with about 200 people and an annual budget of around $20 million. Its founder and leader is Elbert Leander "Burt" Rutan, the architect of *SpaceShipOne,* the first private-venture aircraft to attempt to enter space. *SpaceShipOne* was named *Time* magazine's "coolest invention" of 2004.

By contrast, NASA has an annual budget of over $16 billion. The U.S. government has spent over $370 billion on NASA since the early 1960s—more than the annual wealth that is generated by the gross national product of Greece, Sweden, or Switzerland. Though NASA plays Goliath to Scaled's David, some of NASA's detractors argue that Scaled accomplishes more with less. Granted, comparisons between the two are complicated by their different operations, especially since Scaled focuses on suborbital space flights. In suborbital travel, spaceships travel at speeds faster than 2,500 miles per hour (over 4,000 km/h) to leave the earth's atmosphere and pierce space before beating a hasty retreat back to the earth's atmosphere. NASA's space program has been committed to the far more challenging task of orbital travel since the mid-1970s.

AN EXAMPLE THAT
HITS CLOSE TO HOME

Don't get me wrong, I'm not trying to pick on the folks you've read about thus far in this book. A personal example highlights how I got interested in hubris and what I've learned about the costs of not playing out potentially adverse consequences. In 1987, I worked on a team that underwrote an equity offering for a client. In these types of deals, we would agree to buy the client's shares if we couldn't find other shareholders who would. Usually we had an out clause in these contracts that would eliminate our obligation should the market fall below a certain level. This time our client, a major Australian resource company, asked us not to. Entirely confident that the deal would be successful anyway, we accepted the client's terms, and considered it a relatively trivial concession. Sure enough, the market collapsed after we signed this deal. As a result, we couldn't find shareholders to buy our client's shares at pre-market levels and were forced to buy shares in the client at above-market prices. Rather than hold the shares, we started selling them, losing tens of millions of dollars on a deal that earned us around $100,000 in fees.

Upon reflection, we were brave rather than courageous and that made us needless victims of hubris. I believe that we would have avoided our false confidence if we had enacted the simple framework offered in this chapter. Working with our salespeople, we could have played out—step by careful step—the implications of a distressed sale of our client's stock. We could have made this even more real by working through the financial implications of these consequences on our earnings. Basic forms of insurance, including sharing risk with fellow investment banks, would have mitigated our losses.

Still the contrast between the two is useful because they share the critical and common decision of whether to launch a space flight, and because their different decision-making approaches highlight how vulnerable each is to hubris.

DECISION MAKING AT SCALED COMPOSITES

Scaled Composites is a small and secretive private company that operates in the Mojave Desert, some 100 miles northeast of Los Angeles. Historically, Scaled designed proprietary aircraft for general aviation and military aircraft manufacturers. In fact, since its inception in 1982, it has forged at least 38 new aeronautic designs, creating consistent profitability in a notoriously unprofitable industry. After countless test flights, the firm has never had a pilot die or become seriously injured in flight.

The barren Mojave Desert serves as Scaled's headquarters because it offers more space for flying and a distinctly "low rent district." The desert also elicits greater commitment from engineers, who must sacrifice personal relationships and interests to live in its forbidding environment. "What keeps us in this crummy desert is doing things that are fun," says Rutan, who adds, "I built a house without windows because you don't need to look outdoors here."[8]

Rutan and Scaled are on a crusade to make space flight as commonplace as traveling on an expensive cruise ship, believing that NASA has forsaken its responsibility to make space exploration accessible to everyone. A mantra at Scaled is that NASA is a bloated, gate-keeping government monopoly that has failed to meaningfully innovate for decades. "We haven't had a proper, aggressive space program in this country since 1970," charges Rutan, who further laments that "the flying that America has done in the last 20 years is by far the most expensive way to get to space and the most dangerous."[9]

Rutan wasn't always so dismissive of NASA's accomplishments. In 1961, at age 17, he was transfixed by the radio news of Alan Shepherd and NASA's successful suborbital flight. That kindled an odyssey that eventually led to his commitment to win the Ansari X Prize for manned suborbital flight, a prize established in 1996 by investors to incite such flight in much the same way as the $25,000 Orteig Prize moved Charles Lindbergh to fly across the Atlantic in 1927.

The X Prize rules stipulated that $10 million would be awarded to the first civilian team to carry three people or a pilot and equivalent ballast to suborbital space twice within two weeks on the same spacecraft before the end of 2004. And so it was that *SpaceShipOne* emerged victorious, after two successful suborbital flights on September 29 and October 4, 2004.

SpaceShipOne's design is small enough to fit in a two car garage. The craft begins its journey from the belly of a special purpose cargo plane, the *White Knight,* which unceremoniously drops it from 46,000 feet. Once released, *SpaceShipOne*'s rockets catapult it into suborbit in an ascent that is steered by a pilot (rather than a computer) who takes the spaceship into suborbit for about five minutes before decelerating. Then its tilted, hinged wings are released to a flatter position to "feather" its violent reentry into the earth's atmosphere, in which it glides and lands like a conventional airplane.

Rutan's first and foremost concern is safety. Before starting Scaled, he worked as a flight test controller for the U.S. Air Force, gaining experience at testing and fixing planes that stalled and spun out of control. Spend enough time with him and he will invariably recount the sobering statistic that 18 of the 430 people who have flown into space have died there. Upon naming Rutan its entrepreneur of the year in 2004, *Inc.* magazine recounted some of the daunting safety challenges:

> Scaled Composites had never launched one aircraft from another, never built the sort of flight simulator that would be

necessary for training and testing, never designed a thruster system needed to turn a spacecraft in space, and never put together from scratch an electronic navigation system. Most daunting of all, Rutan and Scaled had never built a rocket motor—the source of fully half of all space-launch failures—and had never had to deal with the nightmarish heat and extreme forces generated from re-entering the atmosphere at high speeds.[10]

What can we learn from Rutan and Scaled's enviable record of managing the consequences of decisions that are highly susceptible to false confidence? Let's explore this question through the lens of the framework outlined earlier in this chapter: Rutan's assessment of whether to launch *SpaceShipOne* reflected an analysis of *what* could go wrong and *when* and *where* problems could materialize. Remarkably, it's also a process that's directly led to a number of simple, though revolutionary, solutions, highlighting that a commitment to safety can foster innovation.

Establishing What Could Go Wrong with a Premature Launch of *SpaceShipOne*

Spaceships usually fail because of faulty rocket motors, whether they are ignited from a launch pad or in the sky. After recognizing that the firm's engineers lacked the time and world-class expertise to develop such motors, Rutan chose to outsource them. Before long, a small Californian rocket maker, SpaceDev, loomed as a natural supplier because it had a design that Scaled's engineers could quickly understand, test, and tweak in-house. For safety reasons, the rocket is powered by two inert substances—nitrous oxide (also known as laughing gas) and rubber—which are far less combustible than the liquid propulsion fuels that power NASA's shuttles.

Spaceships encounter maximum stress upon their launch and their reentry into the earth's atmosphere. The NASA shuttle *Challenger* disintegrated 73 seconds after launch as a result of faulty seals in its rocket boosters. *Columbia* exploded after debris that was created during launch punctured the ship's surface insulation and compromised *Columbia's* ability to reenter the earth's atmosphere. So rather than face a costly and risky launch from land-based rocket boosters, Scaled's simple, low-cost solution was to launch *SpaceShipOne* from the belly of the cargo plane, *White Knight.*

To improve safety during reentry, Rutan had the spaceship built out of a composite material of woven graphite and used a revolutionary set of wings to soften the impact of reentry. Relative to the metal used in shuttles, woven graphite seals better, minimizes the use of seals, and is less expensive to buy and work with. Following standard procedure, backup seals compensate for the possible failure of the primary individual seals. The wings stand upright during ascent to reduce resistance and then flatten out during descent to maximize the surface area of the spaceship that is exposed to the surrounding air. What emerges is a "shuttlecock effect" on descent, which allows the spaceship to both slow down and right itself without pilot intervention.

Acting on Problems That Emerged during *SpaceShipOne*'s Testing

At the front line of the safety initiative are Scaled's pilots who, literally and metaphorically, have *all* their skin in the game. With so much at stake, the pilots are not simply hired guns who flight tested *SpaceShipOne;* they are also engineers and project managers who work on teams that test the spaceship on the ground.

Developing and testing *SpaceShipOne* involved flying it at ever higher altitudes. Much like a runner who undertakes increasingly challenging runs before attempting the marathon, *SpaceShipOne* flew 15 missions before its first suborbital flight. Numerous problems emerged from these increasingly difficult experiments or probes. Amongst other things, *SpaceShipOne*'s tail was too small, causing it to veer out of control before coming under pilot control.

Rutan described the test flight immediately preceding the Ansari Prize attempt as having "the most serious flight system safety problem we have had in the entire program." In fact, a glitch in the flight control system caused the spaceship to drift 22 miles off course. Pilot Mike Melvill vividly recalls:

> . . . right after I lit the motor, the airplane by itself rolled 90 degrees left. I stomped on the rudder pedal and put in some control and it rolled 90 degrees right. And it's never, ever done that before. So at that point, I was kind of reaching for the switch to shut (the engine) down in case I was going to lose control. But I was able to get it back, get it leveled up, and started trimming the nose up to pick up the proper gamma, the angle of climb, which is nearly to the vertical.[11]

Having survived this scare, Rutan refused to let *SpaceShipOne* fly again until the control system was fixed, regardless of the Ansari Prize deadline. Faced with either grounding *SpaceShipOne* or fixing it, engineers and pilots worked around the clock on flight control solutions that could survive harsher tests than *SpaceShipOne* would encounter in space.

With their generalists' knowledge, engineers and pilots tend to reject sophisticated simulations for small, fast, and cheap experiments that test the parts, modules, and systems that comprise the spaceship. What emerges is a holistic decision-making process in which engineers and pilots work together on the *overall* integrity of the aircraft. Generalists also have a bias for simple, cheaper, and faster, "low-tech" solutions over more complex ones. With this approach, more engineers know how to design and build spaceships, identify and fix potential problems, identify overconfident decisions, and communicate the potential consequences. Later we'll see the contrast with NASA, where specialists work on spaceship modules, which leads to fragmented decision making and reduces the likelihood of finding threats to the overall safety of the spaceship.

To illustrate further, Chief Engineer Matthew Gionta believes that the team found a simple solution for the rocket engine because "we were just creative about how we used them (materials and components) together." Hired expressly as a generalist, Gionta and other young engineers experience early leadership roles on challenging projects. "What I had to learn on the job made my formal education pale in comparison, but I had to learn it because no one else was going to do it for me," says Gionta. "The stress took years off my life, but when you get that kind of responsibility, it's hard not to feel ownership."[12]

Embracing failure means treating it as a learning opportunity, as seen in the firm's approach to developing and testing breakthrough innovations. Scaled's unwritten rules dictate that failure is tolerated, even welcomed, provided that it is not so expensive that it can shut down operations, that it leads to improved decisions and actions, and that the same mistake is not repeated. Says Rutan, "I encourage my people to fail because if they're not failing, they're not going to have a breakthrough."[13]

While many factors prepare Scaled's engineers and pilots to act on the potential consequences of decisions that are driven by false confidence, including a premature launch, we cannot overestimate the virtues of:

- A culture that embraces failure and shared responsibility
- Key decision makers, in this case pilots, with skin in the game
- A strong preference for simple, generalist solutions that foster a bias toward action and transparency

Scaled's Backup and Loss-Mitigation Action

Along with this readiness, backup actions are integral to the safety of the X Prize attempt—just in case. As at NASA, Scaled's first line of defense against negative consequences is the control room. *SpaceShipOne's* controls are replicated at the firm's avionics center so that pilots can get constant feedback on their flight trajectory and any emerging problems.

Control room support is reinforced and, where needed, supplanted by abortion procedures at each flight stage. Because the *White Knight* and *SpaceShipOne* are designed to take off, fly, and land together, *White Knight* could return *SpaceShipOne* to base in an abort mode enacted prior to the smaller craft's release. Should *SpaceShipOne*'s rockets fail to ignite after it is released by *White Knight*, the spaceship glides to earth. As Melvill noted earlier, pilots can always shut off the rockets when they are burning, converting the spaceship into a glider. Maximum pilot risk remains at reentry, when pilots rely entirely on the spaceship's structural integrity.

Needless to say, none of this is foolproof. *SpaceShipOne*'s flight depends on pilot skill and, presently, lacks a backup pilot and/or an autopilot capability should the pilot fail. Friction on reentry will always be an issue as well, especially as the team gets more comfortable with successful missions and the spaceships it produces are subject to more use and stress. Issues like these must be carefully managed before the company is ready to begin its space tourism initiative.

Ongoing Challenges: From *SpaceShipOne* to Space Tourism

Even though this is a vastly different enterprise to getting *SpaceShipOne* into suborbit, Rutan boldly, if not overconfidently, asserts, "In 12 to 15 years, we'll have suborbital space tourism that costs as much as a luxury cruise, and very soon after that, you'll be able to spend your vacation in orbit."[14]

Rutan's projections for space tourism could be false bravado. Presently, the current mortality rate of surviving space travel (at 4 percent) exceeds the odds of returning alive from the summit of Mount Everest. But, the plan is for space tourism to become as routine as civilian air travel and, says Rutan, "You can't have an airline that kills 4 percent of its passengers."[15]

Will Rutan's space tourism program be safe? The challenges of building a fleet of spaceships for tourists will differ from those at the experimental *SpaceShipOne*. Apart from anything else, Scaled will have to hire new personnel to assemble the ships. Because the new spaceships will fly numerous missions, they must exceed the standards and capabilities currently at Scaled. And as we've seen in cases of many highly successful CEOs, Rutan's brilliance as an inventor may make him overconfident as a general manager. Will he believe that his obsessive perfectionism will suffice to carry the space tourism program? Or will he be prepared to delegate responsibility for quality assurance, and new processes, to more seasoned manufacturing executives?

Scaled had some luck with *SpaceShipOne* in the light of the dangers that come with spaceflight. At the same time, the firm's engineers, pilots, and leader had a systematic and rigorous approach to safety to establish what could go wrong with the spaceship, they were primed to act on conditions that would result from potential failure, and they had backup *action* in place, just in case. Those are the key ingredients for managing tomorrow today, elements that have been missing in launch decisions at NASA in recent years.

Today, the Scaled team is on its way to making space tourism a reality. Richard Branson, through his subsidiary Virgin Galactic, will invest up to $100 million to build five five-person spacecrafts. Separately, Virgin announced an agreement with the state of New Mexico to build a $225 million spaceport there. So far, 38,000 people have paid a deposit for a seat on its spacecraft, including 100 "founders" who have paid the initial $200,000 to be among Virgin Galactic's first space tourists. Branson, along with Rutan, will be aboard the first flight.

DECISION MAKING AND CONSEQUENCE MANAGEMENT AT NASA

In spite of their differences in size and resources, Scaled's closest comparison point is NASA. NASA's history until the mid-1970s is so splendid that it's worth recapping. NASA was established in 1958 to oversee the public space program of the United States. Its formation was a response to the Soviet Union's successful launch of its space satellite, an event that some U.S. officials perceived as a threat to the country's security and technological leadership. NASA quickly committed to sending astronauts on suborbital and orbital flights. Alan Shepherd's suborbital flight in 1961 and John Glenn's orbital flight in 1962 made for heady days at NASA and the country.

Buoyed by Shepherd's triumph, President John F. Kennedy memorably told the American people, "I believe this nation should commit itself to achieving the goal, before this decade is out, of landing a man on the moon and returning him safely to earth." Kennedy and his successors authorized $25.4 billion for the Apollo program to make this notion, seemingly far-fetched at the time, a reality. Anyone old enough remembers where they were in 1969 when Neil Armstrong and Edwin "Buzz" Aldrin launched their lunar module from Apollo 11 to explore the moon's surface. It was Armstrong, the first man to walk on the moon, who uttered the immortal words, "That's one small step for man, one giant leap for mankind." In spite of the tragedy of 1967 when NASA lost three astronauts on the launch pad, the organization put 12 astronauts on the moon during the Apollo program, which ended in 1972.

Since the 1970s, NASA has invested over $145 billion in the shuttle program, which has dominated its operations, and another $100 billion on the International Space Station, which is intended to establish a near-permanent presence for man in space. Announcing the shuttle program in 1972, President Richard Nixon declared that it would "help transform the space frontier of the 1970s into familiar territory, easily accessible for human endeavors in the 1980s and 1990s. This system will center on a space vehicle that can shuttle repeatedly from earth to orbit and back. It will revolutionize transportation into near space, by routinizing it."

Bravely Underestimating Problems

Five operating shuttles have been built as reusable craft for repeatedly orbiting the earth and providing services and supplies to the International Space Station. Rocket boosters at ground level allow the spaceships to launch vertically until they reach low earth orbit, where the engines are shut down and they enter low earth orbit. Like *SpaceShipOne,* the orbiter converts into a conventional glider for landing, after which it is refurbished for reuse.

The shuttle has three main modules: the reusable spacecraft or orbiter vehicle (OV) with engines built by Rocketdyne; the expendable external tank (ET) that carries the huge amount of fuel the spaceship needs upon launch, which is built by Martin Marietta (now part of Lockheed Martin); and two solid rocket boosters (SRBs), construction of which was outsourced to Morton Thiokol (now part of Alliant Techsystems). The tank and boosters are jettisoned shortly after launch and disintegrate into the ocean.

Yet, the program has been subject to intense criticism for being unsafe. Even though the shuttle has made over 112 successful flights since the *Columbia*'s first launch in 1981, the program has been grounded for extended periods due to safety concerns (including two years after the *Columbia* disaster in 2003).

Ultimately, false confidence of NASA officials in the safety of the missions has not helped their cause, especially after the *Challenger* explosion on January 28, 1986. As part of the Rogers Commission investigation into the tragedy, Nobel Prize–winning physicist Richard Feynman interviewed NASA engineers and their boss to assess the likelihood of future engine failure on the space shuttle. NASA's official launch risk estimate was 1 catastrophic failure in 100,000 launches. That is roughly equivalent to launching the shuttle once a day and experiencing 1 catastrophic accident in 300 years. Perhaps even more telling, subordinate engineers estimated such failure in the range of 1 in 200 to 1 in 300.

False confidence also entered NASA's assumptions about the *Columbia*'s prospective performance. NASA expected that *Colum-*

bia and the other shuttles would make up to 50 flights each per year, when the maximum number of flights achieved by any shuttle over its *lifetime* is 32. NASA grossly overestimated that a $5 billion budget would be enough to build a shuttle that would last for 100 missions at a cost of nearly $8 million per mission. The program has been far more expensive than anticipated; costs presently run at over $1.3 billion per launch.

Nevertheless, such confidence became self-perpetuating after it helped NASA win over the White House and Congress. Sheila Widnall, the first woman to chair an academic department at the Massachusetts Institute of Technology and a former Secretary of the Air Force and member of the Columbia Accident Investigation Board (CAIB), observed in a CAIB inquiry report that the program "was badly oversold . . . . They learned a very bad lesson in the sense that every time they over-promised, they got more money."

The Rogers Commission, which was appointed to investigate the *Challenger* accident, reached the consensus that the disaster was caused by defective O-rings. This disaster, too, may have links to overconfident decision making.

O-rings join segments of the solid rocket boosters and prevent hot gases in the SRBs from escaping and igniting the shuttle's massive external fuel tank. With unusually lower temperatures in Florida on the day of the launch, the O-rings had become especially rigid and failed to seal the joints between the segments of the boosters.

Evidence that NASA knew that the O-rings were a major risk factor includes the following:

- *Early 1977.* First evidence emerges that O-rings leak and erode.
- *November 1982.* O-ring erosion discovered during shuttle flight, prompting NASA to make the O-ring a critical safety issue.
- *January 1985.* Roger Boisjoly, a lead engineer with Morton Thiokol, which was responsible for the SRBs, discovers serious erosion of O-rings from the shuttle *Discovery*.

- *March 1985*. Preliminary tests show that O-rings function more poorly at lower temperatures, when O-ring failure in nozzle joint occurs at launch temperature of 70 degrees. NASA requests a full review of the problem.
- *August 1985*. Thiokol briefs NASA on joint seal problems. NASA concludes that the issue is insufficiently important to ground the fleet—it downgrades the safety threat.
- *January 1986*. Delays to the *Challenger* because of bad weather place added pressure on the shuttle program to launch the orbiter.
- *January 1986*. Engineers have not resolved problems with the O-rings. NASA's Flight Readiness Review meets two weeks prior to launch and downgrades the seriousness of the problem; Boisjoly asks for a teleconference to suspend the launch.

In investigating the *Columbia* shuttle explosion, the CAIB team found evidence of yet more overconfident decision making at NASA. According to the CAIB findings, the cause of the *Columbia* accident was a loose piece of insulating foam. The record shows that NASA had abundant evidence that foam debris could damage *Columbia* prior to its fatal mission, including photographic evidence of foam loss from 65 of the 79 missions that it had photographed for damage. After the *Columbia's* first flight, the ship had sufficient damage to its external surface that NASA had to replace over 300 tiles. In 1990, foam debris was classified as an "in-flight anomaly"; that is, the problem would have to be fixed or engineers would have to prove that it does not jeopardize astronauts.[14]

NASA's Failure to Act on Adverse Conditions: Evidence from *Challenger* and *Columbia*

Both *Challenger* and *Columbia* serve as tragic reminders of the pitfalls of collecting information without being prepared to act on it. Why was it that NASA was not primed—willing and able—to ground these shuttles in the light of all the evidence?

NASA had all the data about faulty O-rings that it needed to establish how they could affect the *Challenger,* for example. But when faced with the choice to ground the shuttle until the O-ring problem was fixed or continue with the planned flight schedule, NASA officials chose the latter. Why?

First, without adequate testing procedures such as those used at Scaled, concerned engineers at NASA would not prove potentially adverse consequences. Former NASA engineer Torarie Durden, describes the decision-making process:

> As an engineer, you are accustomed to the scientific method of problem solving where you create a hypothesis, you do experiments, you get data, and you prove or disprove your hypotheses. But at NASA, the burden of proof, especially for factual data, is leaps and bounds beyond anything I have ever seen. It was hard to create the number of experiments needed to create the data to prove your point.[16]

Unable to marshal the time, resources, and support needed to perform these tests, concerned scientists had to rely on *suggestive rather than conclusive* data. If they chose to present such evidence, they faced criticisms that they were inconclusive, that they were unduly delaying launch progress, and that they were questioning the authority of those who might be better informed. All of that prevents people from speaking up. This failure in NASA's decision-making process is analogous to the drug development process we examined earlier where *proving* that a drug is unsafe requires conclusive results from tests on animals and humans. A key point from the Vioxx case is that suggestive rather than definitive evidence that a product is unsafe must be acted on.

Second, NASA used evidence of prior success as an indicator of future safety. Richard Feynman described NASA's mind-set as "a kind of Russian roulette . . . . [The shuttle] flies [with O-ring erosion] and nothing happens. Then it is suggested, therefore, that the risk is no longer so high for the next flights. We can lower our standards a little bit because we got away with it last time."[17] Flipping a coin and getting heads may increase our confidence that the next flip will be heads, but obviously has no bearing on the true likelihood of such an outcome. Milton Silveira, formerly NASA's chief engineer, believes, "As we started to fly the shuttle again and again, I think the system developed false confidence in itself."[18]

Third, NASA faced commercial and political pressure to launch, especially given that the program was behind schedule. As NASA's commitment to launch escalated, management's concern for safety diminished. When engineers at Morton Thiokol lobbied for a delayed launch on *Challenger*'s ill-fated mission, a senior NASA manager, Lawrence Mulloy, retorted, "My God, Thiokol, when do you want me to launch, next April?"[19] Two NASA engineers told reporters for National Public Radio that they fully expected *Challenger* to blow up at launch ignition.[20]

Devastatingly sudden, the events of the *Challenger* disaster gave NASA no chance of recovering the astronauts and spaceship. Even if the disaster occurred in flight, the consequences would still have been fatal. Overconfident about safety issues, NASA lacked an escape system for the crew on the *Challenger*. Subsequent shuttles also lacked such a system, including the *Columbia,* which was on the 16th day of its 28th mission when it exploded upon reentry on February 1, 2003. *Challenger* and *Columbia* present different scenarios for examining how the failure to manage consequences can lead to hubris.

The CAIB reached consensus that the *Columbia* tragedy happened because a loose piece of insulating foam that detached from the external tank during launch breached the shuttle's left wing. As a result, perilous heat broke the wing during reentry and eventually the spaceship, instantly killing the crew. If, as demonstrated earlier, NASA had ample evidence that the foam insulation on its shuttles became damaged during flight, then why did it fail to act on this knowledge?

Responsibility for *Columbia*'s last mission fell to the space shuttle program's manager, Ron Dittemore (ironcally, now president of Alliant Techsytem's Thiokol division). Reporting to Dittemore was Wayne Hale (now deputy director of the Space Shuttle Program), who ran the launch itself, and Linda Ham, who oversaw the rest of the mission with her Mission Management Team (MMT).

Regarding mission planning, engineers *assumed* that only small pieces of debris would strike, and that the shuttles would withstand minor impact. Damage from foam debris became such an accepted part of shuttle flights that it was regarded as an annoyance rather than a safety risk. Safety expert and CAIB member James Hallock noted, "[shedding foam] became sort of expected. Not only was it expected, it eventually became accepted."[21] In NASA terminology, it was an "in-family" event—one that had been experienced, analyzed, and understood, and an "accepted risk," or one that would not jeopardize missions. Sociologist Diane Vaughan calls this the "normalization of deviance."[22] The idea is that organizations can get lucky and survive errors and indeed misdeeds (flights, production runs, sales efforts, crime), leading them to accept luck as evidence. But, as they do so, their managers come to regard these potential problems as more routine and acceptable, inducing false confidence by softening them to the true challenges.

In both shuttle tragedies, therefore, NASA had ample data about what *could* go wrong, but it failed to act on that knowledge. Gaps of 17 years and 89 flights separated the *Challenger* from the *Columbia* explosions, and with each successful mission, and ever more planning, NASA's leaders became increasingly confident about safety issues. According to Jim Oberg, a former shuttle flight controller, "The NASA team leaders think they're way smarter than their record indicates, and they can use a little more humility and a little more anxiety in the way they approach their profession."[23]

A Failure to Prepare for the Consequences of a Shuttle Disaster

Consider now NASA's loss-mitigation plan—what was the agency prepared to do to minimize the damage of the disastrous consequences of an in-flight system failure? To explore this question, let's focus on the *Columbia*'s in-flight foam damage and subsequent explosion.

In 1990, NASA classified foam loss as an "in-flight anomaly"— an event that could jeopardize a flight—a classification that obliged engineers to eliminate the problem for future missions or else prove that it could not imperil crew members. Neither of these outcomes happened.

Instead, NASA relaxed its classification to an "accepted flight risk." For example, after debris struck the *Atlantis* shuttle in 2002, NASA classified its needed response to the event as an action item rather than an in-flight anomaly. The shuttle could keep flying but engineers were required to find the source of the problem and fix it for subsequent missions. The resolution was that the foam loss was "no higher/no lower than previous flights. The ET [external tank] is safe to fly with no new concerns (and no added risk)."[24]

Senior officials' lack of concern about debris before the launch reduced the likelihood that NASA would make provisions for debris-related damage during the mission proper. Shortly after the *Columbia*'s final launch, Ham was told that the damage seemed more significant than prior strikes, but she could not establish the extent of the damage. Having "gasped" at the size of the debris, Rodney Rocha, a field engineer, began pleading with Ham's team to get better images of the damage from in-space satellites that were operated by the Department of Defense. Even though Rocha co-chaired a Debris Assessment Team (DAT) that was formed shortly after the launch, weak communication links between the DAT and Ham's team prevented him from getting heard. Widnall points to the DAT's vague charter. "It wasn't really clear who they reported to," she says. "I think they were probably unsure as to how to make their requests to get additional data."[25]

Operating in a bureaucratic quagmire, Ham resisted getting the satellite photos from the Department of Defense. To do so would have meant changing *Columbia*'s course to bring the shuttle within range of the satellite's photographic gear. As events transpired, the MMT only told pilots about the problem because they did not want them to be "surprised by it in a question from a reporter," and reiterated that NASA had "seen this phenomenon on several other flights, and there is absolutely no concern for [re]entry."[26]

What "just-in-case" loss-mitigation processes might NASA have had in place to save the crew of the *Columbia* once the foam damage took place? Once Dittemore, Ham, and their colleagues knew about the damage, they had at least four principal options, as elaborated by the CAIB:

1. They could have collected more information in a bid to become more informed about the situation (although with the benefit of hindsight, this option was not itself a viable way of saving the crew).
2. They could have instructed *Columbia*'s astronauts to abort entry into space and thereby avoid the reentry issues.
3. Once *Columbia* was in space, they could have mounted a rescue mission in which the astronauts would make a spacewalk from their ship to the rescuing shuttle, *Atlantis* (the *Columbia* was not capable of docking at the International Space Station). *Atlantis* was scheduled for a March 1 mission, and *Columbia* had sufficient power, water, and air to remain in space until at least then. Later reports described such a rescue as "challenging but feasible," though it risked the potential loss of both orbiters.
4. They could have had astronauts undertake a spacewalk to repair *Columbia*. That may have uncovered the damaged part(s) of the vehicle's protective shield and intensified efforts to fix it.

Even after the disaster, NASA couldn't accept the principal role played by foam debris. According to Dittemore, "It does not make sense to us that a piece of debris could be the root cause for the loss of *Columbia* and her crew."

Accepting that the problem was not serious made it easier for NASA's leaders to live with their inability to fix it, in a form of planning that breeds false confidence. Engineers could never determine the cause of foam debris, let alone a reliable technique to prevent it. Rather than reach outside the organization for a solution, officials adopted a more insular and defensive tactic of dismissing the worriers as "foamologists." Tragically, *Columbia* was the crisis that has finally forced NASA to find a sustainable solution to the problem created by foam debris.

VOICING CONCERNS IN A "MISSION ACCOMPLISHED" CULTURE

In many ways, NASA failed to learn from its earlier *Challenger* disaster. Warning signals were suppressed or ignored by officials who were committed to launch dates. False confidence produced the rhetoric that the shuttle was a routine operational vehicle instead of an experimental vehicle. The organization's culture and decision-making process prevented concerns from being heard and acted upon.

Speaking up about potential problems is unusual at most organizations, including large drug companies and NASA, because it is almost invariably a losing proposition. In most corporations, you need to think twice before spotlighting such problems, and risk being labeled as disloyal to your boss and firm, unless your firm has the right leadership and processes in place. Sherron Watkins, for example, the heroic whistle blower of the Enron scandal, now calls herself unemployable.

To take this further, consider a scenario in which you have a new CEO who is trying to make his mark on your firm. He's committed to a $20 million plant expansion. You're worried that the plant seems unnecessary; your firm doesn't have the money and your CEO lacks any track record in successfully raising capital; and the expansion will disrupt your existing operations. In the worst case, the new plant could bankrupt the firm. Moreover, your CEO doesn't have much skin in the game; his guaranteed pay and stock options will make him wealthy either way.

So let's suppose that you want to voice these concerns in order to have the project postponed or stopped. You will need some time and resources to gather the support needed to make a compelling case. What do you know about customers to demonstrate that the plant is unnecessary? Just because the CEO has never raised capital, does that mean he won't be able to do so in the future? How much will it cost in time and money to delay this launch? *Proving* your case is a long shot. And, without the proof, you won't be able to challenge, let alone budge, colleagues who are invested in and committed to seeing *their* projects through.

Suppose, however, that you decide to speak up—a bad idea in this firm. If you successfully do so, the project may be postponed or stopped. Expect now that when your colleagues pass you in the hallway, that they'll remember you as the killjoy who stalled the project. And, if demand picks up and the firm really does need the capacity, heaven help you. If you speak up, but are unsuccessful in having the project postponed or stopped—a far more likely scenario—you still won't benefit. At that point, the train has left the station and you had better be on it.

Telling people that it's okay to speak up can be just a token gesture in many corporate cultures. Former NASA chief Sean O'Keefe accepts that and notes, "Our pervasive culture for the last 45 years has been one of mission accomplishment, and we really get things done . . . . So you really have to understand all the various, different reasons why people are reluctant to speak up, and I acknowledge that there are very many people that will not speak up."[27]

Because this "mission accomplished" culture can be deeply entrenched, the onus is firmly on leaders like O'Keefe to put people and processes in place to establish norms for speaking up.

Toward that goal, leaders can install and institutionalize simple, commonsense processes, including the designation of problem advocates who are assigned to investigate, track, and mitigate potential project problems. Accountants and scrutinizers can lack a generalist's understanding to make for effective problem advocates. If advocates are perceived as blockers rather than enablers, they won't have the necessary credibility within and access to project teams. Further, *problem advocates* should have joint ownership of the performance of the projects and divisions they work in. If the project wins, problem advocates should share in the benefits—after all, their input prevents a project from blowing up. And if it does, then they bear a heavy responsibility. To be effective, problem advocates must have authority with direct lines of communication to projects and mandates that project leaders *must immediately* act on concerns.

Now, let's look at other concrete processes and techniques any organization can use to implement a framework for managing consequence within its own decision-making process.

Constructing a Process for Establishing What Can Go Wrong

By *experiencing* the conditions in which decisions and actions hurt us ahead of time, we are better able to determine the wisdom of our decisions, and are better prepared to communicate and manage their consequences. Here's how we can do that:

- Study the base factors that have caused us and others in similar situations to fail. This helps to identify, conceptualize, and eliminate high-risk steps.
- Systematically test with low-cost probes and experiments because, as Stanford professors Jeff Pfeffer and Bob Sutton

put it, "If you know by doing, there is no gap between what you know and what you do."[28] (We'll see Dell's approach to this in Chapter 8.)

- Avoid delegating work on managing consequences to consultants; they simply experience those consequences as intensely as you will. And, they won't be on hand if problems arise.
- Find a hypothetical situation that is very similar to your own, and take the team through a "what would we do" exercise. The key here is to try and experience what could go wrong as much as possible.
- Avoid overconfident framing and language, including "failure is not an option" and "we are going to do this so I'm not even going to consider the alternative." They convey confidence but they are also cop-outs that substitute for the hard thinking and work that establishes when we could be wrong.

Priming the Organization to Act on Evidence of Problems

If *Challenger* and *Columbia* have taught us anything, it is that knowing that we *could* be wrong is never enough. So the next phase of the framework requires that we be primed to act on evidence of problems. To accomplish that phase, we can:

- Focus on teams' contributions to the overall effort—for example, developing and launching a new product, making acquisition integration work, and completing the construction project
- Establish and promote a culture that accepts and, at times, embraces failure and shared responsibility for it
- Ensure decision makers have an investment in the process—or "skin in the game"
- Encourage simple, transparent solutions that foster a can-do mentality

- Open lines of communication between those with adverse knowledge and decision makers
- Use a "revolving door" that offers the possibility of new eyes and minds, and asks the question: What would be the right decision if we started afresh, if a new expert set of managers tackled this problem? (Andy Grove's decision that Intel must exit memory chips and commit to microprocessors is an excellent example of this technique in action.)
- Use generalists to avoid fragmented decision making that focuses on the success of components and modules and places the burden of proof on those with concerns
- Also avoid these practices: using prior success as predictor of future outcomes; escalating commitment to a certain course of action; establishing normalization of deviance where we accept errors as normal; and removing decision makers from the source of bad news and the consequences of their decisions

Building a Backup or Loss-Mitigation Action Plan

Then comes the final component of the framework: putting a backup or loss-mitigation plan in place. To accomplish that, we can:

- Designate problem advocates. Ensure they have project team credibility and skin in the game of winning and losing. Ensure that they have real input in decision making, if not the power of veto
- Make action B feasible while action A is getting implemented. NASA officials shut down alternative action that could have saved *Columbia*'s crew because they were overconfident that the spaceship would return safely. Assign responsibility for alternative action—just in case
- Avoid delegating the management of consequences to executives who are committed to plan A or who have expressed token interest in action B

SUMMARY

We're always at risk of making an overconfident decision without knowing it. So, just in case, it pays to manage tomorrow's consequences today by institutionalizing frameworks and processes to prevent overconfident decisions from damaging us. In this chapter, we explored the use of a framework for managing these consequences. These are its elements:

1. First, you must *establish the specific conditions in which your decisions could be subject to false confidence.* This step requires that you play out, rather than plan out, the consequences. Your goal in this stage is to determine all possible ways that your decision could go wrong.
2. In the second stage of the framework, you must be *primed to act on evidence of problems.* Knowing what could go wrong isn't enough, you must be willing and able to act on your knowledge. Success in this stage requires a culture that accepts—and even embraces—failure and a shared responsibility for all outcomes.
3. The third stage of the framework for managing consequence requires that you *have a realistic backup or loss-mitigation action in place.* By designating problem advocates and assigning responsibility for alternative actions, your organization can help mitigate or even avoid potential worst-case scenarios.

When our ego is unchecked, we risk making decisions that we literally can't live with; decisions that can cost lives or impose costly burdens upon us, our families, and our colleagues. In order to check our ego, we need to embrace the potentially adverse consequences of our decisions and have processes in place for dealing with them. The problem is that we often don't consider those consequences because they are problematic, unpleasant, and unappealing. Without the intervention of strong personalities and

leaders, organizations default to a culture of silence about potential problems and outcomes of worst-case scenarios. The solution
is to make speaking up an ingrained part of every organization's
culture by systematically adopting frameworks and processes for
identifying and dealing with the adverse consequences of decisions that are driven by false confidence—just in case.

7

From False Confidence
to Hubris

JEAN-MARIE MESSIER'S
REIGN AT VIVENDI

"Not since Napoleon has France produced an empire builder
as ambitious as Jean-Marie Messier."

CAROL MATLACK, *BusinessWeek* [1]

France's proud history might be even more so without the hubris of certain leaders—men like the Napoleans who did not know when to stop. When Napoleon Bonaparte became ruler of France in 1799, his country was Europe's preeminent power. Initially, Napoleon deployed brilliant military tactics to expand France's influence and empire. When he left office in 1815, however, France was a fallen European power. During 17 years of war, millions of French soldiers had fallen on the battlefield. The country had become bankrupt and begun to lose its overseas colonies. Later, Napoleon Bonaparte's relation by marriage, Emperor Napoleon III, ruled France from 1852 to 1870. In a bid to reassert French supremacy, he led France into the Franco-Prussian War of 1870, which France lost disastrously, and which eventually contributed to the conflict of World War I.

History offers precious few stories of the Bonapartes appreciating the limits of their capabilities, seeking out the advice and guidance of trusted advisors to help manage their empires, using available evidence to accurately read their situation, or acting to manage the consequences of their decisions in a manner that would expose and correct false confidence.

Unfortunately, it does not seem that Jean-Marie Messier took their disastrous experiences to heart. Had he done so, he might have seen some similarities with his own career trajectory. Like Napoleon, Jean-Marie Messier enjoyed a period of spectacular success that, ultimately, ended in a tragic downfall and defeat. In time, Messier would become known for trying and failing to become the godfather of French business, a man whose attempt to build a global media and telecommunications powerhouse undermined his career, the businesses he bought, and the people who trusted him.

Messier's story serves as a cautionary tale of false confidence and hubris. As we have seen throughout this book, excessive pride breeds hubris, and it begins with an inability to accurately assess our capabilities and achievements. We have also seen that executives who fail to get the right help by finding and using a foil to assist with decision making stumble as well. And we have seen how an inability to seek out and absorb bad news—both in the form of negative feedback and concerns raised about the potential outcomes of worst-case scenarios—can be a passport to failure, if not disaster. The career of Jean-Marie Messier serves as a stunning illustration of each of these principles in action. The time line in Figure 7.1 tracks the eight-year rise and fall of someone who was one of France's brightest stars of business.

Granted, there will only be one Messier, but there will never be a shortage of people who succumb to excessive pride. Messier's experience spotlights the downward spiral of poor decision making and hubris that can destroy a successful executive and his firm. We can begin to understand that experience by first exploring the role that Messier's pride played in his decision making.

FIGURE 7.1 *Jean-Marie Messier's Rise and Fall*

1994	Messier joins Compagnie Generales des Eaux (CGE) as managing director, or number two officer.
1996	Messier becomes chairman of CGE.
1998	Messier changes CGE's name to Vivendi.
January 2000	Vivendi and Vodafone launch an Internet alliance called Vizzavi.
June 2000	Messier has Vivendi purchase Seagram.
September 2000	Messier publishes his Internet manifesto, *J6M.com,* just as the Internet boom is coming to an end.
January to September 2001	Messier makes a host of acquisitions, including Morocco Telecom, Houghton Mifflin, and a third generation mobile phone license in France.
September 2001	Messier moves to New York.
December 2001	Messier announces that the French cultural exception is dead.
December 2001	Messier has Vivendi acquire stake in Echostar and acquires Diller's group, USA Networks.
March 2002	Messier tells Vivendi board that he will announce a loss of 13.5 billion euros on 2001 results. He tells them the group's net debt, which was forecast to be 8.5 billion euros, was actually 14.6 billion euros.
May 2002	Moody's downgrades Vivendi's debt to just above junk status.
July 2002	Vivendi's board forces Messier to resign.

MESSIER'S RISING STAR EXPLODES INTO EXCESSIVE PRIDE

Messier was born in 1956 into a middle-class family—his father was a chartered accountant from Grenoble, in the French Alps. In time, Messier would become enormously wealthy and successful after building the global media communications firm Vivendi. And, as we shall see, Messier was forced to resign in disgrace in July 2002 after Vivendi posted a loss of €13.6 billion (over US $16 billion). In the process, his once-glorious position in French society and global business unraveled through self-inflicted hubris.

From an early age, Messier's ambition drove him to make the most of his talents. Initially, he was denied a place at L'Ecole Polytechnique, which for 200 years has been a nursery for high school graduates who aspire to be France's elite business and political leaders. Rather than take a place at a lesser university, Messier successfully chose the more difficult option of studying hard to gain entry the next year. From L'Ecole Polytechnique, he could have gone to Harvard Business School (HBS) but chose instead to go straight to L'Ecole Nationale D'Adminstration (ENA).

ENA takes 120 of France's brightest graduate students each year, who are socialized and trained over 27 months to become the country's preeminent business and government leaders. To call ENA the HBS of France, would be high praise for HBS. Some public commentators call ENA the most privileged club in Europe: To graduate from ENA—to be an *ENArque*—is to join a network of France's leading decision makers, including presidents of the Republic and CEOs of major firms. Messier kept company with men who had the keys to all the right doors.

Messier Takes Charge

When he was 29, the door to the office of France's Inspecteur de Finances swung open for Messier. In that position, he reported directly to Finance Minister Edouard Balladur and handled some of France's most important privatizations, including the bank, Societe Generale, and the building materials company, Saint Gobain. At 32, Messier joined Lazard Freres, becoming the youngest ever partner of France's most prestigious investment bank. With his wealth, status, and connections, Messier seemed to have it all. The problem was that he wanted to be Lazard's CEO and that looked to be out of his reach, since the role was reserved for Eduoard Stern, the son-in-law of the firm's chairman, Michel David Weill.

So in 1994, aged 37, Messier became managing director of Compagnie Generales des Eaux—a venerable 150-year-old firm and France's leading water supplier. Two years later, Messier became the firm's chairman, a position that put him right along-side Bernard Arnault of LVMH and Claude Bebear of AXA at the vanguard of a new wave of progressive French business leadership.

Soon Messier made changes that successfully revitalized and transformed a bureaucratic utility. He focused the firm on its core water utility and communications businesses by selling other businesses. He invested in the water business, developing new capabilities and winning major new contracts in almost every major international market. By 1997 the firm was on a solid financial footing; and Messier's star was rising spectacularly.

Given slowing growth in water utilities, Messier worked to turn his company into a global media and communications pow-erhouse, one that owned media content along with the means to distribute it. The strategy, also followed by AOL/Time Warner, was called *convergence*. In 1998, with the new merger completed and a new corporate identity in place, Messier re-christened the firm Vivendi.

The initial results of the company's convergence strategy were striking. In 1996, the firm made just under €300 million (US $360 million) and by 2000 its earnings were up to nearly €2.3 *billion* (US $2.8 billion). Between 1997 and 2001, Vivendi made acquisitions valued at over €91 billion (US $110 billion). By far the most signif-icant was the June 2000 purchase of the Canadian group, Sea-gram, from the Bronfman family for €36.8 billion (US $44.6 billion). With that deal, Messier controlled the world's largest music company, Universal Music, which today sells close to one in every four CDs purchased worldwide, and Universal Studios, one of the world's premier film makers and owners.

A Love Affair with the Press

And between 1998 and 2000, Messier's close relationships with prestigious business news journalists helped make him a celebrity. In June 1999, for example, the *Financial Times* ran a glowing profile of Messier, hailing him as a "brilliant networker."[2] It opened by remarking, "In conversations about his ability and track record, the word *genie,* or genius, crops up regularly." The leading French newspaper, *Le Monde,* pegged him as Jean "Magic" Messier.

In September of 1999, a senior *Fortune* magazine journalist wrote a major article headlined "Leader of the Pack," describing Messier as "one of the brightest of Europe's new breed of entrepreneurial musketeers."[3] It said:

> . . . he has taken Vivendi from a midget in communications to a titan . . . . Vivendi is the biggest pay TV operator in Europe. It is also the largest private mobile phone company in France and one of the largest in Europe. Messier is bringing his own content to the Net with big deals like this year's purchase of Cendant Software . . . . Messier has found a way to link PCs, cell phones, and television.

At the height of his fame, Messier owned the optimistic, energetic, and irrepressibly confident face of the future of French business. He even starting calling himself and signing his name J6M, which stood for "Jean-Marie Messier, Moi-Meme, Maître du Monde" (Jean-Marie Messier, Myself, Master of the World).[4] *J6M.com* would become the title of his autobiography, which he also intended to be a manifesto for the "new economy." Reveling in media attention, Messier seemed to be making a bargain with journalists: You celebrate me and I'll give you breaking news coupled with riveting headlines. An effervescent and irrepressible extrovert with a bottomless gift for dispensing grace and charm, Messier was deep in his element, rejoicing in journalists' glowing descriptions of his genius.

As his love affair with the press continued, however, some journalists had begun to speculate about what the future might hold for Messier. His meteoric rise to fame also brought attention to the challenges of managing his burgeoning empire. In 1999, *The Economist* concluded a story by crediting Messier with turning General des Eaux into a more vibrant business. It also cautioned that Messier faced the new challenge of growing two separate businesses, concluding that "even a master operator like J6M . . . may find it easier to concentrate on one industry at a time."[5] Supremely confident about his managerial abilities, Messier responded by redoubling his commitment to the engine that built his empire—acquisitions.

MESSIER'S PRIDE CLOUDS HIS JUDGMENT

Messier routinely paid acquisition premiums of over 30 percent, decisions that told the market that he could grow acquired businesses' value by at least that percentage. By 2000, however, Messier needed a blockbuster deal to play on the global rather than European stage, and he found it in Seagram, which he bought for a 46 percent premium over its prebid price. The merger was his crowning glory, the event that put his cherubic face across the front covers of *Newsweek, Fortune, BusinessWeek,* and *Time.* Shortly after the merger, Messier told his shareholders, "Vivendi Universal will enter the new century and millennium as the world leader in communications." (An exaggeration from a revenue standpoint since both Disney and AOL/Time Warner were larger). Messier went on to say:

> What a symbol for our future ambitions. And what a response to the skeptics, the naysayers, and those who want to stay in their own backyard. To all of them, Vivendi Universal will demonstrate that it is possible to be both French and global, and that

defending French culture sometimes means stepping out for a breath of fresh air.[6]

Messier and his team had good reason to be proud about their work from 1996 to 1999. During this period, underperforming assets were sold, costs were cut, the water utility business was more focused and aggressive. Profitability had increased dramatically on a much larger revenue base for the legacy businesses, while debt remained at manageable levels.

The Seagram deal had validated and cemented the convergence strategy. Vivendi's stock price was up almost threefold. Messier received the Legion of Honor in July 2001, a highly coveted honor awarded only to the most esteemed French citizens.

Messier's success and celebrity began to take their toll on his performance, however. In particular, he treated the starting line of buying businesses as though it were the finish line of extracting value from them. In reality, the convergence strategy could only be justified by successfully integrating Seagram and the other deals with the rest of Vivendi—as his Seagram partners kept insisting.

But Messier's addiction to fuelling his pride had to be fed with increasing doses of acquisitions. In short order, he paid $2.1 billion for a 35 percent stake in Maroc Telecom, the main telecommunications company in Morocco; then he purchased the Boston-based publisher, Houghton Mifflin, for $2.2 billion; then a 10 percent stake in U.S. pay television operator Echostar Communications for $1.5 billion; and then USA Networks for $10.3 billion in a combined stock and cash transaction. "With Messier, you'd only have to pass him in the street and he'd say 'I've done a deal,'" said Rupert Murdoch.[7] Vivendi's board of directors approved the deals, but Messier controlled the board's composition and selectively disclosed information.

Not only was Messier making new deals before integrating existing ones, but he was relying on debt rather than his firm's stock to pay for them. Belying his supreme confidence, he believed that Vivendi's stock price was grossly undervalued and, therefore, resisted using it as a currency to buy other firms. Putting his money where his mouth was, Messier bought tens of millions of dollars of Vivendi stock for his own account, convincing himself that the company was worth more than it was.

Because the share price was his daily—even hourly—vote of confidence, Messier kept a vigil over it. When it started falling, he spent over €10 billion (money that was earmarked to repay and service debt) to secretly buy the firm's stock in an attempt to artificially support its price. When Vivendi's chief financial officer, Guillaume Hannezo, told him to stop, he went around his CFO by having middle-level executives purchase the stock.

It was as though he viewed the acquisitions and stock price as monuments to his pride, his way of impressing an audience of business leaders, journalists, and stakeholders in France and abroad. Not content just to build Vivendi, Messier wanted to change the landscape of French business, to make it more progressive and international, less culturally bound. He didn't just want to win the approval of the French elite; he already had that. Instead, his objective was to change the way France's social and business leaders thought, by conforming their global views to match his own. To pull off that transformation, Messier *had* to be the wunderkind leader of a fabulously successful international firm.

SQUANDERED EXECUTIVE RESOURCES: MESSIER FAILS TO HEED INPUT AND DELEGATE DECISIONS

Unreasonable ambition led him to overstate both the performance of Vivendi and his contribution to it. Recall that he had acquired a series of businesses that had been built by other executives; Messier had not contributed materially to their successes. He underestimated the challenges of making those deals work, and he overpaid for them by issuing massive levels of debt that would seriously drain cash flow. Further, he overlooked negative data about the performance of the business and exaggerated results. As he allowed his pride to drive critical decisions, Messier degenerated into a caricature of executives who operate from a foundation of overweening pride—within the fourth quadrant of the matrix of executive pride shown in Chapter 3.

Buoyed by his celebrity, Messier believed that his capabilities would be enough to carry the firm. Hence he stopped listening—let alone deferring—to his trusted senior executive team, even if that team included a number of highly qualified, even brilliant, executives who could have served as foils for his expansion plans—people Messier had worked with for years. It was a team with diverse skills, perspectives, and ambitions, who continue today to successfully lead major French businesses. Among them were:

- *Guillaume Hannezo,* chief financial officer, a fellow *ENArque* who was sometimes referred to in Parisian business circles as the "Mozart of finance" for his towering intellect. With a background similar to Messier, Hannezo became an Inspecteur de Finances and then an advisor to French President Francois Mitterand. Messier and Hannezo had known each other for 20 years, dating from when they were colleagues in the French Finance Ministry.
- *Eric Licoys,* chief operating officer and a former Messier colleague at Lazard.
- *Philippe Germond,* head of Cegetel, the French mobile phone operator, and former head of Hewlett-Packard in France; Germond left Vivendi in 2004 to become COO at Alcatel.
- *Agnès Touraine,* head of Vivendi Publishing; a Columbia Business School Graduate, Touraine was formerly the head of Hachette Consumer Publishing Division and has been described as the most powerful woman in French business.
- *Henri Proglio,* head of the Utilities Business, Vivendi Environnement, and a long-standing executive of CGE. The business was sold in 2001 to raise cash and renamed Veolia Environnement with Proglio as its chairman.

- *Antoine Zacharias,* head of Vivendi's construction business, Vinci (where he remains chairman).
- *Pierre Lescure,* chairman of Canal Plus and a long-standing Canal Plus executive who ran Vivendi Universal's television and film distribution business before Messier fired him in April 2002.

Until 1999, this group had helped Messier to revitalize CGE and form Vivendi. Although each member of the team accepted Messier as the boss, they sometimes persuaded him to walk away from bad deals. They were behind the convergence strategy, and supported the Seagram deal as integral to implementing convergence.

But, after that deal, from the middle of 2000, Messier acted with his mouth rather than his ears. Increasingly, it became irrelevant who was on his board and senior management team. Touraine, for instance, later remarked, "There were many moments when I knew things weren't going well, but I didn't know everything. You can talk and talk but then if your boss says, 'this is how it's going to be' you have to accede."[8]

MESSIER KIDS HIMSELF ABOUT HIS SITUATION BY DISMISSING NEGATIVE FEEDBACK

As a result of the Seagram deal, Messier had saddled the firm with $20 billion of debt, which seemed unsustainable to everyone except Messier. The market was saying Messier lacked a strategy, and his closest advisors and friends were telling him that he was becoming a media caricature, even a laughing stock. Their message was unwavering: He had to stay away from journalists, however addicted he may be to the celebrity. He had to pull back from acquiring so as to focus on generating sustainable cash flow.

Investors echoed those concerns. Their confidence in "new economy companies" in general and Messier in particular was waning well before Seagram. After Seagram, investors started dumping the stock, sending the share price into freefall. Messier's response was to buy more shares. To his increasingly isolated mind, he was right and investors were wrong.

On March 4, 2001, seven months after the Seagram acquisition, Hannezo warned Messier in an e-mail, "Our jobs, our reputations are at stake. What investors want to know right now is the following: Is VU [Vivendi] a total fraud like Enron? Is VU threatened by its debt? Has JMM completely lost it? The problem isn't our business; it's us, or more exactly it's you. The problem we have to solve is your credibility that you're in the process of losing."[9] The next day Messier brazenly stated at a Paris news conference, "Vivendi is in better-than-good health."[10] No matter that the firm's profits were actually declining and it lacked the cash needed to service massive and ballooning debt levels.

Hannezo grew dismayed. By December 2001, he sent a handwritten note to Messier that predicted impending doom: "I've got the unpleasant feeling of being in a car whose driver is accelerating in the turns and that I'm in the death seat. All I ask is that this not end in shame."[11] Messier dismissed the note's message out of hand.

Hannezo now claims that he opposed all of Messier's deals from 2000, with the exceptions of Seagram and USA Networks, to no avail. He continued to warn Messier about the share buybacks, calling them "artificial support. You can't fight the market." When Messier would not listen, Hannezo told his finance officers in a memo, "Henceforth it is forbidden to buy shares in the group without a written authority from the chairman." Hopefully, that would stop Messier from picking up the phone on a whim to place orders. When the memo failed to have the desired effect, Hannezo told his people to cease contact with Messier.

When Standard & Poor's and Moody's threatened to down-grade the quality of Vivendi's debt to junk status, Messier was finally forced to act. A downgrade would mean that the firm would have trouble borrowing and would face higher interest rates. Messier would have to sell assets, and even be forced to take a loss on the billions of dollars of Vivendi shares that he had been buying on the market. He did persuade Deutsche Bank and Goldman Sachs to place the shares (buy them as principal and then sell them to the market), though those banks ended up doing so at material losses. But, the resulting cash was not nearly enough to service the debt that was incurred on the new acquisitions.

Over the years, Messier had purged Vivendi's board of his critics, and now the group was largely left in the dark about the share buybacks and the prospect of the debt rating downgrade. Nevertheless, board members, led by Bronfman, insisted on getting independent external opinions on the firm's financial condition. Having spent three days reviewing the firm's finances, a team from Citicorp concluded that the firm would run out of cash within months. In June 2001, a team from Goldman Sachs reached a similar conclusion. When the Goldman bankers presented their results before the board, Messier got defensive, telling them that Goldman had overstepped its brief by being unduly conservative and pessimistic. Later that month, Messier told analysts that he would continue to lead the firm for the next 15 years.

When journalists turned against Messier toward the end of 2001, they did so with a vengeance. In May 2002, *Le Monde* claimed that Vivendi had been close to bankruptcy for some time. Outraged, Messier filed a libel suit against *Le Monde* and threatened to withdraw his group's advertising from its publisher. Messier's honeymoon with the press had come to a screeching halt.

THE FINAL ACT OF HUBRIS:
MANAGING CONSEQUENCES WITH
FOOLISH BRAVADO

Because Messier had lost the ability to listen, he had also lost the ability to adequately assess his capabilities and situation. His pride coupled with his refusal to heed senior managers blinded him to his true situation. Not surprisingly, he was unable to accept the potential consequences of his increasingly irresponsible decisions—consequences that would include Vivendi's potential bankruptcy and his professional ruin.

A case in point was the manner in which he misjudged the implications of attacking the French cultural exception, *l'exception culturelle française*—a label given to the quotas and subsidies that promote French culture in locally produced film, television, and music content. Considerable funds for and distribution of the French cultural exception derive from the pay-for-television operator Canal Plus, which was required to give 12 percent of its revenues to European film production and 9 percent to French cinema. These rules also demanded that 40 percent of the films the company televised must be French. Together, such restrictions badly hurt Canal Plus's profitability.

Frustrated, Messier launched a rhetorical campaign against the values that France's cultural guidelines represented. Initially, he told French journalists, "We will neither be apostles of U.S. cultural domination, nor of *l'exception française.*" Messier told journalists that he was partly motivated to move to a luxurious apartment on Park Avenue in Manhattan on September 2001 (for which Vivendi would spend over $20 million) because France is just an "exotic little country." Then, in December 2001, Messier appeared triumphantly at a New York press conference to announce his acquisition of USA Networks and partnership with the mercurial Hollywood dealmaker, Barry Diller. French journalists were visibly concerned and wanted to know whether the deal would further Americanize French cinema.

With his endless reserves of panache, Messier could obviously have reassured and disarmed journalists in any number of ways. Instead he asserted that, "as we all understand, the Franco-French *exception culturelle* is dead . . . . The anxiety underlined there is totally artificial and has no basis."[12]

It is one thing to be pompous, presumptuous, and arrogant behind closed doors. It is another to do so in a way that disgusts journalists, hurts shareholders, and makes enemies out of supporters. Furious, French journalists turned Messier's comments into headlines on front-page stories. In one fell swoop, Messier had offended the French cultural establishment, essentially alienating the country against him and the firm. Once "Magic," Messier was now the enemy who put French film under siege.

Messier did not help his cause by ostentatiously using company money for personal purposes. In particular, he had bought an Airbus A319 to fly him and other Vivendi executives to and from France and the United States Messier wanted it fitted with a shower to go with its other opulent fixtures. The problem was that, with a shower, the plane would need tanks to carry hundreds of liters of water, greatly diminishing the plane's ability to store fuel. Without the fuel, the plane could not fly nonstop from Paris to Los Angeles, which was, at least ostensibly, its *raison d'être*. Either the shower or the nonstop Los Angeles flight had to go, and Messier chose the latter.

Inevitably, word got out about the plane and its shower, giving the French press yet another field day. When pressed, Messier denied the plane's existence, saying, "It is time to kill all theses ridiculous rumors. Vivendi does not have an Airbus." Later he conceded that Vivendi did own the Airbus, but the firm did not use it much.[13] He might as well have said that he had tried marijuana without inhaling it. Whatever the metaphor, the effect was to undermine his already weak public credibility and further damage his relationship with the Bronfman family.

Meanwhile, the firm's financial situation was worsening. It seemed to insiders that Messier was either oblivious to the prospect that the firm would become insolvent or he knew that the firm was facing bankruptcy, but wanted to gamble his way out of trouble. If somehow he could prop up the firm's stock price, there was still an outside chance that he could raise cash by selling Vivendi shares. Either way, the firm's situation was desperate and Messier refused to come clean.

Even if Messier was worried about the financial condition of the firm, especially after its credit rating was downgraded, he was not overly concerned about his job. Given that French culture is predicated more on consensus than conflict, cultural norms dictate that board members of major French firms do not fire their CEOs. Instead, as Jo Johnson from the *Financial Times* and Martine Orange from *Le Monde* wrote in their collaboration about the Messier debacle, "the French establishment would take charge. Chief executives would be eased out with a quiet word from a senior figure charged with the delicate operation. There would be no resistance. Discretion was the rule." [14]

But this time, the rule didn't apply. On July 2, 2002, Vivendi's directors forced Messier to resign at a time when the firm had $15.6 billion in debt, €14 billion in losses, and had lost over 80 percent of its peak market value. Upon his resignation, a bitter Messier told journalists, "I hope the market will give my successor what it withheld from me, time to act in calm fashion." The harsh reality was that Messier's firm had severe cash flow problems, and he failed to acknowledge that those problems were the consequences of his own failures as a decision maker.

Messier's reputation has been irreparably damaged. He has spent two days in police detention, has been forced to pay millions of dollars in fines, and has been barred from serving on the board of any U.S.-listed company for ten years. Today, he lives comfortably in exile in New York, having secretly sold millions of dollars of shares in Vivendi in December 2001. Messier says, "I failed. I start again from zero. I take my hat and my cane and I go and see clients." [15] With business contacts, including Barry Diller, for clients, he has set up the modest investment bank, Messier Partners.

For our purposes, his experience dramatically illustrates the classic downward spiral by which false confidence induces the overconfident decisions that fuel hubris. It is a spiral that will play out again and again with different people in business and government unless it can be better understood and checked.

SUMMARY

In Chapter 1, I presented a framework for understanding the sources of overconfidence and hubris, and subsequent chapters have explored each aspect of that framework, as it applies to executive decision making. The story of Jean-Marie Messier's professional rise and fall could have been custom-built on that framework. In fact, I learned about the opportunity to apply this methodology from my Harvard Business School colleague, Rakesh Khurana, who invited me to collaborate with him on a case study about Messier's experiences at Vivendi.

Figure 7.2 summarizes Messier's story of executive hubris in the context of this framework and the four toxic sources of overconfidence: getting too full of ourselves, failing to get out of our own way by letting others decide, kidding ourselves about our situation, and discounting the need to manage tomorrow today.

Managing false confidence and hubris requires that we consider one decision at a time and synthesize the types of decisions that we make over time. In the next chapter, we examine the case story of Michael Dell of Dell Inc., an executive who has learned to manage his overconfidence and hubris somewhat more effectively.

FIGURE 7.2 *Jean-Marie Messier's False Confidence and Hubris at Vivendi*

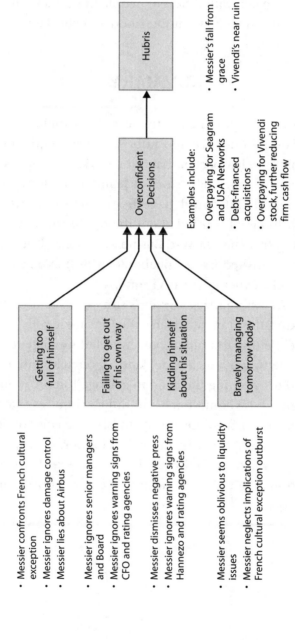

Messier's False Sources of Confidence

- Messier confronts French cultural exception
- Messier ignores damage control
- Messier lies about Airbus

- Messier ignores senior managers and Board
- Messier ignores warning signs from CFO and rating agencies

- Messier dismisses negative press
- Messier ignores warning signs from Hannezo and rating agencies

- Messier seems oblivious to liquidity issues
- Messier neglects implications of French cultural exception outburst

Getting too full of himself

Failing to get out of his own way

Kidding himself about his situation

Bravely managing tomorrow today

Overconfident Decisions

Hubris

Examples include:

- Overpaying for Seagram and USA Networks
- Debt-financed acquisitions
- Overpaying for Vivendi stock, further reducing firm cash flow

- Messier's fall from grace
- Vivendi's near ruin

8

Overcoming Hubris

LESSONS FROM MICHAEL DELL
OF DELL INC.

*"I know my mom would be proud, but I certainly don't feel like we're
the most admired company. I would be relatively dismissive of that
kind of thing and say, 'Well that's really nice, thank you very much.
I'm humbled by that, but we've got a lot of work to do.'"*

MICHAEL DELL (on being told that Dell Inc. was named
Fortune magazine's most admired company for 2005) [1]

Michael Dell has learned to keep his ego in check. Dell, who
turned his start-up into *Fortune* magazine's most admired corporation in 21 years, learned about the perils of executive hubris the
hard way. This chapter looks at the lessons that Dell has gleaned
from some of his costly mistakes.

I started to study Dell in-depth while living in Austin, Texas.
During that time I interacted with Dell senior executives, including Kevin Rollins and Tom Meredith, about whom you'll also read
in this chapter. During those conversations, I was struck by how
Michael Dell had struggled to check his ego, even as he became
one of the world's wealthiest people as the founder of a fabulously
successful multinational firm.

When I dug deeper I learned that Dell's approach was shaped
by a series of mistakes that threatened the life of his firm. Over
time, Dell learned how to rein in his propensity to exaggerate his
capabilities, to develop compelling foil relationships—especially
with Kevin Rollins—and to commit to using feedback and metrics

to make speedy decisions. Finally, having become another victim of disastrous planning, Dell took the task of managing tomorrow's consequences today to heart. Today, even as his firm struggles to sustain its impressive growth, Dell serves as an example of how we can make a fortune doing what we love most, if we can only avoid the dangerous trap of executive hubris.

Steve Jobs might seem like an unlikely comparison point with Dell, even if the two are leaders of the personal computer industry: Jobs is a charismatic visionary who helps to create revolutionary products, where Dell is so introverted and shy that he can appear aloof (when, at least in my experience, he is not). Like Jobs, Dell had the great good fortune of finding work he loved in his early 20s, and then undertook the Herculean effort of building a great business. Jobs could have been speaking for Dell when he told Stanford University's 2005 graduating class, "Your work is going to fill a large part of your life, and the only way to be truly satisfied is to do what you believe is great work."

In 1983 at 18, Dell enrolled in premedical studies at the University of Texas, Austin, much to his parents' delight. Once in Austin, he also started assembling computers in addition to studying medicine. Learning about this choice, his father, an orthodontist, flew from Houston to Austin to intervene. He demanded, "You've got to stop with this computer stuff and concentrate on school. Get your priorities straight," and rhetorically asked, "What do you want to do with your life?" To which his son impertinently answered, "I want to compete with IBM!"[2]

By 1984, Michael founded Dell Computers with $1,000. As I write, the company is suffering from declining margins, slowing international sales, and product quality issues. And yet, the firm has a market value of about $50 billion and Dell owns around 10 percent of that, making him one of the world's wealthiest people. Unable to compete with Dell in personal computers, IBM has long since exited that business. Here, we'll consider how Michael Dell's experiences in pursuit of work that he is passionate about have shaped his skills as a leader and decision maker. And, I believe that the following helps to explain why Dell will recover from its current predicament.

MICHAEL DELL'S GROUNDED PRIDE

In his 1999 autobiography, Dell describes how, as a 12-year-old stamp collector, he disliked paying auctioneers to buy and sell stamps. So rather than pay the middle man his cut, he formed Dell's Stamps, where he would play that role. His tiny operation found people in Houston who wanted to sell stamps and flushed out buyers by producing and mailing a catalogue of those stamps. Dell's Stamps taught him how much the middle man could make, and how much more value customers could get by buying directly.

Before long, Dell developed a passion for computers. He recalls that, as a seven year old, he was captivated by the idea that a calculator "could compute things." Only ten years younger than Jobs, Dell was quickly drawn to Apple's elegant and simple machines. He successfully cajoled his parents into buying him an Apple II, then dismantled it, leaving his parents to wonder why they had paid a small fortune for a set of parts.

Reassembling the Apple II helped Dell appreciate the simple and integral steps involved in making personal computers. Before long, he learned that personal computers were being sold for $3,000, when their nonproprietary components could be bought for about one-fifth that amount. Dell also realized that computers could be easily upgraded. There were no real barriers to his entry into the computer business; he had all the student-customers he needed on his sprawling University of Texas campus. Sure he might have to postpone a possible career in medicine but, other than that, the costs of failing were limited. Dell's strategy was to get his customers made-to-order computers at ever-lower prices.

Dell's grounded pride derives from his ability to deliver just that—over and again for millions of customers.

Struggling to Maintain an Internal Locus of Pride

By and large, Dell reviews sales and customer satisfaction data to appreciate his work and assess his performance. At times, however, he lapses into trying to impress himself and others by dismissively and sarcastically criticizing competitors.

In 1996, for example, Apple's share of the personal computer business was eroding at an alarming pace. When asked what he would do to fix Apple's problems, he replied, "I'd shut it down and give the money back to the shareholders." Nearly ten years later, Apple passed Dell's market capitalization, prompting Jobs to e-mail his executives: "Team, it turned out that Michael Dell wasn't perfect at predicting the future. Based on today's stock market close, Apple is worth more than Dell. Stocks go up and down, and things may be different tomorrow, but I thought it was worth a moment of reflection today. Steve."[3]

In 2001, Dell also acted out of his conservative and softly spoken character by awkwardly and unoriginally calling the data storage company EMC, the "Excess Margin Corporation." It was an attempt to be humorous and clever but it backfired. Eventually, it made sense for Dell's firm to develop a data storage systems alliance with EMC, and his comments only complicated and delayed the process. Overcoming those issues, however, the alliance now generates compelling margins for both firms.

Such slips are rare and uncharacteristic for Dell, who usually avoids public outbursts and self-promotion. In particular, he is suspicious of praise, regarding it as ingratiating and gratuitous. In fact, he notes that people who need praise don't do well at Dell because, within that corporate culture, such need is usually viewed as a sign of insecurity and weakness. (The downside, of course, is that even the highest performing employees at Dell receive limited positive feedback).

Discounting the importance and validity of praise helps Dell to immunize himself and his colleagues against pride that depends on external approval and the need to exaggerate in order to elicit that approval. It is just as well, because his picture glowed, trophy-like from the front cover of *Fortune* magazine for the second time in March 2005. His reaction to the first tribute follows:

> You would think that being featured on the cover of *Fortune* was a great achievement, but I'm quick to remind our team that in 1986 *Fortune* put a big, smiling picture of Digital Equipment's CEO, Ken Olsen, on the cover with the caption "America's most successful entrepreneur: Ken Olsen." [Digital's stock price subsequently plummeted.] Being on the cover of *Fortune* doesn't guarantee you anything."[4]

While there is nothing wrong with celebrity per se, it becomes an issue because, as Dell puts it, "It's easy to fall in love with how far you've come and how much you've done." Early in 2005, a *Fortune* journalist called Dell to say that Dell Inc. had been voted by the CEOs of peer firms as the most admired company in America; and *Fortune* wanted to feature Dell's picture on the cover of the edition that would carry that story, Dell responded by insisting that, if he was going to be on the cover, it would have to be with his chief executive officer, Kevin Rollins.

Where other executives may have basked in the reflected glory, Dell and Rollins used the feature story to tell the public that Dell is an underdog, entering a series of new growth businesses— servers, storage, services, printers—in which it is not the market leader. Overall, their message was that the firm is not nearly as good as it should be.

To get customers value for money, Dell works hard at knowing where technology is today, rather than where it is going to be. When asked about emerging technology that excites him, Dell dodges the question by asserting that the firm tries to determine which markets are sufficiently established to enable Dell to leverage its cost advantage.

Sun Microsystems Chairman Scott McNealy scoffs at Dell for developing me-too servers with dull components and basic applications. McNealy sarcastically calls Dell a great place to go and buy "unassembled ten-speed bikes," calling the firm "the greatest spare parts distributor out there . . . by the way, I can buy a low-cost automobile by buying all the piece parts and not paying for the assembly, labor, certification, and testing."[5] However, as McNealy takes cheap shots that express his pride, Dell continues to take material market share in servers from Sun.

Learning from False Pride

As mentioned in Chapter 5, one source of false pride is erroneous or speculative data, which can—among other things—lead executives to carry excessive amounts of inventory.

Minimizing inventory is imperative at Dell, as it is at any personal computer company. Rollins likens it to unrefrigerated fish: "The longer you keep it, the faster it deteriorates—you can literally see the stuff rot."[6] Today, the firm uses a "direct to order" inventory rule, whereby inventory is ordered in response to demand. It's a rule that Dell learned the hard way.

In 1988, he started making brave assumptions. In particular, he unnecessarily assumed that demand for the firm's computers would explode, computers should be built with existing memory chips, and that supplies of those chips would run out, which, if true, would prevent the firm from meeting demand. Based on those assumptions, Dell had the firm buy large quantities of the chips, only to be stuck with them. Unable to return the inventory at cost, he was forced to sell it for pennies on the dollar, undermining cash flow and profitability. Scared for the life of the firm, he wondered whether he "might be in over my head."[7]

Exaggerating our capabilities is another major source of false pride; and Dell has not been immune here either. Through a series of hard lessons, Dell has learned that his firm's fabulous success at selling computers directly to customers does not automatically translate into success at selling indirectly through retail outlets, nor does it mean that Dell Inc. can successfully lead customers with new products and technologies. Dell also has painfully seen that the firm can't simply extrapolate the success of its direct model in the United States to international markets.

In 1990, the firm entered the retail market by selling through large outlets such as Wal-Mart. At first glance, the new strategy seemed like a huge success with retail growing to 10 percent of all sales within months. What this apparent success belied, however, was customers' confusion about where they would get the best prices and how their purchasing experience (including after-sales support) would differ between the channels. When top managers looked more closely, they found that the new sales would never generate the same returns that were available from direct selling.

"Exit retail" became the new strategy, one that was easier to say than to do. Retailers wanted the business, and they presented a barrier between the firm and its customers that prevented the company from establishing customer satisfaction. Because retail gave Dell more business, it also helped the firm negotiate larger discounts from suppliers. And Wall Street loved the growth.

While costly, the decision to exit retail highlights one of Michael Dell's strengths: When an initiative fails to meet expectations, he resists the temptation to tweak it. Instead, his bias is to more fundamentally ask whether the firm is acting in the best interests of customers or whether it is trying to make a quick buck. When he discovers that it is the latter, as with the retail initiative, exit swiftly follows.

Establishing what's in the best interests of customers is particularly tricky for computer makers given that technology is incessantly changing. The temptation for executives like Dell is to try to lead customers into new technologies by persuading them about new applications. That premise led him to champion the Olympic project to design and develop a computer that served as a "desktop, workstation, and server" all in one box. The firm's engineers heroically built the Olympic to specification and deadline, allowing salespeople and senior managers to showcase it at industry events. In the end, however, customers refused to buy it. Where other leaders may have reacted by redoubling their commitment to the project—launching an aggressive advertising campaign or insisting on technology improvements—Dell again asked whether and how the Olympic benefited customers. Lacking a compelling answer, the firm decisively ended its Olympic campaign.

It was an expensive lesson in knowing one's limits and, unfortunately, Dell's pride blocked his learning. Getting caught up in the Internet bubble in 1999, he sponsored the development of a low-price Web appliance for distributed computing, called the WebPC. It was designed to help customers tap applications and processing capacity on the Web, which they could do after taking delivery of their computers rather than have applications preloaded upon purchase. Again customers rejected it, forcing the firm to pull it from the market.

At about the same time, Dell started investing in "bleeding edge" applications and components, rather than end products. Senior Dell executives still cringe when I remind them about acquiring a small technology firm, Convergenet, for $348 million in 1999. Convergenet was developing emerging hardware and software to connect different types of storage devices to any operating system or platform. Upon announcing the deal, Tom Meredith, then the firm's CFO, hailed Convergenet for being at the "leading edge of research and development of data class storage for storage-area networking." In reality, Convergenet lacked the technology that Dell thought that it had. In fact, the technology was nowhere near ready for the market, and the firm lacked the relevant expertise to accelerate its development. Worse, the acquired engineers were a bad fit in Dell's low cost, pay-for-performance driven culture. The investment essentially had to be written off.

A similar initiative at the time was Dell's move to lead his firm into venture capital investing. The motivation for Dell Ventures was to "get in early on technology curves" and profit as early investors in technologies that would eventually be incorporated on Dell machines. Again, he overshot his capabilities and his firm's strengths. The plan offered limited if any direct value to customers, the investments ultimately failed to generate strong returns, and the operation folded. Perhaps Dell's success and pride made him believe that he could be a technology visionary, and that he could lead his firm into bold new ventures. Through this series of unsuccessful ventures, however, Dell has learned that he and Dell Inc. excel at getting customers more value from money out of products with standardized components that have already been accepted by the market. Now he's quick to point out that is where Dell can best leverage its cost advantage.

Consider also whether Dell has exaggerated his own and his firm's capabilities in foreign markets. It's a crucial issue since Dell's growth, which has been sluggish in recent years, depends on international sales. The firm's present revenue growth rates in Europe, Southeast Asia, and China are close to 20 percent, 30 percent, and 45 percent, respectively, which far exceed those in the United States. The firm has been fabulously successful in important foreign markets. It entered the UK early and is easily the market leader there. It also has market leadership positions in Canada, Ireland, and Sweden, among other countries.

Yet, the firm's performance in other key markets—Italy, Japan, and Spain to name a few—remains disappointing after years of trying. In fact, the firm has less than 10 percent market share in overseas markets that together comprise around 50 percent of global computer sales. And, even though the firm is growing rapidly in China, its overall market share there is 9 percent compared with about 30 percent in the United States.

Dell's confidence in his ability to transplant the direct model from the United States to foreign markets may have contributed to underperformance in those markets. With early success in the UK, for instance, Dell and his team believed that the direct model could be rolled out throughout Europe. In Germany, though, customers resist placing orders directly by phone or through the Web, preferring instead to do business with dedicated salespeople. Or as Dell puts it, "The customer initiates an expression of interest by filling out something on the Web site or faxing us," undermining the firm's ability to win unsolicited sales by phone or on the Web.[8] Similarly, Italians have a deeply ingrained history of using personal contacts and networks to do business, through brokers or *agente*. Slowly, Dell is learning that much more direct and expensive sales intervention is needed in both markets.

Investing in corporate buyers is also critical to win large Asian accounts. Regardless of the quality and price of one's products, selling to Japanese firms, for example, requires finding and pitching to the right buyers. This happens through membership in a Keiretsu, the club or network of large Japanese companies, in which members feel an obligation to take calls and review proposals from other members. Obviously, the firm is not a member of a Keiretsu.

So the alternative is to have salespeople carefully, courteously, and patiently cultivate relationships with prospective buyers. Because it is difficult to get access to senior buyers, relationship building must often start with middle-level buyers, which is an investment that bears fruit after those buyers get promoted to more senior buying positions. Return on investment must be measured over years, an approach that clashes with Dell's culture of transparency and impatience for results. After ten years, the firm's overall market share in Japan is 15 percent, driven mainly by server sales to smaller businesses, results that are well below the firm's aspirations.

GETTING THE RIGHT HELP: MICHAEL DELL TURNS TO LEE WALKER AND KEVIN ROLLINS

Dell's experience in Japan highlights the need to get the right help, particularly input from people with knowledge of local market conditions. Over the years, he has consistently shown that he can do just that—get the right help or get out of the way. Consider, for example, his ability to find and work effectively with the right foils, dating from the firm's first years.

For some entrepreneurs, like Dean Kamen, transferring control of their ventures to professional managers—who have not lived through the birth pains of venture creation— is like giving up one's baby for adoption to the wrong people. Unlike other entrepreneurs, though, Dell knew that he lacked the experience, time, and skill to establish the controls and processes that can ensure profitable growth. His self-directed question was, "What are the things that I'm able to do, and what are those things that I really need help with." [9]

Bringing in Experts to Help a Changing Business

In 1986, Dell hired Lee Walker, a venture capitalist and experienced executive, as the firm's president. Even though Dell continued to drive the firm's day-to-day activities, Walker buffered it by being a mentor and sounding board for him, raising capital and shaping the board of directors. At Walker's insistence, Dell demoted or fired many of the friends who started the firm with him, but who lacked the skills and experience to manage a rapidly growing venture.

To strengthen the board, Walker brought on two of Austin's more respected and seasoned executives: George Kozmetsky, cofounder of a successful technology firm and Dean of the University of Texas School of Business; and Bob Inman, formerly CEO of a large defense firm. Already highly successful, Kozmetsky and Inman began immediately to help the firm by speaking up, especially by questioning rather than endorsing Dell's interest in emerging opportunities. Kozmetsky, for instance, was adamant that retail was a bad initiative, and was instrumental in getting the firm out of that channel.

Their help was a great start, but it was not nearly enough, especially after Walker left in 1989. By 1992, the firm was growing too fast for its own good and Kozmetsky and Inman lacked the time to take hands-on responsibility. Dell recalls:

> We were pulling in more than \$2 billion in revenue but we still had the infrastructure of a \$500 million company. Just about every system we had installed a couple of years before was now unable to support our business. We had outgrown our phone system, our basic financial system, our support system, and our parts numbering system. Our factory systems were all stretched well beyond their original capacity.[10]

With these systems near breaking point, the firm could not produce and deliver high-quality products on time, let alone provide adequate after-sales support. Customer satisfaction began to plummet.

Unable to fix the problems, Dell turned to Tom Meredith, who was dealing with similar issues as treasurer of Sun Microsystems. Meredith warned Dell that the firm would be unable to successfully fill orders, causing it to "hit the wall." After becoming convinced that Meredith had the experience to fix the problems, Meredith was hired as the firm's CFO. Dell reflected, "The challenge in building a business like ours is that you're constantly confronted with situations no one has ever seen before . . . . The best *combination* is a management team that has *both experience and intellect,* and can respond quickly in a dynamic and constantly changing executive."[11]

Sharing Power and Delegating Decision Making

To gain operating experience, Dell also brought in Mort Topfer, a senior Motorola executive, as vice-chairman in 1994. Even though Motorola is not a computer company, Topfer had considerable experience in launching new products, managing product life cycles, and transforming a functional organization into one organized around business segments (based on product lines) that are led by general managers. As the firm's number two officer, Topfer was responsible for operations, sales, and marketing. Dell retained control over external relations, technology, and firm strategy. Topfer's role evolved into managing Dell's internal operations, including planning and developing the right infrastructure, and finding future leaders. (Topfer remains a revered figure at Dell, with an Austin factory named after him.)

One of those leaders was Kevin Rollins, who had helped Topfer and Dell as an external consultant at Bain & Co. In 1997, Rollins was hired to lead Dell Americas. After working closely with Rollins on the firm's operations and strategy, Dell made him the firm's second ever chief executive officer in July 2004. At the time, Dell had not yet turned 40, was in perfect health, and was the CEO of one of America's most successful companies.

It was a major surprise. In fact, months before being appointed CEO, Rollins publicly answered his own rhetorical question "Would I like to be CEO? . . . Sure. Next question. Because I'm not going to be."[12] In this arrangement, Dell is chairman of the firm and shares power with Rollins over all aspects of the firm. Today, they sit on opposite sides of a 40-foot wide room and both like to say that they have never closed the sliding glass partition that divides their office.

Such power-sharing arrangements (Dell and Intel call them "two in a box") are unusual because one leader usually begins from a more powerful position than the other, and doesn't like to give up power. Even when both begin from an equal footing, the arrangement usually triggers a power struggle, leading to polarizing relationships ("who are you with: me or him"), turf wars ("I own that business"), bad communication, and missed assignments.

Scott McNealy, for example, cofounded Sun in 1984. Since then he has autocratically remained the firm's chairman, and, until recently, has resisted opportunities to share power with talented executives. For instance, the firm's long-standing and highly

respected president and chief operating officer, Ed Zander, left
the firm in 2004 to become Motorola's CEO, while McNealy was
blocking his path to CEO at Sun. Zander is now staging a remarkable turnaround at Motorola (think the RAZR cell phone) while
Sun's share price is a quarter of what it was five years ago. When
McNealy announced that he would step down from the company
as CEO, after yet another loss-making quarter, Sun's market capitalization increased by almost $2 billion. The firm's employees and
shareholders were left to wonder why it took so long and why
McNealy remains as chairman.

Leveraging Differences in Collaborative Decision Making

McNealy could have taken heed from Jack Welch's predecessor at GE, Reg Jones. Explaining his decision to appoint Welch as
CEO, Jones told the 1982 Harvard Business School graduating
class that "the first thing that you do when you're looking for a successor is, don't look for someone like you."[13]

Along the lines of Jones's advice, Dell and Rollins are very different. Whereas Dell is a college dropout, Rollins has an MBA
from Brigham Young University. Dell has only worked at his own
firm, while Rollins worked as a partner at Bain and Co. Dell is Jew-
ish; Rollins is Mormon. And Rollins is 12 years older.

How does the relationship work? According to Joe Tucci,
EMC's CEO, "What breaks these kinds of relationships is where
two individuals don't see the future the same, where there's a
power struggle or where there's a problem over 'Who gets the
press?' But if you talk to Kevin and Michael, you know that they see
the future the same way. There's no ego thing."[14]

According to Dell, power sharing is a natural solution to the
reality that one person lacks the time to best run a large firm
because it results in better, more grounded, decisions. He says:

Because each of us comes up with ideas that aren't fully developed, we work through them together, and we end up with better decisions . . . . When Kevin makes a decision by himself or I make decision by myself, it's never quite as good as if we make decisions together.[15]

Rollins also regards decision making as a complementary process. In describing the debates between himself and Dell over issues as such the firm's printer rollout or its alliance with EMC, Rollins says:

[I]t's not as though one of us always plays the optimist and one the pessimist. In both cases, we each talked a lot about the issues and our concerns and got the other comfortable. Then we proceeded as a team.[16]

Rollins's appointment as CEO highlights Dell's ability to check his ego, to put his pride to one side to ensure that he is getting the right input and getting out of the way where necessary. Sure the two strongly disagree at times, but they tolerate the disagreements because the firm is better for having both of them screen decisions.

ENSURING THAT EXECUTIVES USE EXTENSIVE AND TIMELY FEEDBACK

Dell and Rollins also rely extensively on general managers who thrive in Dell's discipline-driven, metrics-oriented culture. Dell is often hailed for its best practices for devising and using metrics to drive costs out of its value chain. General managers have detailed and real-time profit and loss information about how their respective businesses are performing. But, as NASA's experiences remind us (see Chapter 6), there is often an enormous and exceptionally costly difference between having good information and acting on it.

Five ingrained principles give Dell and Rollins confidence that general managers will act on the metrics:

1. *A culture of openness and early disclosure, reinforced by penalties (which can include getting fired), for not speaking up.* According to Michael Dell:

    > The worst thing you can do as a leader at Dell is to be in denial—to try to convince people that a problem is not there or play charades . . . . The manager who covers up and says it's not really as bad as it looks—he'll have a big problem.[17]

    General managers' profit-and-loss results are presented in a standard, online format. Because they are transparent to every senior manager, there is limited scope to game the system by hiding results in the unrealistic hope that they might get better.

2. *An openness to criticism and fundamental questioning from the top down.* According to Michael Dell:

    > Challenging the current state of affairs ensures that you don't get too wrapped up in your success. By now, self-criticism is ingrained in the Dell culture—we're always ready to question our own ideas, looking for ways things can be improved. We try to model this behavior from the top down. We hire for, and develop, leaders who are open minded and can accept being disagreed with publicly or corrected when they've got their facts wrong. This helps promote open debate and encourages an intellectual meritocracy.[18]

3. *A governing rule that decisions must be made quickly and with the best data.* According to Rollins:

    > The first rule is: Make your decision fast—even if you don't have complete data. Get the best data you

can, because making a decision with no data is a sin. But delaying a decision while you overanalyze the data is not good.[19]

Because the firm does everything possible to minimize management layers, communication flows fluidly and transparently within and between business units.

4. *A no-excuses culture.* Dell and Rollins reject the notion that a business doesn't have to make money, say, because it subsidizes another business or because it is expected to turn around at another stage of the economic cycle. Granted, this results in potentially damaging impatience, as seen with Dell's slow development of its Japanese business. But such trade-off is tolerated because Dell wants every executive to be biased toward acting on prompt, performance-driven feedback.

5. *Incentives and pay raises that are tied to metrics.* "Tell Dell" metrics give managers 360-degree feedback (a multisource performance feedback system that enables people to compare the assessment of others to their own self-assessment) on how their colleagues think they are performing.

A criticism of the firm is that its over-reliance on business metrics makes it impersonal and soulless. Acutely aware of this, Dell and Rollins have recently become more sensitive to personal feedback. Dell personally takes 360-degree feedback seriously—whether it comes from his personal assistant, Rollins, or another member of his senior team. 360-degree feedback cannot be credible unless it applies to and is acted on by each employee, from the receptionist to the CEO. Rollins describes how this starts from the top:

Michael and I share the 360 feedback, good and bad, with all our direct reports. They have a free shot at telling us what they don't like about us and what they think we could do bet-

ter. They wanted more feedback. They wanted an opportunity
to participate more in the decision making. They wanted us to
be more open. We were maybe not as friendly as we could have
been in making them want to stay here socially.[20]

Dell divulged that the feedback showed him to be cold, impersonal, and unfriendly. "I also learned from the 360 degree reviews
that I needed to do a better job of connecting with people—relating to people as human beings who want connection and recognition, not mere abstract objects doing work," says Dell. "I've always
really enjoyed business problems and didn't feel as much need for
connection as our team clearly wanted. It took me a while to see
how important this quality of relationship is in building loyalty to
the company."[21]

   With his success, wealth, and power, Dell could dismiss the criticism out of hand. Instead he's taking concrete steps to socialize
with his colleagues by making work social functions a higher priority and leading more training sessions.

MANAGING TOMORROW THROUGH TODAY'S DECISIONS AND ACTIONS

   The final way that Dell and Rollins try to avoid false confidence in decision making is to manage the consequences of decisions, such as whether to enter new businesses, ahead of time.
Decision making that surrounded entry into the printer business
illustrates how the firm tackles this, through what I call an "elevator" approach. Here, the firm has an end goal in sight and works
backwards from there, establishing one level of commitments
before proceeding to the next level.

   According to Dell, "The biggest mistake I've made was not getting into printers sooner." Why did the firm wait until 2003 to do
so? Rollins, who notes that he was instrumental in delaying entry,
says that it's because the firm has a lot of "fish to fry." I take the fish

with a heavy helping of salt, given that, in 2006, the size of the global printer hardware market is roughly $60 billion, and the printer consumables market (ink, toners, paper) is at least that again. Further, the printer market is dominated by Dell's fiercest competitor, Hewlett-Packard (HP), which uses profits from its printer business to subsidize other businesses, including personal computers.

A more realistic explanation of the firm's late entry is that Dell and Rollins agonized and disagreed over the best way to deal with some key challenges. For them, the cost of conservatively managing tomorrow today was delaying entry into such a lucrative market.

Entering a New Market: Managing What Could Go Wrong

Dell and Rollins knew that if the firm launched its own line of branded printers, it would lose its lucrative business distributing HP printers. But that was only one of several challenges that the firm needed to face for the entry to succeed.

First, printers are a technology-intensive business; HP spends $1 billion a year on research and development in improving imaging and has at least 100 patents on its low-end printers alone, with another 9,000 patents for imaging and printing technologies. Because the firm lacked the time, expertise, and inclination to develop the technology necessary to launch a line of printers, it could not compete with HP on quality. The question was whether the firm could develop a sufficiently robust, high-quality machine that could be produced and sold in large volumes.

Dell also had to decide whether to produce those printers in-house or outsource them. On the one hand, it would take the firm years to develop printer technology and manufacturing expertise. On the other hand, using third-party machines would prevent the firm from leveraging its manufacturing and supply chain capabilities and would make the firm dependent on that supplier.

Also, profits from selling printers are usually dwarfed by profits from selling printer consumables. Invariably the business invokes a comparison with Gillette, which sells razors inexpensively in order to make money from razor blades. This comparison belies some key differences, however. Whereas printer cartridges are less differentiated products that can be readily imitated, Gillette's razors are supported by hundreds of millions dollars of research and development and a well-established brand—factors that drive high margins. If Dell could not differentiate its printer consumables, that business would be vulnerable to competition from knock-offs. And, whereas Gillette razors are sold through retail outlets, Dell would have to convince customers to buy printer consumables directly, either online or over the phone, because Dell has vowed not to return to retail channels. After considering these challenges, Dell and Rollins ultimately decided to outsource printers, relying initially on Lexmark to produce printers that would be sold under the Dell brand.

Defusing Potentially Negative Consequences

Given the complexities and uncertainties involved, Dell and Rollins resisted a major launch. Instead, to manage the above challenges, they embarked on a three-part staged decision-making process:

Stage 1. Manage the quality of Dell's branded printers
Stage 2. With the demands of Stage 1 met, control costs to ensure competitive advantage
Stage 3. Once stage 2 is met, differentiate the product from the competition and diversify product offerings to create and increase profits

The governing principle in Stage 1 was that any failure in quality would undermine the firm's ability to be a credible competitor to HP, and so would quickly outweigh benefits of lower-priced printers. To manage quality in its line of branded printers, a final step was to adopt Lexmark printers internally to verify their quality on a wide range of printing jobs.

In the second phase of Stage 1, Dell used its direct model to sell Lexmark printers for the end of 2002 holiday season. The idea was that the firm wanted to test printer quality under Lexmark's name. Third, once Dell was satisfied with the quality in the first two phases, it entered a new phase where it sold Lexmark workgroup, small business, and personal imaging products under the Dell label, testing printer quality on smaller clients before rolling out the launch with major customers. A key component was to test customers' willingness to order consumables online through built-in software that alerts customers when ink is low in the toner and directs them to the right cartridge on the firm's Web site.

Within 12 months of launching the business, the firm had sold 1.5 million inkjet printers, making it the fifth-largest seller of printers in the United States. Even though revenue exceeded expectations and the firm has eroded HP's margins, the business was barely above breakeven. Now was the time to move to Stage 2 of the decision-making process.

Along with improving quality, the firm carefully examined supply chain management for consumables and its nonexclusive relationship with Lexmark. To reduce dependence on Lexmark and squeeze better terms out of original equipment manufacturers in general, the firm also sources printers from Samsung Electronics, Fuji Xerox, and Eastman Kodak.

By 2005, Dell printers was ranked number one in overall customer satisfaction among 1,600 business users polled by J.D. Power. With over 5 million printers sold, the firm has 15 percent of the U.S. printer market by volume.

Still, the vast majority of sales remain in low-margin sales to individuals and small businesses. In Stage 3 of the decision-making process, the firm must differentiate and diversify its product line, expanding from inkjet printers to laser printers, and from lower capacity printers to higher capacity ones. With these product offerings, the firm can now aggressively pursue larger clients with contracts for servicing and replenishing a customer's printer fleet, including supplying toner kits. Recently, the firm anounced a major printer servicing contract with Boeing worth tens of millions of dollars.

In following this model, the firm must successfully complete each stage of the decision-making elevator before proceeding to the next. To ensure that the firm is not overconfident about aggressive cost reductions, it ensures that the quality justifies the cost effort. As the firm considers adding differentiated features, it first ensures that the quality and cost of existing features are at least good enough. With quality, cost, and differentiation capabilities in place, the firm examines further diversification into high-end imaging and digital photography.

The decision-making elevator highlights how conservative Dell and Rollins have become. Nowhere is that conservatism more pronounced than in the firm's approach to managing the consequences of potentially overconfident decisions. In a recent *Harvard Business Review* interview, Dell mentioned, "We think about failure all the time. We've been able to simulate failure in our minds . . . and avoid extinction or disastrous consequences because we've worked through all the bad things that could happen."[22] Staging entry into a new business helps establish the consequences of decisions ahead of time, providing the data needed to inform more extensive product launches.

SUMMARY

Over the years, Michael Dell has developed a decision-making approach that makes him less susceptible to the false confidence that produces hubris. It's an approach that can be deduced from his decisions over the years, even though you won't find it codified anywhere at the firm. Through the various techniques described in the chart in Figure 8.1, he has managed to avoid (1) being too full of himself, (2) getting in his own way, (3) kidding himself about his firm's situation, and (4) incurring the costs of not managing tomorrow today.

Of course, it hasn't always been that way: In the past, his false pride has prevented him from passing the first test. What's noteworthy about Dell's experience is that he's usually—not always—used input and feedback to stop those types of decisions in their tracks, preventing overconfident decisions from translating into outcomes that are difficult to recover from.

FIGURE 8.1 *Michael Dell: Learning How to Manage False Confidence and Hubris at Dell Inc.*

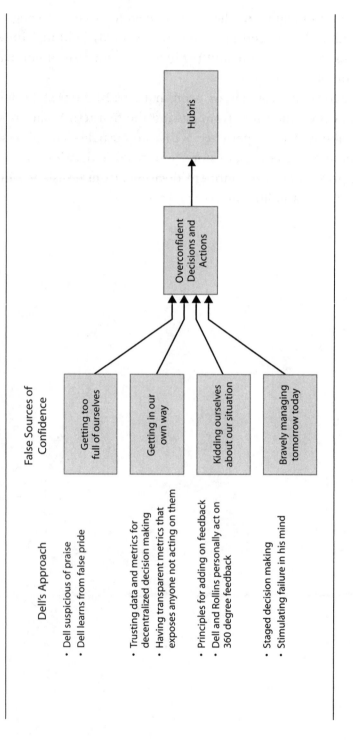

Some
Closing Comments

Michael Dell's story—along with those of Jean-Marie Messier, Meg Whitman, Steve Jobs, Warren Buffett, and the many other executives who are portrayed in this book—keenly illustrates the value of following an ego check framework for grounded decision making. It is one that can stop hubris in its tracks in all walks of life.

In spite of my personal bias toward being overconfident, however, this book will not be enough to stop the false confidence that yields hubris. Hubris will be with us for as long as there are people who think they have all the answers, whether it is in your business or mine, and whether it is in the running of your country or mine. And those people won't have much time for this book. But you will know who they are before and after they strike: They will be the ones who will decide with undue pride, those who are unable to let the right people decide, those who fail to listen and act on needed feedback, and those who, at all costs, avoid acknowledging—let alone experiencing—the consequences of their decisions, especially on others, ahead of time.

So let me close by asking: Do you have all the answers? Or are you ready to rise to the challenge of remaining highly confident without succumbing to hubris? Please take the time to check your ego; it will help prevent you from needlessly falling victim to humanity's cardinal sin.

Glossary of Terms

Terms are listed according to their appearance in the book.

confidence is the level of belief in what we know, what we can do, and what the future will hold.

authentic confidence is confidence derived from the best available evidence.

false confidence is confidence derived from contrived evidence.

overconfidence is overestimating what we know, what we can do, and what the future will hold, whether driven by authentic or false confidence.

hubris is the damaging consequences of overconfident decisions and actions that arise from false confidence.

grounded pride arises when we intrinsically appreciate ourselves and colleagues based on the best available evidence of what we are doing.

excessive pride is when we purport to be more than we are or someone who we are not. It arises when we develop an inflated view of ourselves based on our need for certain outcomes and approval, and our tendency to use self-serving data rather than the facts to support positive self-impression. Dependent, exaggerated, and overweening pride are the three forms of excessive pride.

dependent pride arises when our pride depends on future outcomes rather than present work, including how we want others to perceive us.

exaggerated pride arises when we have an intrinsic locus of pride but base that pride on self-serving data about our performance; say, because we believe what we want to rather than what the facts tell us.

overweening pride arises when our sense of pride is driven by potential outcomes, including how we want others to perceive others, and is supported by self-serving data about our performance.

foil is someone who shares our agenda and helps us with decisions and actions through complementary perspectives and ambitions.

grounded judgment arises where we are highly motivated to make decisions that are based on high-quality feedback about our situation.

selective judgment arises when we have high-quality feedback but we selectively use it to make decisions that please us (i.e., fit our preconceptions of our situation and how we would like it to be).

speculative judgment arises when the best available feedback is inadequate, and we try to make the best of such feedback.

hapless judgment arises where we are faced with inadequate feedback about our situation; and we are not motivated to act on such feedback, say, because that limited feedback does not fit our preconceptions or aspirations.

Notes

Introduction

1. A. Cooper, C. Woo, and W. Dunkelberg, "Entrepreneurs Perceived Chances for Success," *Journal of Business Venturing* 3 (1988).

2. Brainy Quote Web site, *www.brainyquote.com* (accessed August 1, 2006).

3. M. Morrison, "Herb Kelleher on the Record, Part 3," *BusinessWeek*, December 24, 2003.

4. L. V. Gerstner, *Who Says Elephants Can't Dance?* (New York: HarperCollins, 2002), 15.

5. J. Collins, *Good to Great* (New York: HarperCollins, 2001), 36, 39.

6. J. Boorstin, "The Best Advice I Ever Got," *Fortune*, March 21, 2005.

7. All the following quotes are from Brainy Quote Web site, *www.brainyquote.com* (accessed August 1, 2006).

8. J. O'Loughlin, *The Real Warren Buffett* (London: Nicholas Brealey, 2003), 124.

Chapter 1

1. J. Krakauer, *Into Thin Air* (New York: Anchor, 1999).

2. Ibid.

3. S. Watts, *The People's Tycoon: Henry Ford and the American Century* (New York: Knopf, 2005).

4. T. Verducci, "Who's your Papi?" *Sports Illustrated*, June 19, 2006.

5. Padraig Harrington, Sports Illustrated online, *www.pga.com/pgachampionship/2005/news/harrington080905.html* (accessed August 1, 2006).

6. M. Symonds, *Softwar: An Intimate Portrayal of Larry Ellison and Oracle* (New York: Simon & Schuster, 2003).

7. J. Welch, *Jack—Straight from the Gut* (New York: Warner Business Books, 2001).

8. Symonds, *Softwar.*

9. Michael Dell, *Direct from Dell* (New York: Harper Business, 1999).

10. D. Leonard, "All I Want in Life Is an Unfair Advantage," *Fortune,* August 8, 2005.

11. Ibid.

12. Ibid.

13. Ibid.

Chapter 2

1. Dan Rather, "The Next Big Thing," *60 Minutes,* August 27, 2003.

2. Ibid.

3. J. Heilemann, "Reinventing the Wheel," *Time,* December 10, 2001.

4. M. Legace, "Not a Scooter, Not a Vehicle: Make Way for Segway," Harvard Business School Working Knowledge, February 25, 2002, *http://hbsworkingknowledge.hbs.edu/archive/2795.html* (accessed August 1, 2006).

5. S. Kemper, *Code Name Ginger: The Story behind Segway and Dean Kamen's Quest to Invent a New World* (Boston: Harvard Business School Press, 2003).

6. Ibid.

7. Ibid.

8. *www.segway.com* (accessed August 1, 2006).

9. Kemper, *Code Name Ginger.*

10. Ibid.

11. Cooper et al., "Entrepreneurs Perceived."

12. R. Kramer, *The Harder They Fall* (Boston: Harvard Business Review Press, 2003).

13. J. VanDerhie, Employee Benefit Research Institute's annual retirement confidence survey, 2006.

14. B. Barber and T. Odean, "Trading is hazardous to your wealth: the common stock investment performance of individual investors," *Journal of Finance* LV, no. 2 (April 2000).

15. B. Barber and T. Odean, "Boys will be boys: Gender, overconfidence and common stock investment," *Quarterly Journal of Economics* 116, no. 1 (February 2001).

16. Index Funds AdvisorsWeb site, *www.ifa.com* (accessed August 1, 2006).

17. J. Spencer, "Lessons from the Brain Damaged Investor," *Wall Street Journal,* July 21, 2005.

18. See J. Yates, *Judgment and Decision Making* (Englewood Cliffs, N.J.: Prentice Hall, 1990) for the evidence on sore throats. D. Dunning, C. Heath, and J. Suls, "Flawed Self-Assessment: Implications for Health, Education, and the Workplace," *Psychological Science in the Public Interest* 5 (2004) provides an excellent review of these and other relevant studies.

19. J. Linder and R. Stafford, *Journal of the American Medical Association* 286 (2001).

20. S. Zwart et al., "Penicillin for Acute Sore Throat in Children: Randomized, Double Blind Trial," *British Medical Journal* 327 (2003).

21. CSIRO Web site, *www.csiro.au/* (accessed August 1, 2006).

22. Z. Tomlin, C. Humphrey, and S. Rogers, "General Practitioners' Perceptions of Effective Health Care," *British Journal of Medicine* 318 (1999).

23. J. J. J. Christensen-Szalanski and J. B. Bushyhead, "Physicians' Use of Probabilistic Information in a Real Clinical Setting," *Journal of Experimental Psychology* 7 (1981).

24. Ibid.

25. D. A. Risucci, A. J. Torolani, and R. J. Ward, "Ratings of Surgical Residents by Self, Supervisors and Peers," *Surgical Gynecology and Obstetrics* 169 (1989).

26. J. M. Tracey et al., "The Validity of General Practitioners' Self-Assessment of Knowledge: Cross Sectional Study," *British Medical Journal* 215 (1997).

27. D. Streitfeld, "Mixed Views of Doctor at Heart of FBI probe," *Los Angeles Times,* November 11, 2002.

28. Ed Bradley, "Unhealthy Diagnosis," *60 Minutes,* July 27, 2003.

29. Ibid.

30. College Board, Student descriptive questionnaire, 1976–1977 (Princeton, N.J.: Educational Testing Service).

31. P. Cross, "Not Can but Will College Teaching Be Improved?" *New Directions for Higher Education* 17 (1977).

32. Linda Wertheimer, "Harvard Grade Inflation," *All Things Considered*, National Public Radio, November 21, 2001.

33. A. Williams, "Inflation, Apathy," *The Daily Northwestern*, April 2003.

34. H. Mansfield, *The Chronicle Review*, April 6, 2001.

35. Ibid.

Chapter 3

1. Dell, *Direct from Dell.*

2. L. Butcher, *Accidental Millionaire* (New York: Paragon House Publishers, 1988).

3. Ibid.

4. Ibid.

5. "Striking It Rich: America's Risk Takers," *Time*, February 15, 1982; and "Inside the Apple Microsoft Deal," *Time*, August 18, 1997.

6. A. Hertzfeld, *Revolution in the Valley* (Sebastopol, Calif.: O'Reilly, 2005).

7. O. W. Linzmayer, *Apple Confidential* (San Francisco: No Starch Press, 1999).

8. Hertzfeld, *Revolution in the Valley.*

9. Ibid.

10. *http://news-service.stanford.edu/news/2005/june15/jobs-061505.html.*

11. J. Sculley, *Odyssey* (New York: HarperCollins, 1987).

12. Ibid.

13. Ibid.

14. Ibid.

15. Ibid.

16. Ibid.

17. Ibid.

18. D. McGinn, MBA Jungle Palm Case Study: Handy Andy, December 2001/January 2002.

19. Ibid.

20. Ibid.

21. Linzmayer, *Apple Confidential.*

22. D. Goodman, Interview with John Sculley, *Playboy*, September 1987.

23. J. Useem, "Happiness and the Downwardly Mobile CEO," *Inc.,* May 1999.

24. A. Deutschmann, *The Second Coming of Steve Jobs* (New York: Broadway Books, 2000).

25. Ibid.

26. J. Nocera, "Stevie Wonder," *GQ,* October 1993.

27. J. S. Young and W. L. Simon, *iCon Steve Jobs* (Hoboken, N.J.: John Wiley & Sons, 2005), 276.

28. L. Kahney, "Inside Look at Birth of iPod," *Wired News,* July 22, 2004.

29. "Apple Presents iPod," Apple press release, October 23, 2001.

30. D. Vasella and C. Leaf, "Temptation Is All around Us," *Fortune,* November 18, 2002, 109.

31. U. Malmendier and G. Tate, "Superstar CEOs," working paper, Stanford University, 2006.

32. W. Buffett, "Berkshire Hathaway Annual Report to Shareholders," February 26, 1982.

33. S. B. Shephard. "Gerald Levin Looks Ahead," *BusinessWeek,* November 6, 2000.

34. See, for example, A. Agrawal, J. Jaffe, and G. Mandelkar, "The Post Merger Performance of Acquiring Firms," *Journal of Finance* 47 (1992).

35. M. Hayward and D. Hambrick, "Explaining the Premiums Paid in Large Acquisitions: Evidence of CEO Hubris," *Administrative Science Quarterly* 42 (1997).

36. J. Welch, *Jack—Straight from the Gut.*

37. M. Hayward, V. Rindova, and T. Pollock, "The Causes and Consequences of CEO Celebrity," *Strategic Management Journal* 25 (2004).

38. See, for instance, the Web site of the Commonwealth Club, *www.commonwealthclub.org/archive/01/01-11welch-speech.html* (accessed August 1, 2006).

39. B. Groysberg, A. Nanda, and N. Nohria, "The Risky Business of Hiring Stars," *Harvard Business Review* 82 (2004).

40. B. Groysberg, A. McLean, and N. Nohria, "Are Leaders Portable?" *Harvard Business Review* 84 (2006).

Chapter 4

1. P. Sellers, "The 50 Most Powerful Women in American Business," *Fortune,* October 12, 1998.

2. C. J. Loomis, "Why Carly's Big Bet Is Failing," *Fortune,* February 7, 2005.

3. Ibid.

4. C. J. Loomis, "How the HP Board KO'd Carly," *Fortune,* March 7, 2005.

5. Ibid.

6. Symonds, *Softwar.*

7. Ibid.

8. Ibid.

9. Ibid.

10. Ibid.

11. Ibid.

12. Ibid.

13. Ibid.

14. Ibid.

15. Ibid., 159.

16. Ibid., 160.

17. Ibid.

18. Warren Buffett, *1994 Berkshire Hathaway Annual Report to Shareholders.*

19. Warren Buffett, *2004 Berkshire Hathaway Annual Report to Shareholders.*

20. Warren Buffett, *2003 Berkshire Hathaway Annual Report to Shareholders.*

21. Warren Buffett, *2005 Berkshire Hathaway Annual Report to Shareholders.*

22. Ibid.

23. C. Hymowitz, "A Tech Manager Shares Advice on Weathering Business Cycles," *Wall Street Journal,* March 23, 2006.

24. E. J. Lyman, "I Will Survive," *Advertising Age,* February 27, 2006, 1.

25. D. Rushe, "I'll See You in Court," *Sunday Times,* February 26, 2006, 5.

26. P. Sellers, "Most Powerful Women in Business," *Fortune,* October 18, 2004.

27. L. A. Hill and M. T. Farkas, "Meg Whitman at eBay, Inc.," (A) Harvard Business School case, 9-401-024.

28. Ibid., 7.

Chapter 5

1. Brainy Quote Web site, *www.brainyquote.com* (accessed August 1, 2006).

2. C. Camerer and D. Lovallo, "Overconfidence and Excess Entry: An Experimental Approach," *American Economic Review* 89 (1999); quoting "Going After the Big One," *Los Angeles Times,* December 31, 1996, F1.

3. T. Zenger, "Why Do Employers Only Reward Extreme Performance? Examining the Relationships among Performance, Pay, and Turnover," *Administrative Science Quarterly* 37 (1992).

4. See the terrific article by J. Kuger and D. Dunning, "Unskilled and unaware of it: How difficulties in recognizing one's own incompetence lead to inflated self-assessments," *Journal of Personality and Social Psychology* 77 (1999).

5. J. McCallum, "Point Guard from Another Planet," *Sports Illustrated,* January 30, 2006.

6. Ibid.

7. Ibid.

8. Ibid.

9. B. M. Staw, "The Escalation of Commitment," in Z. Shapira, ed., *Organizational Decision Making* (New York: Cambridge University Press, 1997), 191–215.

10. M. E. P. Seligman and P. Schulman, "Explanatory Style as a Predictor of Productivity and Quitting among Life Insurance Agents," *Journal of Personality and Social Psychology* 50 (1986).

11. Ibid.

12. See M. E. P Seligman, *Learned Optimism* (New York: Simon and Schuster, 1998). See also Seligman's Positive Psychology Web site, *www.ppc.sas.upenn.edu.*

13. J. Simons, D. Stipp, and R. Parloff, "Will Merck Survive Vioxx?" *Fortune,* November 1, 2004.

14. G. D. Curfman, S. Morrissey, and J. F. Drazen, "Expression of Concern Reaffirmed," *New England Journal of Medicine,* March 16, 2006.

15. A. W. Mathews and B. Martinez, "Warning Signs: E-Mails Suggest Merck Knew Vioxx's Dangers at Early Stage; as Heart-Risk Rose, Officials Played Hardball; Internal Message: Dodge; Company Says 'Out of Context,'" *Wall Street Journal*, November 1, 2004.

16. R. Langreth, "Drugs: Merck's Health Hinges on Sales of Its New Pain, Arthritis Pill," *Wall Street Journal*, April 14, 1999; and J. Simons, "Will Merck Survive Vioxx?" *Fortune*, November 1, 2004.

17. J. Simons, "Will R&D Make Merck Hot Again?" *Fortune*, July 8, 2002.

18. Langreth, "Drugs."

19. Simons, "Will Merck Survive?"

20. B. Meier and S. Saul, "Marketing of Vioxx: How Merck Played Game of Catch-Up," *New York Times*, February 11, 2005.

21. H. A. Waxman, "The Lessons of Vioxx: Drug Safety and Sales," *New England Journal of Medicine* 352 (2005).

22. G. D. Curfman, S. Morrissey, and J. F. Drazen, "Expression of Concern: Bombardier et al.: 'Comparison of Upper Gastrointestinal Toxicity of Rofecoxib and Naproxen in Patients with Rheumatoid Arthritis,'" *New England Journal of Medicine* 343 (2005).

23. Mathews, "Warning Signs."

24. Langreth, "Drugs."

25. FDA Advisory Committee, "Vioxx Gastrointestinal Safety," briefing document, NDA 21-042 s007 (Rockville, Md.: Food and Drug Administration, 2001).

26. Langreth, "Drugs."

27. Ibid.

28. D. J. Graham, et al., "Risk of Acute Myocardial Infarction and Sudden Cardiac Death in Patients Treated with Cyclo-Oxygenase 2 Selective and Non-Selective Non-Steroidal Anti-Inflammatory Drugs: Nested Case-Control Study," *Lancet* 365 (2005).

29. Simons, "Will Merck Survive?"

30. Ibid.

31. A. W. Mathews and S. Hensley, "Merck May Return Vioxx to Market: Move Depends on Whether FDA Panel Decides Risks Exist in Similar Medicines, *Wall Street Journal*, February 18, 2005.

32. A. Berenson, "Chief Executive Quits at Merck: Insider Steps Up," *New York Times*, May 6, 2005.

33. K. McKoy, "Merck CEO Sets Sights on Change: Clark Calls His Turnaround Plan a Mission 'to Save This Company,'" *USA Today,* February 27, 2006.

34. J. Kruger and D. Dunning, "Unskilled and unaware of it: How difficulties in recognizing one's own incompetence lead to inflated self-assessments," *Journal of Personality and Social Psychology* 77 (1999).

35. H. W. Tesoriero et al., "Side Effects: Merck Loss Jolts Drug Giant, Industry; In Landmark Vioxx Case, Jury Tuned Out Science, Explored Coverup Angle; 'Shadow' Plan at McDonald's," *Wall Street Journal,* August 22, 2005.

36. Professors Peter Salovey and Jack Mayer coined the term emotional intelligence. They divided up emotional intelligence into five component abilities:

1. *Self-awareness.* Observing yourself and recognizing feelings as they happen
2. *Managing emotions.* Handling feelings so that they are expressed and acted on appropriately, realizing what is behind a feeling, finding ways to cope with fear, anxiety, anger, and sadness
3. *Motivating yourself.* Using emotions to help achieve goals, self-control, delaying gratification, overcoming damaging impulses
4. *Empathy.* Sensitivity to other people's feelings and concerns, being able to see things from their perspective, appreciating differences in other people's viewpoints
5. *Handling relationships.* Managing emotions in others, social skills, the ability to handle conflict and difficult issues

37. J. Pfeffer and R. I. Sutton, *Hard Facts* (Boston: Harvard Business School Press, 2006).

Chapter 6

1. S. Covey, *7 Habits of Highly Effective People* (New York: Simon & Schuster, 1999).

2. J. Diamond and D. Moniz, "War Critics Rile Rumsfeld, Myers," *USA Today,* April 1, 2003.

3. Associated Press, "Ex-FEMA Chief Says Bush Was Overconfident," March 1, 2006.

4. M. Bloomberg, *Bloomberg by Bloomberg* (New York: John Wiley & Sons, 2001).

5. R. Buehler, D. Griffin, and M. Ross, "Exploring the 'planning fallacy': Why people underestimate their task completion times," *Journal of Personality and Social Psychology* (1994).

6. K. Freiberg and J. Freiberg, *Nuts! Southwest Airlines Crazy Recipe for Personal and Business Success Broadway* (New York: Broadway Books, 1998).

7. G. Hamel and G. Getz, "Innovate—Inexpensively," *Harvard Business Review,* July 1, 2004.

8. D. H. Freedman, "Entrepreneur of the Year," *Inc.,* January 2005, 58.

9. M. Martinez, "Space Pioneer Predicts 3,000 Astronauts in 5 Years," *Chicago Tribune,* November 21, 2004.

10. Freedman, "Entrepreneur of the Year."

11. W. Harwood, "SpaceShipOne Rockets into History," *Spaceflight Now,* June 21, 2004.

12. Freedman, "Entrepreneur of the Year."

13. Martinez, "Space Pioneer."

14. G. Gugliotta, "A Rocket Flight for the Common Man?" *Washington Post,* June 12, 2004.

15. C. Skrzycki, "Giving a Fledgling Industry Space to Breathe," *Washington Post Online,* May 3, 2005; *www.washingtonpost.com* (accessed August 1, 2006).

16. Quote appearing in R. Bohmer, A. Edmondson, and M. Roberto, "Columbia's Final Mission," Harvard Business School case 9-304-090, 2004.

17. "Report to the President by the Presidential Commission on the Space Shuttle Challenger Accident (Rogers Commission)" (Washington, D.C.: Government Printing Office, June 9, 1986, vol. 2, appendix F.

18. Columbia Accident Investigation Board, final report August 26, 2003 (Washington, D.C.: Government Printing Office, 2003).

19. H. Berkes, "Challenger: Reporting a Disaster's Cold, Hard Facts," NPR, January 28, 2006.

20. Ibid.

21. Columbia Accident Investigation Board report.

22. D. Vaughan, *The Challenger Launch Decision: Risky Technology, Culture, and Deviance at NASA* (Chicago: University of Chicago Press, 1997).

23. "NASA Promises to Break Culture of Silence," *The Black Vault,* July 29, 2003.

24. Columbia Accident Investigation Board report.

25. Ibid.

26. Ibid.

27. K. Cowing, "People Is Hard: NASA Seeks to Fix Itself," *SpaceRef.com,* April 14, 2004; *www.spaceref.com/news/viewnews.html?id=943* (accessed August 1, 2006).

28. J. Pfeffer and R. Sutton, *The Knowing Doing Gap* (Boston: Harvard Business School Press, 2000).

Chapter 7

1. C. Matlack, "The Stars of Europe," *BusinessWeek,* June 11, 2001.

2. D. Owen, "A New Style Networker with a Radical Edge," *Financial Times,* June 7, 1999.

3. S. Tully, "Leader of the Pack," *Fortune,* September 6, 1999.

4. Jean-Marie Messier, *j6m.com* (Paris: Hachette Litteratures, 2000).

5. "Neat but Not Yet Tidy," *The Economist,* September 25, 1999.

6. Messier, j6m.com.

7. J. Johnson and M. Orange, *The Man Who Tried to Buy the World* (New York: Portfolio, 2003).

8. A. Touraine, luncheon speech to European Professional Women's Network, April 2004.

9. G. Hannezo, Submission to the Commission des Operations de Bourse investigation, October 2002.

10. J. Carreyrou and M. Peers, "Damage control: How Messier kept cash crisis at Vivendi hidden for months," *Wall Street Journal,* October 31, 2002.

11. Hannezo, Submission to the Commission des Operations de Bourse investigation.

12. A. Riding, "Remark by Vivendi chief unnerves the French film industry," *New York Times,* December 24, 2001.

13. Johnson and Orange, *The Man Who Tried.*

14. Ibid.

15. Ibid.

Chapter 8

1. A. Serwer, "The Education of Michael Dell," *Fortune,* March 7, 2005, 73.

2. Dell, *Direct from Dell.*

3. J. Markoff, "Michael Dell Should Eat His Words, Apple Chief Suggests," *New York Times,* January 16, 2006.

4. Dell, *Direct from Dell.*

5. "On the Record: Scott McNealy," *San Francisco Chronicle,* September 14, 2003.

6. B. Breen, "Living in Dell Time," *FastCompany,* November 2004.

7. Dell, *Direct from Dell.*

8. Ibid.

9. Ibid.

10. Ibid.

11. Ibid.

12. C. D. Neilsen, "Chief of Dell," *Marriott Alumni Magazine,* Fall 2004.

13. J. Useem, "20 that made history," *Fortune* (2005).

14. W. J. Holstein, "Dell: One Company, Two CEOs," *The Chief Executive,* November 2003.

15. T. A. Stewart, "Execution without Excuses," *Harvard Business Review,* March 2005.

16. Ibid.

17. Ibid.

18. Dell, *Direct from Dell.*

19. Stewart, "Execution."

20. D. Kirkpatrick, "Dell and Rollins, the $41 Billion Buddy Act," *Fortune,* April 19, 2004.

21. Stewart, "Execution."

22. Ibid.

Index

Share the message!

Bulk discounts
Discounts start at only 10 copies and range from 30% to 55% off
retail price based on quantity.

Custom publishing
Private label a cover with your organization's name
and logo. Or, tailor information to your needs with
a custom pamphlet that highlights specific chapters.

Ancillaries
Workshop outlines, videos, and other products are
available on select titles.

Dynamic speakers
Engaging authors are available to share their expertise
and insight at your event.

**Call Kaplan Publishing Corporate Sales at 1-800-621-9621, ext. 4444,
or e-mail kaplanpubsales@kaplan.com**

PUBLISHING